Jerry Baker's

FIX IT
FAST
and Make
It Last!

www.jerrybaker.com

Other Jerry Baker Books:

Jerry Baker's

FIX IT
FAST
and Make
It Last!

2,175
DIY secrets, shortcuts, and solutions to keep your home in tip-top shape!

www.jerrybaker.com

Published by American Master Products, Inc.

Executive Editor: Kim Adam Gasior
Managing Editor: Debby Duvall
Writer: Vicki Webster
Copy Editor: Nanette Bendyna
Design and Layout: Alison McKenna
Illustrator: Deborah Cowder
Indexer: Mary Pelletier-Hunyadi

Publisher's Cataloging-in-Publication
(Provided by Quality Books, Inc.)

Baker, Jerry, author.
    Fix it fast and make it last! : 2,175 DIY secrets, shortcuts, and solutions to keep your home in tip-top shape! / Jerry Baker.
    pages cm
    Includes index.
    ISBN 978-0-922433-25-4

    1. Home economics--Equipment and supplies.
2. Do-it-yourself work.   I. Title.

TX298.B35 2016   643'.7
           QBI15-600241

Printed in the United States of America
4 6 8 7 5 3 hardcover

CONTENTS

Chapter 4 Heating & Cooling

Chapter 5 Cabinets & Countertops

PART 2 OUTSIDE YOUR HOME

Chapter 6 Exterior Walls

Chapter 7 Doors & Windows

Chapter 8 Roofs

Chapter 9 Outdoor Structures & Systems

PART 3 THE STUFF IN YOUR LIFE

Chapter 10 Appliances

Chapter 11 Furniture

Chapter 12 Home Furnishings

Chapter 13 Clothing & Accessories

Chapter 14 Automobiles

1 2 3 4 5 6 7 8 9 10 11 12 13 14

Your Home Sweet Home

For well over half a century now, I've been preaching the gospel of solving small problems before they turn into big ones. That's a smart strategy to practice in every aspect of life. But it's an absolute must inside and outside your home, where a tiny spot of trouble that's left unattended can quickly escalate into a budget-busting repair project—or even a major disaster.

TIPS, TRICKS & INSIDER SECRETS

If you're tired of emptying your wallet to repair or replace your treasured belongings, then you've come to the right place! These super solutions show you exactly how to solve—and, better yet, prevent—all kinds of interior and exterior woes without shelling out big bucks for professional help. For instance, you'll learn how to:

▶ **Detect and repair minor water leaks**—before the elixir of life becomes the potion of death for your walls, floors, or roof (chapters 3 and 8)

▶ **Deliver fast first aid for cracks** in drywall, plaster, stucco, and brick—so they don't expand into craters that make your walls come tumblin' down (chapters 1 and 6)

▶ **Stop electrical glitches** at the starting gate—to prevent potentially deadly fires (Chapter 2)

▶ **Keep your heating and cooling systems** humming along—and avoid one of the costliest household projects of all: installing a new furnace or central AC system (Chapter 4)

▶ **Perform quick and easy repairs** to your driveway, deck, and other outdoor structures—which will boost your home's curb appeal and resale value (Chapter 9)

And that's just the tip of the iceberg! I'll also clue you in on a whole lot of fast fixes and practical ploys that can prolong the life of everything from the appliances in your kitchen to the clothes in your closet and the car in your garage. For example, you'll discover how to use common household products to:

- ▶ Put the bite back in a blender's blades (page 270)
- ▶ Refinish disfiguring gouges in wood furniture (page 278)
- ▶ Erase stubborn stains from clothes and accessories (page 335)
- ▶ Remove sticky road deposits from your car—without damaging the paint (page 362)

In every chapter, you'll find plenty of illustrated step-by-step instructions for fix-it projects that would cost you a bundle—if, that is, you could find someone to do the work. These jobs are a piece of cake if you do 'em yourself. Just to whet your appetite, you'll learn how easy it is to reface your kitchen cabinets (see "About!—Face!" on page 123), re-cover a lamp shade (page 314), and unstick a stuck suitcase handle (page 341).

Wait—the terrific tips don't stop there! This book is also filled with fantastic features like An Ounce of Prevention, which contains simple secrets for stopping trouble in its tracks. For example, cutting back on the amount of detergent you use can keep your washing machine in tip-top shape for many years to come (page 255). And if you simply keep your foot off your car's brake pedal while you're driving, you'll dramatically cut wear and tear on the brake pads (page 361).

In Rehab • Revamp • Revive, you'll discover creative ways to turn would-be trash into treasure. A couple of examples: To fix worrisome wounds in your wooden paneling or trim, just mix coffee grounds or used tea leaves with spackling compound or white glue (page 11). On a more urgent note, when a water or drain line is leaking, a piece of old garden hose can save the day. Just slit it lengthwise, slip it onto the cracked pipe, and secure it with C-clamps, duct tape, or large binder clips. It'll keep the scene clean until your plumber arrives (page 86).

Well, Whaddya Know! is just for fun. These fascinating factoids and tantalizing tidbits relate to the subjects at hand in each chapter. Just to pique your curiosity, here are two trivia questions you can toss out at your next neighborhood barbecue:

Who invented the dishwasher? The answer: A Shelbyville, Illinois, housewife named Josephine Cochrane. For her amazing saga, see page 73.

What momentous fashion event occurred on May 15, 1940? The answer: Nylon stockings first hit store shelves all over the U.S.A. You'll snag the full scoop on page 346.

Finally, my Powerful Potions are fabulous formulas that'll solve or prevent household problems of all kinds. Two cases in point: Dandy Deck Cleaner will spruce up your deck, porch, fence, or any other wooden surface without any of the harsh chemicals that you'll find in those pricey, toxic commercial products (page 212). And my Automotive Anti-Frost Formula will keep your car's windows ice- and frost-free on even the most frigid nights (page 365). So let's dig in...

While this book is chock-full of sensational strategies for taking charge of your home's health and well-being, there are times when you just can't, or shouldn't, go it alone. These features spell out—loud and clear—when you need to forget DIY measures and summon professional help. At best, your well-intentioned fiddling could wind up costing you a lot more money than you'd have to pay an experienced expert. At worst, getting in over your head (for example, with a potent force like electricity) could be deadly. So know your limits, and always err on the side of caution!

PART 1

INSIDE YOUR HOME

As the old adage goes, there's no place like home. Generally, we interpret the saying to mean that no place can give you more pleasure than your very own humble abode. But your treasured surroundings can also offer up their fair share of trouble, and resolving even basic problems can often cost you a pretty penny—if you have to bring in professional help. The good news is that with some basic tools and my quick and easy DIY tips and tricks, you can solve a whole lot of your interior woes without shelling out bundles of your hard-earned bucks—and actually have fun doing it. In this section, you'll learn how to make timely repairs to inside structural features and the systems that keep everything humming along. I'll also share some super-simple tips for maintaining all those surfaces and moving parts so that they're less likely to go belly-up before their time.

Walls, Ceilings & Floors

These flat surfaces suffer more wear and tear than any other parts of your home's interior. You walk on your floors, drag things across them, and spill everything from red wine to salad dressing (and worse) on them. You drive nails and screws into your walls and ceilings to hang heavy objects. All that abuse takes its toll. With the insider secrets in this chapter, you'll learn how to act fast when trouble strikes—and to deliver some basic TLC that can keep collateral damage to a minimum.

WALLBOARD

Wallboard Enemy Number One

Wallboard (a.k.a. drywall, gypsum board, plasterboard, and Sheetrock®) is sturdy stuff. But one thing can send it to the building-material grave-yard *fast*: good old H_2O. So keep an eye out for moisture in your walls —not only obvious wetness, but also brown or blackish spots, which are almost certain signs of water damage. Pinpoint the source first, and fix it ASAP. Then direct your attention to the water damage. These are the most common culprits:

- Ice dams that form under rooftop snow
- Leaks in your roof or eaves
- Leaky pipes
- Persistent splashing or overflow from sinks, showers, or tubs
- Poorly grouted or caulked seams in tiles or tub surrounds

Note: *Plaster walls are also sitting ducks for water damage.*

First Aid for Holes and Cracks

Tiny holes and cracks (up to ½ inch wide) in wallboard (or plaster) are a snap to fix. Simply enlarge the opening slightly, using a sturdy knife. Then clean out the dust, and fill the hole or crack with commercial spackling compound, using a small putty knife. Let the compound dry, sand it smooth, and touch up the paint. That's all there is to it!

Note: *Use this same technique to fill small dings in a wallboard ceiling—let's say, for example, screw holes that were left when you removed an overhead pot rack.*

4 Quick and Quirky Hole Fillers

When you need to fill a nail hole or other small gouge in a hurry and you have no spackling compound on hand, reach for one of these handy homemade fixers:

- ▶ **Baking soda and white glue.** Mix 'em together, starting with roughly equal parts, and add more glue or soda until you get a workable consistency.

- ▶ **Chewing gum.** Chew it until the sweetness vanishes, then pull off as much as you need to do the job.

- ▶ **Soap.** Simply rub the bar over the hole until it's filled up.

- ▶ **Toothpaste.** Using the traditional white kind (not gel), squeeze a dab onto your finger or a cotton swab, and go to town.

Stuff your filler of choice firmly into the gap until it's even with the wall surface, and wipe off any excess using a damp sponge. Wait until the spot has dried thoroughly, and then touch it up with paint that matches your wall. No leftovers from your last paint job? Don't fret—just grab a crayon or felt-tip marker that's the right color.

CALL A PRO

Just about anyone can repair cracks, holes, and dents in wallboard using the tips in this chapter, but major water damage is a whole other kettle of fish. When a lot of water has found its way into your walls or ceilings, call an experienced contractor, who can assess the extent of the trouble and replace the soaked panels. And hurry because a small water problem can turn into a big water disaster in the blink of an eye!

Patching Bottomless Pits

Mending gouges that go all the way through wallboard is a more complex process than filling tiny dings (see "First Aid for Holes and Cracks" on page 3). But it's still easy enough for a novice do-it-yourselfer. Here's the nine-step routine:

STEP 1. Cut out a rectangular section of the wallboard around the hole, using a small saw or large knife. Make sure that the new opening extends to a stud on either side. To ensure an easy fit, use a T square to be certain that you've got straight lines and 90-degree angles.

STEP 2. Measure the opening, and cut a new piece of wallboard the same size.

STEP 3. Set the patch into the opening, trimming it with a utility knife.

STEP 4. Attach it to the studs on either side with 1 ¼-inch drywall screws, and trim away any loose paper or gypsum.

STEP 5. Spread a coat of joint compound over the seams.

STEP 6. Cover the seams with joint tape, being sure not to overlap the tape where it meets at the corners.

STEP 7. Draw a scraper across the tape at an angle to squeeze out most, but not all, of the compound.

STEP 8. Let the compound set until it's dry, then apply a second coat that extends 6 inches beyond the first. When it dries, sand it smooth, and add a third coat, extending out another 6 inches.

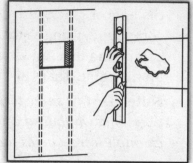

Cut a rectangular opening that extends to a wall stud on either side.

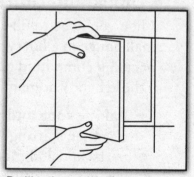

Position the patch in the opening, and screw it to the studs.

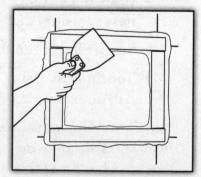

Apply joint tape over the compound, and scrape to squeeze out most of the compound.

STEP 9. When the final coat has dried, sand lightly with fine sandpaper. Then remove the dust, using a slightly damp sponge, before priming and painting over the patch.

Note: *Ceilings are made of thicker, sturdier drywall than the kind used on walls, and the material is far less vulnerable to damage. When large holes or cracks do appear, they could be a sign of major trouble above the ceiling, and you may have more on your hands than a simple patch-up job.*

Deep-Down Relief

If you've got a hole that's too deep to fill with spackling compound or one of its substitutes (see "4 Quick and Quirky Hole Fillers" on page 3), but not deep enough to be treated like a bottomless pit, try one of these amazing alternatives:

- **Chalk.** Push it into the gap, and break it off even with the wall.
- **Cork.** Find a cork that's the right diameter, and insert it firmly into the opening.
- **Steel wool.** Break or cut off small chunks of the stuff, and fill the cavity in the wall with them.

Whichever filler you've used, spread spackling or joint compound over it, pushing it in around the edges. Then let it dry, sand and wipe the surface smooth, and brush on some paint.

PLASTER

Don't Dawdle over Dings

Solid plaster walls are far stronger and more durable than those made from wallboard. But when major damage does occur, it can cost a small fortune to fix it. So when you spot even a tiny hole or crack, spring into action immediately. Unlike wallboard wounds, small punctures in plaster can turn into big-time trouble. That's because the weight of the damaged plaster creates extra stress that loosens the surrounding material. Unless you act quickly, that little, easy-to-fix flaw will turn into a big, gaping hole before you know it.

Cast a Clear Eye on Cracks

When you find diagonal hairline cracks in your plaster, especially above doors or windows, or in areas that have been recently repaired, don't fret. Most likely they're stress cracks—which are no big deal. Just patch 'em up following the same procedure you'd use for little flaws in wallboard (see "First Aid for Holes and Cracks" on page 3). But cracks that are longer than a few inches, uneven in width, or recessed into the wall may be a sign of structural damage. Your best bet is to have a contractor or structural engineer take a look at the area and correct any underlying problem before you repair the plaster.

3 Steps to Perfect Plaster Patching

Although modern spackling compound works fine for filling tiny gouges in plaster walls, repairing anything larger than ½ inch or so demands a different technique and different materials than the ones you use on wallboard. If your damage covers an area that's more than 6 inches across, call a professional plasterer. But for anything smaller than that, you can deliver relief yourself using patching plaster, in either powdered or premixed form. It's as easy as 1, 2, 3!

STEP 1. Clean the loose plaster from the cavity, including the stuff between the lath strips at the back. Staple a piece of hardware cloth to the wood to provide a solid grip.

STEP 2. Moisten the area, and apply the patching plaster in three thin coats. Use a joint knife that's narrower than the opening, and let each coat dry before adding the next one.

STEP 3. Apply a very thin, feathery layer of wallboard joint compound using a joint knife that's wider than the patch. Let it dry, then sand it smooth, and paint over it.

Stop Stress Cracks in Their Tracks

Whenever you or your hired helpers make wall or ceiling repairs— whether the surface is made of plaster, wallboard, or wood, there's a simple way to avoid future trouble. Just spray the patched area with an elastic coating like Good-Bye Cracks® before painting the surface.

Sagging Ceiling Surgery

Everything on earth is governed by the law of gravity. And plaster ceilings have to fight against nature's force with all of their might—standing firm against footfalls, dropped objects, and occasional floods from above.

One of the first signs of trouble is a slight bulge that you may think is no big deal. Wrong! That bump is a clear indication that the plaster has separated from its lath supports—and unless you act fast, your ceiling will start falling to the floor. If the projection is less than 18 inches in diameter, and the plaster moves quickly back into place when you push on it, it's an easy fix. Just get some plaster washers (a.k.a. ceiling buttons) and 1½-inch drywall screws, and proceed as follows:

Carefully remove any loose plaster. Then drive the screws through the washers into the ceiling joists (use the less stable lath only as a last resort). Don't try to pull the plaster tight all at once, or it may crack. Instead, start a few screws in strategic places, then slowly tighten each of them so that the plaster gradually pulls snug against the joists.

▶ Spread a thin coat of drywall joint compound on the patched area, cover it with joint tape, and scrape the tape to embed it in the compound. When it has dried, apply another thin coat, and let it dry.

▶ Once the compound has hardened completely, sand it smooth, remove the dust, and inspect the site. If any imperfections remain, apply one or two more thin coats of compound, and sand again.

▶ Apply a primer to your repair job, and then paint. (Wallboard compound is quite porous, so it may take at least two coats of latex paint to give you the coverage you need.)

Note: *While your plaster is less likely to push out from a wall, it can happen. If it does, use this same routine to win the battle of the bulge.*

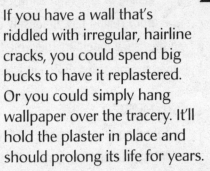

AN OUNCE OF
PREVENTION

It Looks Like a Road Map!

If you have a wall that's riddled with irregular, hairline cracks, you could spend big bucks to have it replastered. Or you could simply hang wallpaper over the tracery. It'll hold the plaster in place and should prolong its life for years.

Overhead-Tile Trade-Ins

Speaking of sagging ceilings, ceiling tile comes in two types. Suspended (a.k.a. drop) ceiling tiles fit loosely inside a metal grid. Attached tiles are flanged, so they slide together. They're either glued directly to the ceiling or stapled to wood furring strips. Both kinds are a cinch to replace. Here's the how-to routine:

SUSPENDED

- Standing on a sturdy stepladder, lift up the tile with both hands so that a gap appears at one end of the tile. Then tilt it to one side, and slip it through the opening in the grid.

- If the original tile was custom-made for your ceiling, use it as a template to mark and cut a new one with a straightedge and utility knife. On the other hand, if you've got standard-size tile, proceed directly to the next step.

- Flip the replacement tile on its side and slip it through the opening lengthwise. Then hold it on the level, and slide it into position. It'll drop right into its support tracks.

ATTACHED

- Using a straightedge and utility knife, cut a line 1 inch from each edge of the damaged tile to make a square. Pry it out with a putty knife, and scrape away any adhesive.

- Cut a square of the same size from the replacement tile (removing the flanges in the process).

- If the tile was glued in place, put a golf-ball-size blob of ceiling-tile adhesive about 2 inches from each edge, and press the new tile into position. It should bond almost instantly.

- For a furring-strip system, spread carpenter's glue on the strips and the corresponding areas of the new tile, and press the patch into place.

- With the glue securing the tile, drive two 1-inch nails through each corner and into the wood. Then sink the nails just below the surface with a nail set.

WOOD PANELING

Make Scrapes and Scratches Scram

Whether your wood-paneled walls are covered in the real deal or (as is usually the case today) hardboard topped with wood veneer, the mending process is the same. The difference comes in the degree of damage.

- ▶ **Light scratches.** For scratches that go no deeper than the finish, apply a coat of clear wax using a soft cotton cloth (material cut from an old T-shirt is perfect). Make sure you rub with the grain.

- ▶ **Deeper scratches.** Some damage reaches through to the wood or hardboard. If you have a box of crayons on hand, simply pull out the one that matches the color of your wall, and rub it on until the mark has vanished. No crayons? Then use a furniture marker or wax stick that's specially designed for the job.

- ▶ **Large scrapes.** Dip a fine-grit sanding sponge in mineral spirits, and sand the damaged area, making sure you go with the grain. Then wipe it clean with a soft cotton cloth dipped in mineral spirits. When it's dry, cover the spot with a matching-color wood stain, removing any excess with a soft, dry cotton cloth. Let the stain dry, and then apply a thin coat of spray lacquer.

5 Clever Cover-Ups

When a scrape goes only deep enough to remove the surface color from your paneling—or anything else that's made of wood—any of these household staples can save the day (at least temporarily):

- Coffee
- Iodine
- Shoe polish (either paste or liquid)
- Steak sauce
- Tea

Just choose the remedy that most closely matches the color of the wood, and dab it onto the surface using a cotton ball or swab. (If necessary, add water to your "stain" to lighten the color.)

Rein In Runaway Paneling

When your paneling and your wall begin to part company, here's how to force a reunion in a hurry:

STEP 1. Use pliers to pull out any loose nails.

STEP 2. Insert the flat end of a small pry bar under the loose edge of the panel, and gently pry it upward. Put a scrap of wood, wrapped in a piece of soft cloth, under the pry bar to increase your leverage and to protect the in-place paneling. Then slide your wood scrap into the pried-up area to keep it wedged open.

STEP 3. Shoot a generous bead of paneling adhesive onto the wall or the wooden (a.k.a. furring) strip behind the wayward panel. Keep it propped up until the adhesive gets tacky (10 minutes or so).

STEP 4. Remove the wedge, push the panel back in place, and hammer over the edge using a rubber mallet with a piece of cardboard under it to avoid marring the paneling.

STEP 5. Drive color-matched paneling nails along the glued edge at 5-inch intervals. Just don't use the old holes!

POWERFUL POTIONS

WOOD-PANELED WALL CLEANER

An occasional dusting will keep paneled walls looking great, but when they demand a more thorough cleaning, reach for this DIY formula. (Just multiply the recipe as necessary to suit the size of your room.)

> **1 cup of white vinegar**
> **¼ cup of lemon juice**
> **2 cups of water**

Mix the ingredients in a pail. Bunch up a handful of old panty hose, dip it into the solution, and wipe the paneling clean. For best results, work from the bottom of the wall upward to avoid messy runs, drips, or errors. **Note:** *The texture of panty hose provides the perfect abrasive, yet gentle, scrubbing action for this job.*

A Paneling Myth Debunked

True or false? If your so-called wood paneling is really only hardboard covered with wood-grained plastic or vinyl, you can't paint it because paint will not adhere to those materials.

Absolutely false! Despite what many do-it-yourself books tell you, you can paint over plastic or vinyl paneling. The secret to success lies in using a top-of-the-line maximum-adhesion primer. Most of the premium paint brands (including Kilz®, Sherwin-Williams®, and Zinsser®) make them, and they bond tightly to even the slickest surfaces, including plastic tile, plastic laminate, glass, fiberglass, and glazed brick. And there's no sanding necessary, either before or after you apply the primer. Just buy your supply from a reputable paint store, and tell the clerk exactly what you'll be painting and the conditions the surface "lives" in. Also ask for help in choosing the best type of paint to use over this miraculous undercoat.

Note: *This tip applies to any surface you intend to paint, indoors or outdoors.*

Believe it or not, the remnants of your favorite morning wake-up beverage can repair worrisome wounds in your wooden paneling or trim. Just mix coffee grounds or used tea leaves with spackling compound or (in a pinch) white glue until you get the color just right, and shove the mixture into the crack or hole. Smooth it over with a damp cloth, and you're good to go!

Paint Those Panels!

You say you've bought a house with wood-paneled walls that you don't like one little bit? Well, think twice before you tear the paneling out. There's no telling what's behind it, and you may be asking for a bigger—and more expensive—project than you can even imagine. Painting over the wood (or pseudo-wood) will give you a whole new look at a fraction of the cost, with no risk of unpleasant surprises.

If you're not sure what your paneling is made of, the first step is to sand a small, inconspicuous spot (say, an area that's normally hidden by furniture). Vinyl or plastic will flake; wood will not. Once you know the nature of the beast you're dealing with, ask your local paint store staff to recommend the appropriate no-sand primer and paint (see "A Paneling Myth Debunked," at left). Then plunge in, following these guidelines:

STEP 1. Wash the walls with a solution of warm water and a no-rinse detergent, such as trisodium phosphate (TSP).

STEP 2. Apply the primer (before you fill any imperfections) according to the directions on the label, and let it dry. If you choose to leave the grooves intact, prime them using a brush, then continue with a roller to cover the overall surface.

STEP 3. Fill the grooves and any holes or gouges with spackling compound. When it's dry, sand it, and wipe the dust away.

STEP 4. Proceed with one or two finish coats, as needed.

MOLDING & TRIM

2 Tricks to Making Trim Stay Put

When your wood molding parts company with the wall, you might think that you can simply pound the loose nails back in place and be done. Unfortunately, that approach rarely works because reused nails tend to ramble again. These timely tips will help you do the job right:

- Always use new nails, and drive them in beside their loosened counterparts. Then either pull out the old nails with pliers or use a nail set to sink them—it's your call.

- To avoid splitting the molding, predrill holes that are the same size as the nails you'll be driving in. After you've pounded the new nails into place, use a nail set to sink them slightly below the surface of the wood. Then fill the new and old holes with wood putty that matches your trim, and smooth it out.

Say "Nuts!" to Scratches

To remove scratches from dark woodwork, reach for some nuts. Brazil nuts, pecans, and black walnuts work best. Simply rub the nutmeat directly into the scratch, being careful to keep it away from surrounding areas (so as not to darken them). As you might imagine, this ploy also works on furniture, floors, or any other dark-toned wood surface.

Close the Gaps

Decorative molding that fails to come together at corners—whether it's on baseboards or door and window frames—doesn't pose structural problems, but it sure is unsightly, and it's not going to fix itself! Your fix-it game plan depends on where the opening is.

Baseboards. First, try to squeeze the two ends together by hand. If you can't make the edges meet, it means that the installer cut the pieces too short. So fill the opening with caulk or wood putty, and paint over it as necessary. If the gap does close under pressure, then drive a trim screw right through each section of the baseboard into the framing at the corner of the wall, following the procedure in "Nix the Nails—Maybe" (see page 14). Cover the screw heads with wood putty, and touch up the spots.

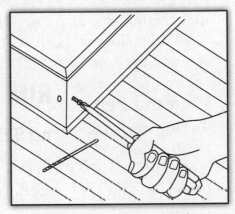

Driving screws into baseboards

Door or window frames. Buy a miter clamp at a home-improvement or hardware store, and then:

- Slide a piece of thin cardboard behind the trim to protect the wall, and set the miter clamp in place.

- Shoot a drop of wood glue into the gap, and tighten the clamp to bring the corners together.

- Drill a hole through the side and top of the frame so that a 1½-inch nail can go through one piece and into the other.

- Drive the nail into the hole, remove the clamp, and touch up the spot.

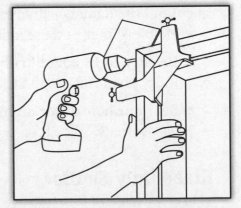

Drilling hole in door frame with miter clamp in place

Nix the Nails—Maybe

When it comes to attaching or reattaching molding, trim screws have a couple of major advantages over nails: They hold more securely—especially if the molding is warped—and they don't bend as you're screwing them into the wood, as thin nails are prone to do. The downside is that the heads are larger and more conspicuous. On the bright side, while the installation process takes a little longer, it's a snap to perform. Drill shallow depressions in the wood (a.k.a. countersinks) that are the same diameter as the screw heads and slightly deeper. Then drill pilot holes that are the same diameter as the screws' shanks, screw in the screws, and fill the indentations with wood putty.

Plug the Punctures

To plug small nail holes in trim—or anything else that's made of wood—dip a toothpick in white glue, and shove it into the opening. Slice it off flush with the surface using a utility knife or a single-edge razor blade. Sand the spot smooth, and touch it up with paint or stain.

WALLPAPER

A Duo of Dandy Ways to Cast Off Crayon Marks

When a budding Pablo Picasso or Georgia O'Keeffe uses your wallpaper as a coloring book, don't despair—and don't think you have to cut out the damaged areas and repaper them. As long as the paper is washable, either of these spic-and-span solutions will work.

- ▶ **Brush a light coat of rubber cement** onto the crayon marks, let it dry, then roll it—and the colorful wax—off with your fingertips.

- ▶ **Set your hair dryer on high,** and hold it on the marks until the wax softens. Wipe it off using Murphy® Oil Soap on a damp cloth.

Erase Ugly Scuffs

When the back of a chair leaves a blemish on your wall, take it off with a white eraser. Either the soft rubber or the crumbly gum kind will remove most scuffs without hurting either wallpaper or paint. Whichever kind you use, just make sure it's white. An eraser that's pink (or any other color) may leave a new stain that's even tougher to remove.

Wallpaper Repair in 3 Simple Steps

Don't cry over torn, gouged, or permanently stained wallpaper. As long as you've saved some scraps from the original job, it's a piece of cake to patch up the damage. Here's the easy three-step process:

STEP 1. Grab one of your scrap pieces, and make sure the repeating pattern matches up. Then carefully tear (don't cut!) a replacement patch that's slightly larger than the area you need to cover.

STEP 2. Cut away any damaged paper that's sticking out from the wall, and sand the edges smooth if necessary.

STEP 3. Align the piece to match the pattern, and paste it onto the wall using (surprise!) wallpaper paste.

And why, you may ask, is it important to tear, rather than cut, your wall's "bandage"? Because torn edges are thinner than cut versions, so they'll smooth out more snugly against the wall—thereby blending in better with the existing paper.

Grease, Go Away!

To remove a grease mark from wallpaper, put a piece of brown paper over the spot, and hold a dry, warm (not hot) iron on it for a minute or so. Shift the paper so that a clean portion covers the stain, and press it again. Repeat the process until all of the grease has been absorbed into the paper.

Please Pass the Bread

Looking for a simple way to clean your nonwashable wallpaper? Check your bread box. Plain old white bread makes a first-class wallpaper cleaner. Just cut off the crusts to lessen the chance of scratching the paper, then wad up the slice in your hand and rub it over the dirty areas. They should come right off. (Of course, this trick works just as well on wallpaper that you *can* wash, so use it for those times when you simply don't care to fuss with sprays or buckets of water.)

PAINTED SURFACES

Issue a Correction

If you think that typewriter correction fluid went extinct years ago, think again. Not only is it still "alive" and kicking, but it's one of the most useful items you can have in your honey-do tool kit—that is, if you have any white-painted walls, ceilings, trim, or furniture in your home. Whenever you see a small stain or spot, simply dab it with fluid and say, "Bye-bye, blemish!" When you're touching up glossy surfaces, let the cover-up dry, and then give it a coat of clear nail polish.

Lock In Lead Paint

Lead paint can be dangerous, but you don't necessarily need to remove it. If your house was built before 1978 (when lead-based paint became illegal), simply scrape off a chip of paint, and mail it to a testing lab. If the test results come back positive, apply two coats of high-quality paint over the old stuff. As long as your new top coat remains intact, the lead will pose no danger to you or your family.

Note: *You'll find testing labs listed in the Yellow Pages and on the Internet.*

Don't Pinch Pennies

With paint, as with most things in life, you get what you pay for. In the long run, investing in top-of-the-line paint will save you big bucks—and a whole lot of hassle. For one thing, cheap paint generally requires at least twice as many coats to cover what's on the wall, thereby raising your cost big-time right from the get-go. Furthermore, poor-quality latex paint gets chalky as it ages, so you'll need to repaint sooner than you would if you'd forked up only a few more bucks for the really good stuff.

Kill the Stains

When your walls or ceilings are sporting water marks or other indelible stains, don't count on even premium paint to perform a solo act. Always coat any discolorations with a high-quality stain killer to keep them from seeping through to the surface. Check with your local paint store pros to find the best product for your particular wall material and the marks you need to cover.

When you need to paint hard-to-reach places, like the inside edges of a radiator or the back of a pipe, use an old—but hole-free—sock. First, put on a rubber glove (because the paint will seep through the fabric), and slip the sock over that. Then dip your hand into the paint, reach for the object of your painting spree, and slide that slender "brush" right along until the surface is covered to your satisfaction.

3 Paint-Project Foil Feats

Whether you're setting out to paint a whole room or just embarking on a round of touch-up jobs, make sure you've got plenty of aluminum foil on hand. Here's a trio of ways it can make the project a whole lot easier—and neater.

- ▶ Before you start to paint, mold foil around any hardware that you don't want to cover, such as doorknobs, drawer pulls, and coat hooks.

- ▶ To keep a crust from forming on leftover paint, try this trick: Set the paint can on a sheet of aluminum foil, and trace around the bottom of the can. Then cut out the disk, lay it on the paint surface, and close up the can.

- ▶ Instead of cleaning your brushes when you call it a day, wrap them (still wet) in aluminum foil and stash them in the freezer. When you're ready to paint again, defrost the brushes for an hour or so, and they'll be good to go.

AN OUNCE OF
PREVENTION

Paint Storage 101

If you want your leftover paint to be in good shape at touch-up time, do yourself a favor, and transfer it from the opened cans to smaller lidded containers as soon as possible. Fill them all the way up, so that as little paint-destroying air as possible can get to the contents. Clear plastic milk jugs or glass canning jars are ideal because they let you see at a glance what colors you've got. Attach a label showing the date and the paint formulation (in case you have to buy more), as well as the room or rooms you used it in.

Then store your jugs or jars—as well as any unopened cans of paint—in a dry, cool (but not freezing!) place that's off the ground or a concrete floor. Full, unopened cans of latex will remain usable for up to 10 years. Oil-based and alkyd versions can easily last as long as 15 years. Paint from previously opened cans is best used within two years.

Stop the Drops

Do you need to brush-paint some overhead woodwork or part of a ceiling? Here's a way to catch the inevitable drips: Slice a hollow rubber ball in half, cut a slit in one of the halves, and slide it over your brush handle, hollow side up. Got no ball on hand? Then use a plastic lid from a coffee can or similar container. Whichever you use, you'll finish the job with paint-free hair and arms!

A Quick Nick Trick

Whenever you finish a paint job, pour some of the leftover paint into a small glass bottle with a tight cap. Use a rubber band to fasten an inexpensive craft brush to the bottle, and store it following the instructions in "Paint Storage 101" (at left). Then, when any painted surface needs a minor touch-up, reach for the bottle, and deliver fast first aid.

Chase Away Chips

Let's face it: No matter how careful you are, the paint on woodwork and wood floors gets chipped from time to time. When that happens, jump into action this way:

- Dust or vacuum the surface to remove any dust or soil. Then wipe the wood with a sponge dampened with a solution made from a few drops of dishwashing liquid mixed in 2 cups of water.

POWERFUL POTIONS

POWERFUL PAINTED WALL & FLOOR CLEANER

This formula works every bit as well as any store-bought cleaner—and a lot better than many—at a fraction of the cost!

1 cup of borax
2 tbsp. of dishwashing liquid
1 gal. of warm water

Mix the ingredients in a bucket. Gently rub the solution onto the wall, using a natural sponge. Start from the bottom and work upward, tackling one section at a time and slightly overlapping the just-cleaned areas. Rinse with clear water, and dry with an all-cotton towel.

Although most modern paints can be washed with no problem, don't take chances: Test this on a small, out-of-the-way spot before you tackle a larger area.

- Lightly sand the chipped area, gently feathering the edges so that it blends into its surroundings.

- Apply wood putty to deeper dings, smooth it off so that the filler is flush with the surface, and wipe off any excess with a damp cloth. When the filler has dried, sand it smooth and wipe away any dust.

- Brush a thin coat of primer over the spot. When it's dry, cover it with matching paint, using long, even strokes so it blends into the rest of the surface. Let the paint dry; top it with a second coat.

WOOD FLOORS

Restore the Shine

If your wood floor has lost its luster, don't assume that you need to refinish it—at least not before you try this simple shine perker-upper: In a handheld spray bottle, thoroughly mix equal parts of vegetable oil and white vinegar. Then spray the formula onto the floor in a thin mist, and rub it in well using either soft, clean cotton cloths or a wax applicator that you can get from the hardware store. Remove the excess with clean cotton cloths, and buff with fresh ones to restore that old, familiar glorious glow.

A Fast Fix for Worn Spots and Scratches

There's no getting around it: No matter how well you care for the surfaces in your home, over time they pick up signs of wear and tear. When scuffs, dings, and other marks appear in your wood floor, they're a snap to conceal. Just dip very fine steel wool in floor wax, and rub in the direction of the wood grain until the colors blend in.

Knot a Problem!

Got a knot that's come loose in your wood floor? Don't replace the floorboard—just shove the knot back into place and secure it with high-quality carpenter's glue. It should hang in there for the long haul.

Hide Holes in Plain Sight

Wood putty is the go-to choice for filling small floor holes. The trouble is that no matter how carefully you apply the stuff, the patch will never be invisible. But you can make it look like a natural part of the floor. How? Just use putty that's slightly darker than the surrounding wood. It'll look like a tiny knot rather than a poorly matched mending job.

Scratch Me Not!

You can buy commercial furniture sliders that enable you to safely move heavy furniture across a floor (Moving Men™ and EZ Sliders™ are two popular brands). But you can also reach for a couple of thick, clean towels (dirty ones could scratch the floor). Fold them over, and shove one under each end. Then slide that baby right along. Use four towels, one under each leg, if a single one won't span the distance on each side.

A Cleaning Crew in a Box!

One of the most helpful home-upkeep aids you'll ever find comes in a bright orange box. It's none other than baking soda! It's been helping folks keep their houses clean and trouble-free for more than two centuries. Here are four common troubles that the strong arm can help you solve:

Painted wood surfaces (including floors). Make a solution of 1 teaspoon of baking soda per gallon of hot water. Apply it with either a mop or a sponge, then wipe the surface dry with a soft cloth. (To dry a wooden floor, wrap the cloth around the business end of a dust mop.)

Scuffed floors. To remove black shoe-scuff marks from a bare floor, rub them with a paste made from 3 parts baking soda to 1 part water.

Dirty wallpaper. Wipe it with a sponge or soft cotton cloth dampened with a solution of 2 tablespoons of baking soda per quart of water. To remove grease stains, mix 1 tablespoon of baking soda with 1 teaspoon of water to make a paste. Rub it onto the spot, wait 5 to 10 minutes, then wipe it off with a damp sponge.

Grout between ceramic tiles. Wet down the  grout with a cloth or sponge, then dip a toothbrush in baking soda, and scrub the dirt away.

Silence the Squeaks

Squeaking floorboards rarely pose any threat to life and limb, but they can drive you up a wall. Before you call a contractor to shore up the floor—or a doctor to prescribe tranquilizers—try one of these silencers:

▶ Douse the offending area with talcum powder, cornmeal, cornstarch, or baby powder, and work it into the cracks. In the case of a squeaking stair, sprinkle a bit of powder into the seam at the back, between the tread and the riser.

▶ Pour liquid floor wax between the floorboards—but only if your floor has a waxed finish. Do not use wax on a varnished floor!

VINYL, LINOLEUM & CORK FLOORS

Blister, Begone!

An air-filled bump that suddenly springs up on vinyl or linoleum tile can make your whole floor wear unevenly—and therefore wear out before its time. So fix it now. Here's how:

STEP 1. Cover the bubble with an old T-shirt, and hold a warm iron on the spot until the vinyl is soft and pliable. (Increase the heat gradually if necessary, but be careful not to burn the tile.)

STEP 2. Slit the blister and about ½ inch of the tile on either side with a utility knife fitted with a brand-new blade.

STEP 3. Pull up each edge of the slit (gently!), and force a water-based flooring adhesive under the bubble with a nozzle or a putty knife. Wipe off any seepage with a damp sponge.

STEP 4. Cover the area with wax paper, and weigh it down with a stack of books or a heavy object for 24 hours.

STEP 5. Apply liquid seam sealer (available in hardware and home-improvement stores) to the cut to make it all but invisible.

Gouge Removal Made Easy

Got a ding in your vinyl floor? Just grab a tile scrap that's the same color as the damaged section, then make a batch of powder by sanding an edge of the tile's surface, either by hand or using a Dremel® tool. Mix the powder with enough clear nail polish to make a very thick paste. Surround the hole with masking tape to protect the undamaged floor, and spread the paste across the wound with a putty knife or plastic scraper. When the patch has dried completely, sand it with ultra-fine sandpaper until it blends in with the original tile once you remove the masking tape.

Flatten Curly Tiles

When a linoleum or vinyl floor tile curls up at one or more corners, cover the trouble spot(s) with a cotton hand towel or doubled-over dish towel. Then set a steam iron on low and move it back and forth over the covering to soften the adhesive underneath. Carefully pull up the loosened area(s), apply fresh adhesive, and press the tile back into place. Wipe away any seepage. Then cover the tile with wax paper, and weigh it down with whatever heavy objects you have on hand until the adhesive has dried and is firmly set.

LINOLEUM: The Quicker Fixer Upper

If your linoleum floor tile gets a "boo-boo," you're in luck: While most vinyl-tile patterns are merely printed on the surface, the true colors of linoleum go all the way through. So if your floor gets scratched, a light sanding will send the mark packing. To mend a deeper gouge, (say, one from a dropped knife), just scrape some shavings from a leftover piece, mix them with wood glue, and work the paste into the crack. Bingo—end of blemish!

Replacing Damaged Floor Tile

When a vinyl or linoleum tile is damaged beyond repair, follow this six-step removal and replacement process:

STEP 1. Warm and soften the tile by moving a steam iron in circles back and forth over a cotton towel that you've spread on top of the damaged area.

STEP 2. Use a broad putty knife to pry out the damaged tile, being very careful not to touch or damage any of the adjacent ones.

STEP 3. Scrape off the old adhesive, and remove any remaining dust from the floor with a vacuum cleaner.

STEP 4. Check the fit of the replacement tile. If clearance is tight, trim the tile with a utility knife and straightedge, or lightly sand the edges with a sanding block.

STEP 5. Spread a light coat of adhesive on the floor, set the new tile in place, and wipe away any residue.

STEP 6. Weigh the newly installed tile down with books or another heavy object until the adhesive has dried.

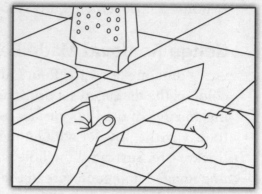

Warm and pry out the damaged tile.

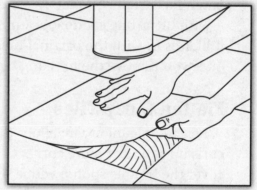

Apply adhesive to the floor, and put the new tile in place.

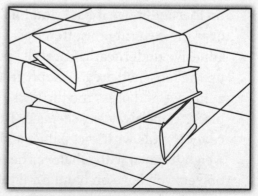

Weigh the tile down with books or other heavy objects until the adhesive has dried.

"No Wax" Means "*Don't Wax!*"

You may think that a "no-wax" label on vinyl tile simply means that you don't *have* to wax it in order to retain the shine. Think again, my friend: That shine comes from a clear coat of polyurethane, and wax simply will not adhere to it. If you decide to boost your floor's glow by waxing it, you'll wind up with a royal mess that you'll have to strip off. So forget that idea. Instead, whenever your no-wax floor starts to look dull, follow this routine:

- Clean the floor with a cleaner that's made for no-wax vinyl.
- Follow up with a sealant that's also made for no-wax vinyl (the package directions will tell you how many coats you need to apply).

Routine mopping should keep the floor shiny bright for a year or longer.

De-Wax Your Do-Wax Vinyl

You say you've got an older vinyl floor that does require waxing—but the wax has built up way too much? No worries! Just open the windows to ventilate the room, scrub the floor with a solution of 3 parts water to 1 part rubbing alcohol, then rinse thoroughly.

AN OUNCE OF
PREVENTION

4 Ways to Curtail Floor-Tile Casualties

The soft texture that makes linoleum and vinyl easy on your feet also makes these materials prone to damage from kitchen furniture and appliances. Here's a quartet of ways to guard your hardworking floors:

Install protective mats under your oven, fridge, and dishwasher.

Outfit the feet of heavy stationary furniture, like hutches and large tables, with individual floor protectors.

Attach felt pads to the feet of chairs so they slide safely over the floor.

Use floor glides to move large appliances. They're made to let you push your hefty helpers smoothly—and safely—from one spot to another.

Note: *You can find all of these dandy devices in hardware and home-improvement stores and (of course) on the Internet.*

Cork made its floor-covering debut in 1889, but it's been making folks' lives easier in one form or another since 2500 BC. The earliest cork products included fishing floats, bottle stoppers, and shoe soles. Fast forward to the 21st century, when, in addition to still performing in those conventional roles, cork is used to form anti-vibration joints in NASA's space shuttle boosters.

Here's another corker of a fact for you: The source of cork, an oak by the botanical name of *Quercus suber*, is the only tree that can actually regenerate itself after each harvest. In fact, the outer bark must be stripped off periodically in order for the tree to thrive. Workers use a specially designed hatchet to do the job. Nine years later, they can come back for more. The process is repeated every 9 or 10 years for a full century and a half before the tree must finally be replaced by a new one.

More than half of the world's cork supply comes from Portugal, but the trees are also grown in six other Mediterranean countries: Algeria, France, Italy, Morocco, Spain, and Tunisia.

Conquer Cork Catastrophes

Cork is one of the most durable floor coverings you could ever hope to find, but even it can suffer scrapes and gouges. When that happens, go to your local hardware store, and buy a wood filler that's the right color. Then fill in the dents and dings. Once the stuffing has dried completely, use fine-grit sandpaper to smooth it out so that it's level with the floor's surface. Then apply a matching stain using a soft cotton cloth.

Note: *Before applying a filler, test it on a hidden spot to make sure the color is right. If it isn't, either replace the filler with one that's the shade you need, or mix it with one of the DIY color helpers in "5 Clever Cover-Ups" (see page 9).*

Keep the Classics Clean

A classic floor covering like cork deserves an equally classic cleaning routine: Once a month, mop the floor with a solution made from ½ cup of apple cider vinegar per gallon of warm water to cut through grease and dirt and leave the air smelling sweet. P.S. This works as well on rubber, wood, and ceramic-tile floors as it does on the other classics.

CERAMIC TILE

Got a Chip Off the Old Tile?

If so, just cover the spot with a marker or paint that matches the color of the tile, and then cover it with clear nail polish. If the ding is too deep to conceal that way, fill it with epoxy and let it dry before you go to work with your marker or paintbrush.

When "Close Enough" Won't Do

If you're replacing tiles in an out-of-the-way spot, like under a sink or behind a door, a not-quite-perfect match might work just fine. But in a more visible area, the new tile will stick out like a sore thumb. So what should you do if you can't find quite the right shade? It's simple: Pick out a contrasting accent color, and replace a number of tiles throughout the room, creating a varied color scheme.

Timely Tricks for Grout Replacement

Crumbling or cracked grout can lead to as much trouble as broken tiles. So it's important to correct any damage ASAP. Here's all you need to do:

- ▶ Remove the damaged grout with a grout saw, vacuum up the debris, and clean the surrounding area (see "Easy Does It," below).

- ▶ Apply the grout according to steps 5 and 6 in "Go for Broke" on page 28.

- ▶ Apply caulk as necessary if the tile adjoins a bathtub or sink.

Easy Does It

By and large, glazed ceramic tile is what my Grandma Putt called an "easy keeper." But if you want it to last and keep its good looks for the long haul, you need to treat it gently at cleaning time. In particular, never clean ceramic-tile floors or walls with abrasive scouring pads or powders because they will dull the finish. Instead, use either a commercial tub and tile cleaner or (Grandma's cleaner of choice) ¼ cup of white vinegar mixed in a bucket of warm water.

Go for Broke

A single cracked or broken ceramic tile can make a visual mess, and it can also let damaging moisture seep through to the underlying wall. With very little effort, you can make that marred surface look as good as new. Here's your six-step game plan:

STEP 1. Remove the grout around the damaged tile using a grout saw or cordless tile saw. If the tile is adjacent to a bathtub or sink, remove the caulking with a screwdriver or chisel.

STEP 2. Wearing sturdy work gloves and safety glasses, use a hammer and cold chisel to break the tile and remove the pieces.

STEP 3. Scrape off the old adhesive with your chisel or putty knife.

STEP 4. Spread mortar onto the back of the replacement tile,* press it firmly into place, and let it dry overnight.

STEP 5. Force the grout into the joints with a float, holding the tool at an angle and drawing it across the tile diagonally. Immediately wipe away any excess grout with a damp sponge. When a haze appears on the grout, rub it off with a soft, clean cloth. Wait 24 hours before touching the tile. If necessary, apply caulking.

STEP 6. Two to three weeks later, apply a grout sealer. (The waiting time varies, so follow the directions on the package.)

If you don't have any tile left over from the original installation, take one of your broken pieces to a tile store, and find the closest match that you can.

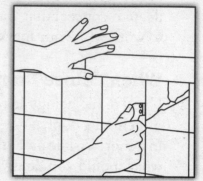
Remove the grout surrounding the damaged tile.

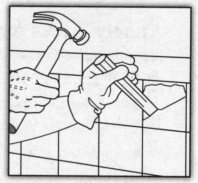
Carefully break and chisel out the tile.

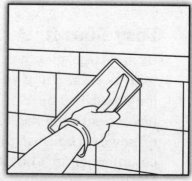
Apply grout using a float.

Great Grout Maneuvers

Wiping down your tile on a regular basis should keep the grout clean, too. But the secret to an attractive floor is clean grout. So for those times when your grungy grout needs a little extra attention, use a commercial grout cleaner or—for even tougher dirt—scrub it away with a mixture of ½ cup of household bleach per half gallon of water. (A retired toothbrush makes a dandy tool for this job.) Let it sit for 10 to 20 minutes, then rinse thoroughly with clear water, and dry with a soft, clean cloth. Once the grout has dried thoroughly, follow up with a silicone sealer, keeping these two guidelines in mind:

- If your tile is the glazed variety, be careful to keep the sealer only on the grout because it can stain the tile.

- On the other hand, if you have porous tile, such as slate, stone, or unglazed terra-cotta, seal it right along with the grout by applying a combination tile and grout sealer.

It Sure Doesn't *Look* Like a Car!

After you clean ceramic wall tiles, let them dry thoroughly, and then give them a good going-over with liquid car wax. They'll shine like the sun, and soap scum, cooking splatters, and other gunk will have a hard time taking hold, making your cleaning job a whole lot easier next time.

Note: *Don't try this slick trick on ceramic floor tiles, or you could wind up falling flat on your fanny!*

AN OUNCE OF PREVENTION

Cushion the Blows

Weighty objects that fall onto ceramic tile are all but guaranteed to crack or chip the fragile material. Your simple protection plan: Put area rugs or cushioned mats in front of any cupboards that hold canned goods, small appliances, cooking pots, or other stuff too heavy for your tiles to handle.

CARPETING

2 Crafty Cures for Carpet Burns

When your carpet has a run-in with a hot assailant like a cigarette, a burning candle, or a toppled steam iron, deliver damage control in one of these two ways:

▶ Pull off as much of the blackened residue as you can with your fingers. If the fibers are sizzled or melted, snip off the worst of the damage with a pair of manicure scissors—but don't take off too much, or you'll end up with a bald spot in your rug. Then use your fingers to comb the neighboring fibers over the spot.

▶ Rub the mark away with fine sandpaper or steel wool. Work with a light, circular motion, and keep at it until the spot disappears.

POWERFUL POTIONS

CARPET SCORCH LIFTER

Light scorch marks on carpet will come right out when you treat them with this fantastic formula.

1 cup of white vinegar
¼ cup of unscented talcum powder
2 onions, coarsely chopped

Mix the ingredients together in a pot, and bring the mixture to a boil, stirring constantly. Let it cool to room temperature, then spread it on the stain with a sponge. When the spot is dry, brush or vacuum away the residue. Your carpet should look as good as new!

Color Stains Gone

You say you've tried everything in the book, but the stain in your carpet refuses to budge? Or maybe it's a bleach spot that stands out like a sore thumb. Before you do a cut and patch-up job, try this trick: Find a crayon that matches the color of your floor covering, and hunker down on your knees to color over the spot. Then lay a piece of wax paper over it, and iron it on low heat. If the shade isn't quite dark enough, repeat the process as needed.

Fluff Up Carpet Dents

Rearranging the furniture can freshen up a room's appearance, no question. The only drawback is the deep impressions that remain where the heavy pieces used to stand. Don't let the dents drag you down. Just use one of these two methods to get those sinkholes on the level again. You can choose from hot or cold.

- **The hot method.** First, comb the sunken area to loosen the carpet fibers. Then soften them by holding a hot, steaming iron over the area for a few seconds. (Don't let the iron touch the rug because the heat could burn natural fibers or melt synthetic ones!)

- **The cold method.** Put an ice cube on the spot, and let the ice melt.

Whichever tactic you've used, finish by brushing the spot with a stiff, clean brush until the carpet strands are on the up-and-up again.

Repair a Torn Carpet

The vast majority of carpet tears occur along a seam, where sections have been sewn or glued together. Most often, the damage is caused by furniture or other heavy objects being dragged across the floor. To close the gap, first thread heavy nylon fishing line through a large, curved upholstery needle. Push it through the carpet about ½ inch from the edges of the tear, spacing your stitches roughly ½ inch apart. Keep your stitches parallel to the wound on top and diagonal on the underside.

Note: *If the seam was glued rather than sewn, it might be hard to force the needle through the old glue tape. So use needle-nose pliers to provide the essential push power.*

Out of the Cookie Jar...

And into the carpet. Thanks to a dandy carpet-repair kit that looks—and works—much like a cookie cutter, it's a snap to replace a small section of carpet that's so badly stained or burned that you can't fix the damage. The tool, which you can buy online and in home-improvement stores, features a sharp cutting blade that rotates on a center pivot, along with a supply of double-faced tape. All you do is cut out the damaged area, then cut a patch from a piece of matching carpet. Stick some tape on the bare spot, and press the patch into place. If you don't have any scraps handy, cut your repair "cookie" from a hidden area, like the inside of a closet.

Tuck in New Carpet Tile

One of the reasons that so many home (and business) owners choose carpet tile over the broadloom version is that damaged tiles are easy to replace. Shove the edge of a metal scraper or putty knife under one corner to loosen it. Grab it with pliers or gloved hands, and pull the tile off the floor. Scrape away any adhesive residue, and check to make sure the replacement tile fits the space. Trim it a tad if necessary, then remove the backing, and press the new carpet chunk into place.

INTERIOR DOORS

Put the Hush on Hinges

Got a squeaky door hinge that's driving you nuts? The secret to peace and quiet is waiting in your kitchen or bathroom. Just leap into action with one of these nifty noise reducers:

- **Hair conditioner.** Add a drop or two to the moving parts using a medicine (a.k.a. eye) dropper.

- **Nonstick cooking spray.** Take aim at the hinge, and push the button on the can—but make sure you have paper towels on hand to wipe up the drips.

- **Petroleum jelly.** Rub a fingertipful of the stuff into the hinge, and open and close the door a few times to work the jelly in.

- **Vegetable oil.** Apply it to the scene of the commotion using the same technique recommended for hair conditioner.

It Just Won't Stop!

If you've tried lubricating the hinges, and your door still sounds like a baby bird squawking for its supper, the most likely culprit is dirt or rust on one or more hinge pins. Go at it with this four-step process:

STEP 1. Prop the door closed with a heavy object, like a toolbox, a laundry basket of clothes, or a few heavy books.

STEP 2. Tap out the hinge pin with a chisel and rubber mallet.

STEP 3. Scrub the pin with fine-grade steel wool; wipe off any residue.

STEP 4. Rub or spray some lubricating oil onto the pin, and then tap it back into place.

While you're at it, repeat the procedure with the remaining hinge pins even if they're not squeaking. It's all but guaranteed that they're harboring as much debris as the first one, and they'll probably let you know it sooner rather than later!

More Help for Misbehaving Hinges

Not all hinge problems announce themselves vocally. This duo is not so loud—but still as annoying as all get-out:

- **Sticking hinges.** Either rub the lead part of a pencil along the spine, or dampen a soft cloth with light oil, and wipe it over the hinge. Then push the door back and forth until it moves freely.

- **Loose hinges.** Replace the screws with ones of the same diameter, but about an inch longer, so that they'll penetrate farther into the door frame.

Loose Hinges, Take 2

If you have no replacement screws on hand and you're in a hurry to tighten up your door, go with this alternative method: Remove the screws, then round up several wooden toothpicks or matchsticks. Dip them in wood glue, and shove them into the hole so that they fill it completely. When the glue has dried, slice off your fillers, and sand the area so it's level with the surface. Then drive the screws into place through the hinge plate, and you'll be back in business.

Fit to Be Tied

Got a door that slams shut with a bang every time a gust of wind blows through an open window? If so, this tip will ease your frazzled nerves: Tie a length of twine to one doorknob, run it around the door edge, and attach it to the other knob. The door will still close, but the friction provided by the string will cushion the blow. If you want your traveling door to remain open, simply use thicker cord.

Painting or cleaning the bottom edge of a door is all but impossible without removing it from its hinges—that is, unless you have some carpet scraps handy. Cut a piece to a size that's comfortable to hold in both hands, and top the pile side with paint or your cleaner of choice. Slide the "brush" back and forth under the open door until the area is covered with paint or free of dirt.

Holy Moly—Save That Door!

Heaven knows it's easy to put a hole in a hollow-core door. But, contrary to what you may think, it's also pretty darn easy to repair the damage—so don't even think of sending the victim off with the trash! Instead, remove the splintered wood around the hole, and then pack it tightly with steel wool or a wad of aluminum foil. Then work wood putty into the opening, making sure that all gaps in the stuffing are filled. Use a putty knife to smooth out the surface, wait until it's dry, and sand it. Then prime and paint either your patch-up job or the whole door.

BASEMENT

Get the Damp Demons Outta Dodge

It's no secret that moisture is the most common of basement bugaboos, often stemming from conditions outside your house. But a number of interior factors could be contributing to your wetness woes. Here's a handful of simple measures you can take to help resolve the problem:

▶ **Dry the air.** Install a dehumidifier, and run a plastic tube from the unit to a drain so that the collected water will run right away.

▶ **Stop the water flow.** Fix any leaky faucets or plumbing connections, and insulate sweating pipes with foam tape or pre-slit sleeves.

▶ **Evict man-made moisture.** Vent clothes dryers to the outside. And make sure the laundry room, bathroom, and any hobby or workshop areas that use water are vented to the great outdoors, too.

▶ **Improve ventilation.** Use fans year-round. Then open windows during cool, dry weather and close them in hot, humid conditions.

Waterproof Your Basement...

Maybe. A white powdery substance on your basement walls or floor is a sign that water is seeping through the concrete—or has seeped through in the past and left soluble salts behind. To find out whether the seepage is active, remove the white stuff using a stiff nylon-bristled brush. If the powder returns, buy an epoxy or latex waterproofing mixture that's specially made for treating concrete walls and floors, and apply it following the manufacturer's instructions on the label. Make sure you give the surface two coats— a single coat will not correct the problem under normal conditions.

De-Dampen the Floor

And spruce it up at the same time. How? With an acid-free penetrating stain that waterproofs, strengthens, and colors concrete—indoors or out. Depending on the brand, you can choose from dozens of colors, some of which give you full, blemish-hiding coverage and others that provide a more natural-looking translucent finish. There are several brands. Some, like LastiSeal®, are available online. Others, including Sherwin-Williams H&C®, can be picked up at your friendly neighborhood paint store.

Water, Water—Everywhere!

Even the driest of basements can suddenly turn into a soaking-wet mess. All it takes is a burst pipe, a clogged drain that overflows, or a window that breaks during a rainy downpour. So buy a water alarm. These dandy (and inexpensive) devices send out a loud signal when they detect even the smallest amount of moisture, and you can rush into action before any serious damage is done.

CALL A PRO

If you've taken all of the measures described here and your cellar is still wet, call an experienced contractor. It's all but guaranteed that you have serious drainage problems, either inside, outside—or both. Trying more DIY solutions probably won't solve your problem—and they could wind up costing you more time, effort, and money that you'll have to shell out for expert help.

Winning the War on Mold and Mildew

These foul fungi can cause major damage to just about every surface in your home. The sinister spores can also wreak havoc on your health—and cause serious trouble before you have a clue that anything has gone awry. Your best battle plan for demolishing the demons depends on where they are:

Basement floors. Sprinkle them with chlorinated lime (a.k.a. bleaching powder), which you can find in your supermarket's laundry section. Let it sit for 24 hours, then sweep it up with a broom. Put the stuff in a plastic bag, close it tightly, and dispose of it outdoors. If the musty odor persists, it means that the spores are still alive and kicking, so the floor should be covered with a concrete sealer.

Nonporous surfaces. In the case of ceramic tile, painted walls, varnished floors, pipes, and bathroom fixtures, use a solution made from ¾ cup of household bleach per gallon of water. Open up as many windows as possible throughout your house, and (especially in the bathroom) keep the fan running. Clean shower and tub drains with the formula in "Cut the Clog" (see page 75).

Basement walls. Mix 2 ounces of household bleach per quart of water in a handheld spray bottle, and spritz the surface. Then scrub the walls with a sturdy nylon-bristled brush. Whatever you do, don't use a metallic brush because the metal fibers will get trapped in the concrete and rust—leaving you with another messy problem!

Porous materials. Immediately remove, discard, and replace porous materials such as carpets or wallboard.

Grout between ceramic tiles. Soak three or four paper towels in white vinegar, and lay them over the grout. Press the towels firmly to ensure full contact. Splash the paper with more vinegar occasionally to keep it saturated. After eight hours, remove the towels, and use an old toothbrush to scrub away any remaining crud. Then rinse with cool, clear water.

Your Electrical System

Does the thought of trying to fix an electrical problem strike terror in your heart? You're not alone. Lots of folks are convinced that anything involving electricity is so complicated that it takes a pro to handle it. Well, I'm here to tell you it just ain't so. Yes, there are complex and dangerous tasks that demand the services of a licensed electrician. But there are also plenty of things you can safely and easily tackle yourself—with help from the electrifying tips and tricks in this chapter.

WIRING, FUSES & CIRCUIT BREAKERS

Electricity 101

People have known about electricity since the days of ancient Greece. In fact, the word comes from *electron*, the Greek word for the mineral amber, which, when rubbed, makes static electricity. Fast forward to 1752, when Ben Franklin began his famous experiments that led to work by Alessandro Volta, Georg Ohm, and (of course) Thomas Edison, who fully harnessed this amazing natural force. Fortunately, you don't have to be a scientific mastermind to understand the general concepts that keep your superpowered domicile humming along. Here's the gist of it:

▶ **The basic principle.** Electricity is simply the flow of subatomic particles called electrons through a conductor—a material that has low resistance to electrical flow. Copper ranks among the most efficient conductors, which is why it is so widely used in home wiring. Conversely, rubber and plastic are highly resistant to electric current, which is why they make such efficient insulators.

▶ **An electric circuit** is a continuous stream from a power source (like your local power station) through a utility transformer, to your electric service panel, and into a power-using device (like a lightbulb), and then back to the source. A switch between the panel and the appliance acts as a gatekeeper. When the switch is closed, the power is turned on (yes, I know that sounds odd), and the multitude of electrons in the hot wire flow toward a lower supply in the neutral wire. The resulting current makes a lamp light or a TV set turn on. When the switch is open, the current flow stops, and the power goes off.

▶ **Electricity enters your home** through your main service panel. There, it is divided into individual circuits that supply power to the various areas of your house. The circuits are protected by either circuit breakers or fuses.

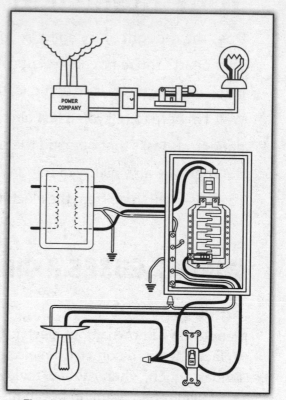

Electric current flows from a power source through a transformer to your service panel and a switch to a power-using device, like a lamp.

How to Read Your Electric Bill

When your electric bill arrives each month, you'll see several line items, including delivery and distribution charges, generation and delivery riders, and taxes. But the key item—and the one that is within your control to the greatest extent—is the one listed as kWh. Those letters stand for kilowatt-hours, and the corresponding number represents the total wattage of all the electrified gear that you used during the billing period and the length of time you used it. For example, if you used a total of 1,000 watts for one hour, you've racked up 1,000 watt-hours, or 1 kilowatt-hour.

Write All About It

The first step in fixing any problems in your home's electrical system comes when you first move in. That is, you must check the electric service panel to see whether the inside of the door has a list telling you which fuse or circuit breaker controls the power to which part of your house. If all you see is a list of numbers that coincide with the ones on the breakers or fuse outlets, then have a friend help you fill in the blanks. No pal on hand? No problem. Plug in a radio or a vacuum cleaner and turn it on. Then, one by one, trip circuit breakers or pull out fuses until the sound goes off. On the appropriate line, write the location in your home that's covered by the fuse or breaker.

Note: *While each circuit normally covers more than one outlet or hardwired fixture, large appliances often have one or more designated circuits. If you're performing a solo act, you may have to turn them on, then trek up from the basement to the kitchen or laundry room to see whether they've turned off.*

Coming to Terms with Electricity

Are you baffled by the terms used to measure electricity? This simple glossary will clear up any confusion.

Amperes (a.k.a. amps): The electrons' rate of flow

Ohms: Resistance to electrical flow

Volts: The amount of pressure that forces the electrons through a conductor

Watts: The amount of power delivered by those electrons

These properties are all interconnected, so if you know the figures for any two of them, you can determine the third using these formulas:

- Volts ÷ ohms = amps
- Volts x amps = watts
- Volts ÷ amps = ohms
- Watts ÷ amps = volts

Read All About It, Too

It seems crazy (at least to me) that the circuit numbers on electric panels are stamped into the metal in tiny type that's all but invisible to the naked eye. So do yourself a favor: Grab a permanent marker, and re-enter those crucial identifiers with digits that are big enough to spot at a glance *without* your reading glasses. Or, if you prefer, get some stick-on numbers that are as large as the available space permits, and slap those onto the panel in the appropriate places. If you find yourself in a situation where every second counts, those visual aids could save your house—and maybe even your life!

Give It Space

It's crucial that you and every adult and adolescent in your household can reach your electric panel and its innards quickly. So never stack storage boxes in front of it, even temporarily, and keep the space around the door clear so that the door can open freely. Also, check to see that everyone can reach all parts of the panel. If not, station a footstool or small ladder within grabbing range. If necessary—for example, if someone in your home is confined to a wheelchair—have an electrician move the box to an easily accessible location. (Your peace of mind will be well worth the cost!)

Take Its Temperature

Every once in a while, lightly touch the back of your hand to the circuit breaker switches and several other spots on your electric panel. If any area feels warmer than room temperature, you may have a wiring problem that's generating heat. If so, call an electrician to

CALL A PRO

Electricity can be—and frequently is—deadly. If there is even the tiniest doubt in your mind that you can safely and accurately make an electrical repair or conduct a test, then turn the job over to a licensed electrician. You'll rest easier knowing the job was handled by a pro.

investigate immediately. Don't try to play detective and remove the panel cover yourself! One simple slip of your hand could cause an explosion called an arc flash—with potentially disastrous results.

When Your Service Panel "Speaks Up"

Your fuse or circuit breaker panel is your home's first line of defense against an electrical fire. Fuses are designed to blow and circuit breakers to switch off when you have either an overloaded circuit or a short circuit. So don't pass off the darkness as just an inconvenience. Hop to it—check your service panel ASAP! Regardless of the cause, a circuit breaker will have moved to midway between the "on" and "off" settings. On the other hand, a blown fuse gives you a clue as to what caused the problem. If the glass window is clear, but the metal strip inside is broken, the circuit is overloaded. A discolored window generally signals a short circuit.

A Trip That Could Save Your Life

Once a year, you should make it a point to trip all of your circuit breakers. By turning them off and back on periodically, you'll prevent corrosion from setting in. Why is that so important? Because in the event of an emergency, a breaker that's corroded may not budge from its "on" position. I shouldn't have to tell you how disastrous that could be!

Circuit Overload!

An overloaded circuit simply means (surprise!) that you're using more watts than that particular section of wiring can handle. Your best plan of action depends on how the problem presents itself. If:

- **A new, power-hogging appliance** gets turned on, and the room suddenly goes dark, immediately unplug the monster or switch it off. Then, if possible, move it or several smaller devices to a less busy circuit to free up space for the big bruiser. If you absolutely must use all of this apparatus in the same area, call a licensed electrician, who can safely upgrade your circuitry.

ELECTRIC SHOCK

When you see someone being shocked, your natural instinct may be to grab him and pull him to safety. Don't! The current could flow through his body into yours. Instead, follow this four-step procedure:

1. Turn off the power at the disconnecting switch or circuit breaker. If you can't find it, pry or pull the victim away from the power source using an insulated object such as a dry wooden board, a length of non-metallic conduit, a rubber hose, or an electric cord.

2. Call 911!

3. Check for breathing and pulse. Perform CPR as necessary.

4. Continue checking vital signs, and keep the victim warm and comfortable until help arrives.

The danger of electric shock does not end after initial medical treatment. Shock victims remain at risk for heart trouble up to several hours after the event.

- **The power goes off for no apparent reason,** unplug all devices and turn off all lights in the area the circuit serves. Replace the blown fuse with a new one of equal amperage. Or flip the circuit breaker "off," then back on. Once you've restored power, check the circuit's load capacity by turning on each light and plugging in each appliance one at a time. If the first switch you turn on triggers another blackout, it means you have a serious problem, so call an electrician right away.

Make Short Work of a Short Circuit

A circuit shorts out when a worn hot wire touches another worn wire, the ground wire, or any grounded metal, triggering a dangerous surge in current. Here's your two-part fix-it plan:

- Check all cords and plugs for frayed or exposed wires.

- If you find any, leave the culprit unplugged, and replace the fuse or flip the circuit breaker back on. If Lady Luck is with you, you can simply repair or discard the "guilty party." But if the fuse blows again, call an electrician. The short is probably in your wiring system.

Bigger Is Not Better!

If you replace a blown fuse with one that handles more amps, you'll solve your overloaded circuit problem lickety-split, right? *Wrong!* The number on top of each fuse specifies the amperage that the wires it controls are designed to support. A new fuse that sports a higher digit will accept a bigger load—and the excess power will create heat that could set your house on fire. So, whenever you buy fuses, make sure that the amp value noted on the box matches that of your current supply!

Stop Trouble at the Starting Gate

Heavy power tools, as well as large appliances like clothes dryers and air conditioners, gobble up considerably more power when they start up than they consume once they're in full operating mode. While these initial loads are business as usual for circuit breakers, the sudden jolts often blow ordinary fuses. The simple solution: Pinpoint the problematic circuits, and replace your standard fuses with time-delayed versions, which are designed to handle start-up power surges without blowing.

Foil Four-Footed Feasters

No doubt you've noticed that when the evening news reports a house fire, very often it is officially designated as a conflagration "of unknown origin." Well, statistics suggest that a great many of those mystery blazes are actually started by rodents chewing on household

WELL, WHADDYA KNOW!

Today, most of us take electricity for granted—that is, until the power goes out for even a few hours, and our whole world turns upside down. In reality, though, this amazing energy source has been at our beck and call for only a little more than a century—since 1879, to be precise, when Thomas Edison invented the first practical electric lightbulb. A few years later, in 1882, he built the world's first electric power plant, the Pearl Street power station in New York City. It sent electricity to a whopping 85 buildings in the Big Apple. And the rest, as they say, is history!

ULTRA-SAFE MOUSE AND RAT BAIT

This rodent bait is fatal to mice and rats, but if a child or pet should swallow a mouthful of the stuff, the worst-case scenario would be a little belching.

1 cup of baking soda
1 cup of flour
1 cup of sugar

Mix the ingredients in a bowl. Put a table-spoon of the mixture into jar lids or similar containers, and set them where you've seen droppings or other signs of rodent visitations. The baking soda will mix with their stomach acids to create carbon dioxide. Because the critters can't burp, their tummies will swell up and squash their lungs.

wiring. That means that one of the most important steps you can take to safeguard your home—and your family's lives—is to control mice and rats. So stay on the lookout for the vile varmints, and at the first sign of their presence, bid them adieu with the Ultra-Safe Mouse and Rat Bait (at left). And, of course, keep the little hellions out by sealing up all the gaps in your home's walls and foundation. You'll find everything you need to know on that score in Chapter 6.

Words to the Wise about Extension Cords

Extension cords are handy things to have around the house, but if you don't use them properly, you could wind up with a heap of trouble. To avoid blown circuits—or even a fire—keep these guidelines in mind:

▶ **Watch the watts.** Most extension cords are labeled to show the maximum number of amperes and watts they can handle. If the capacity is not marked, assume that it is 9 amperes, which equals 110 watts, and nothing you plug in should exceed that.

▶ **Note the diameter.** An extension cord that is thinner than the cord of the device to which you attach it could overheat in a hurry.

▶ **Give them short-term jobs.** Extension cords are intended to be used on a temporary basis—not as permanent parts of your home-wiring scheme. When they stay in place for the long haul, it's all but guaranteed that they'll wind up holding too many plugs. The result could be a dangerous circuit overload.

Stay Off the Road to Overload

Thanks to a couple of handy helpers from the hardware store, it's easy—and cheap—to ramp up your plug-in capacity, right? *Wrong!* Steer clear of outlets that screw into light sockets, as well as those "octopus" plugs that convert a single outlet into six or even eight of them. Both of these "conveniences" can easily overheat and start a fire.

An Outlet Adapter Could Kill You

Outlet multipliers aren't the only instant electrical "upgrades" that can lead to tragedy. Those little adapters that let you insert a three-prong grounding plug into a two-prong receptacle can also be big disasters waiting to happen. So if your home has only two-prong outlets, replace at least some of them with receptacles that can safely handle grounded plugs. For step-by-step instructions, see "Replace Two-Prong Outlets with Three-Prong Versions" on page 52.

A collection of off-duty extension cords can quickly turn into a jumbled mess. So try this nifty trick: Fan-fold each cord, slide it into an empty toilet paper tube, and use a felt-tip marker to write the length and maximum amp load on the cardboard. Then tuck the tubes into a drawer in your workshop. When you need to extend your wiring's reach, you can grab the right helper in a flash.

BACKUP GENERATORS

Two of a Kind

More and more homeowners are acquiring generators so they can keep things functioning on an even keel during power outages—which seem to be occurring more frequently and lasting longer every year. If you're thinking of adding one of these safety nets to your household, you need to determine which type is best for you. These are your choices:

- **Portable generators** are meant to be stored indoors and hauled out to your yard on an as-needed basis, and they run on gasoline.

POWER LINE DOWN!

When you spot a downed power line, there is only one right way to respond: Get outta Dodge pronto, and call 911 or your local electric provider! Don't even think of going anywhere near the line because it's all but guaranteed to be fully energized. To put that danger into perspective, consider these sobering stats: It takes only 100 volts of electricity to deliver a deadly shock, and residential power lines carry 7,200 volts. Even downed phone lines can do you in because they carry up to 120 volts.

When a storm is due, you set the generator up on a level place in your yard, fill the gas tank, and start the engine. Then you run extension cords to your various appliances and electronic devices. A portable unit may be just fine if power outages are rare, your electrical consumption is fairly low, and you don't mind trekking outdoors to refill the gas tank—which, depending on the model, could be as often as every 3 to 10 hours.

• **Standby generators** run off your home's natural-gas line or a propane tank that can be easily installed underground. When the power goes out, a transfer switch automatically starts the generator, which kicks all of your circuits into action—even if you're not home at the time. The downside of an at-the-ready system is that it will cost you considerably more than a portable model. Not only is the equipment itself more expensive, but it also needs to be installed by a licensed electrician. Still, if your area is hit by frequent, long-lasting blackouts, you want to ensure that you can run all of your electrical devices—from your toothbrush charger to your whole-house AC—or you simply prefer the convenience that a standby system offers, then this is your baby.

Take Stock

Regardless of whether you opt for a portable generator or a standby system, your first shopping decision is how much backup power it needs to pack. To make that call, simply decide which appliances and systems you want to keep running when the power goes kaput, and then add up their total wattage. The websites of major generator manufacturers, including General Electric®, Generac®, and Kohler®, feature electricity usage calculators that make the chore a snap. But to give you a sneak preview, the list below indicates the wattage requirements of some common appliances. To figure the total consumption (a.k.a. watt-hours), multiply the watts used by the hours the device is in operation.

▶ 10,000-Btu air conditioner: 1,500 watts

▶ Laptop computer: 250 watts

▶ Microwave oven: 600 to 1,200 watts

▶ Refrigerator: 700 to 1,200 watts

▶ Television: 300 watts

▶ Washing machine: 1,200 watts

AN OUNCE OF
PREVENTION

Back Up with Caution

A portable generator is a handy thing to have when the power goes out. But the comfort it offers comes with a couple of potentially huge price tags:

Carbon monoxide. Portable generators can produce CO fumes that can kill people in no time flat, and they do so frequently. In fact, statistics show that when a natural disaster strikes, more people die from CO poisoning from gasoline-powered generators than from the event that caused the power outage. The takeaway: Never use a portable gas-powered generator indoors. Keep the unit at least 10 to 25 feet away from and downwind of your home, and—just to play it extra safe—make sure you have a battery-powered CO detector inside the house to alert you to any trouble.

Back feed. When an improperly connected generator begins feeding electricity back through the power lines, it can kill anyone who happens to be near the wires. To avoid tragedy, never connect a portable generator directly to your home's main electric panel. Instead, have an electrician install a subpanel off your main circuit panel, with a dedicated inlet to power it. Be aware—this is not a DIY project!

WALL SWITCHES & RECEPTACLES

Mind the Main!

Whenever you're fixing anything that's connected to your electrical system, and you don't know which circuit controls that part of the house, don't take any chances: Turn off the main switch for electricity in the building. On a circuit breaker system, you'll see a marked switch, usually at the top of the panel. A fuse box may have a lever switch, also marked, that you can turn off. If not, look for the main fuse block, which is generally also at the top of the panel. Grab the metal handle, and give it a tug. It should slide right out. (You may want to wear gloves—the handle and other metal parts could be hot!)

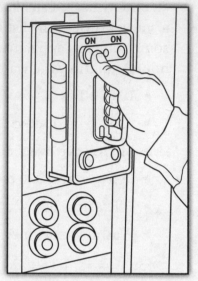

If your fuse box has no lever switch, pull out the main fuse block.

This Is Only a Test

Even if you think you've tripped the relevant breakers or pulled the fuses, it's a good idea to go one step further: Before you work on any switch, receptacle, or fixture, always make absolutely certain that there is no power in the circuit. All you need for that job is a noncontact voltage tester (a.k.a. power pen), which is a small battery-powered device. When it comes in contact with a hot (a.k.a. live) wire, it either lights up or sounds off, depending on the model. Before you put your tester to work, check the batteries by inserting the tip into a live electrical socket or holding it against a lit-up lightbulb. If the gadget's light comes on, or you hear chirps or beeps, you're good to go. So turn off power to the circuit, and proceed as follows:

▶ **Light fixture.** Turn the light switch on, remove the bulb, and touch the tip of the tester to the center socket button. If the light is on a three-way switch, conduct your test with one switch set in both the up and down positions.

▶ **Power switch.** With the switch in the "on" position, remove the cover plate, then touch the tip to the screw terminals on either side of the electrical box.

▶ **Receptacle.** If the outlet is connected to a wall switch, make sure it's turned on. Then insert the tester tip into every plug slot. (This is important to ensure an accurate reading because sometimes individual plugs are wired separately.) Next, confirm the no-juice diagnosis: Unscrew the receptacle, pull it out, and test all the plug wires directly, along with any others that you can reach from the back of the receptacle.

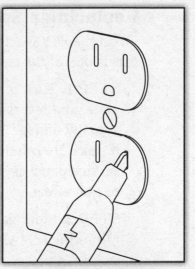

When a voltage tester lights up or makes chirping sounds, it means that the circuit is live.

Note: *Noncontact voltage testers can't penetrate metal conduit or sheathing. So if your problem resides in that kind of wiring, turn the job over to a pro.*

AN OUNCE OF
PREVENTION

Hands-On Testing

Ground fault circuit interrupter (GFCI) outlets are designed to shut down when they sense leaks of electric current that could cause a potentially deadly shock. They do a first-class job of it, too—except when they go on the fritz. For that reason, it's a good idea to test all of your GFCI outlets once a month. Here's how to do it:

• Press the Reset button (it's the upper one).

• Plug in whatever electrical device you have on hand.

• Push the Test button. Your "guinea pig" device should turn off.

• Hit Reset again. The power should come back on.

If any GFCI in your home flunks its test, replace it ASAP. Do it yourself, using the same routine that's required for replacing a two-prong outlet with a three-prong version (see "Replace Two-Prong Outlets with Three-Prong Versions" on page 52).

Replacing a Switch

Of all the DIY electrical fixes you can perform around your home, this is one of the easiest. Here's the simple seven-step process:

STEP 1. Turn off the power to the circuit. Then remove the cover plate, and test the screw terminals to make sure the power is actually off (see "This Is Only a Test" on page 48). To play it safe, if there are other people in the house, hang a note on the electric service panel saying, "Work in Progress—Do Not Touch," or words to that effect.

STEP 2. Remove the two mounting screws that hold the switch in place, and gently pull the switch out of its box to fully expose the wires.

STEP 3. Loosen the screw terminals and disconnect the wires, then use colored pens or tape to indicate which wire came from which screw.

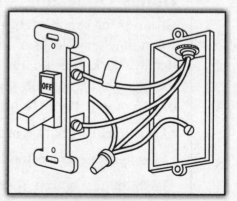

Pull the old switch out of its box and disconnect the wires.

STEP 4. Take the switch to a hardware store and buy a new one exactly like it.

STEP 5. Back home, hold the new switch up to the wall, and attach the bare leads of the wires to the screws according to the colored tags you made in Step 3.

STEP 6. Push the wires into the box and drive the mounting screws back into their slots.

Attach the wires of the new switch to the screws in the box.

STEP 7. Reattach the switch cover, turn the power back on, and flick the switch. The lights should pop right on.

Give Metal Plates a Pass

Metal switch and outlet faceplates are all the rage in home-decorating circles—and granted, they do look classy. But if a loose hot wire comes in contact with the metal, you could be in for a painful shock. Fortunately, safe alternatives go way beyond the basic plastic plates you see in hardware stores. Craft stores, many home-furnishing stores, and websites galore sell faceplates that are made of ceramic, wood, resin, and leather, as well as highly decorative plastic. So do yourself a favor and spruce up your walls, with no risk to your fingers! (An Internet search for "decorative faceplates" will bring up scads of sources.)

Be Well Connected

The key to a successful electrical installation or repair job lies in getting the relevant wires connected in just the right way. Here's a trio of the basic techniques that you need to master:

Stripping. Before you join two wires, you generally need to remove about ¾ inch of insulation from each end. Just insert the wire in the appropriate notch of a multitool, then close the handles and rotate the gadget to cut through the insulation. It'll slide right off. **Note:** *Be very careful not to nick the wire while you're stripping it. A nick could create a hot spot that could loosen the connection over time.*

Splicing. To connect solid wires, simply hold the stripped ends together, and twist a plastic wire connector (a.k.a. wire nut) on clockwise. When you're working with stranded wires, twist the bare ends together, and then screw on the connector.

Hooking. This technique is most often used to connect the end of a wire to a screw terminal. Bend the stripped end of the wire into a loop using needle-nose pliers. Then wrap the loop around the shank of the screw, and tighten the screw.

Replace Two-Prong Outlets with Three-Prong Versions

If your home has a shortage of three-prong outlets, here's good news: As long as an outlet box is grounded, you can safely and easily retrofit it with a three-prong version. Just follow these steps:

STEP 1. Kill the power to the circuit and confirm its demise using a noncontact voltage tester (see "This Is Only a Test" on page 48). Remove the cover plate, and pull the old receptacle partway out.

STEP 2. Check for ground by inserting one prong of a two-prong circuit tester* into the receptacle's shorter (a.k.a. hot) slot and touching the other prong to the box. If the tester does not light up, it means the box is not grounded, and you should stop reading now and call an electrician. If you do see light in the little window, proceed to Step 3.

STEP 3. Unscrew the old receptacle from the box and disconnect the wires.

STEP 4. Attach the hot (black or colored) wire to the brass terminal and the neutral (white) wire to the silver terminal.

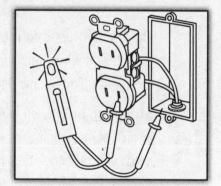

Use a two-prong circuit tester to see if the box is grounded.

STEP 5. Insert a green grounding screw* loosely into a pre-threaded hole in the back of the box. Hook one end of an 8-inch green grounding wire (a.k.a. pigtail)* around the screw, and tighten it. Secure the other end to the green grounding terminal on the new receptacle.

STEP 6. Gently nudge the new receptacle into the box, and turn on the power. Then test to confirm that current is flowing.

These parts are available in hardware and electric-supply stores.

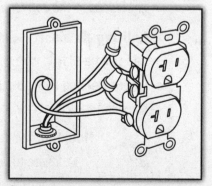

Connect one end of the grounding wire to the box's grounding screw and the other end to the grounding terminal on the new receptacle.

CEILING & WALL LIGHT FIXTURES

Do the Tater Twist

We've all been there before: Somehow, you manage to break a light-bulb that's still in its socket. So how can you get the thing out without cutting yourself? It's a snap! First, make sure the power to the fixture is turned off. Next, push half of a potato onto the glass, with the cut side against the broken bulb. Turn the spud just as you would to unscrew a whole lightbulb. Once it's out of the socket, don't try to remove the bulb from the tater—just toss the whole shebang into the trash.

Got no spuds on hand? No worries! Simply use a halved apple or orange instead. This trick works just as well with floor and table lamps as it does with hardwired fixtures. And make sure the lamps are unplugged before you apply your produce of choice!

When a Long-Life Bulb Dies Early...

It probably means that it was living in a place that's subject to a lot of vibration—for example, in a workshop where you use power tools, or near a door that slams frequently. The simple solution: Replace your regular long-lifers with rough service bulbs. They're designed to survive the bumps, shocks, and jolts in places like subway tunnels and factories, so they're bound to sail right through whatever "heavy weather" your home can deliver.

The Secret to Longer Lightbulb Life...

Is in the socket. To be specific, it's the little brass tab on the bottom that makes contact with the base of the bulb. When that tiny piece of metal is either dirty or bent, it interrupts the flow of current, which causes the bulb's filament to flash on and off. These flashes happen so quickly that you can't even see them, but they shorten the bulb's life. Your life-lengthening mission is simple: Every few weeks, switch off the circuit breaker (or unplug the lamp), and clean the tab with a cotton swab moistened with rubbing alcohol. Then use a little screwdriver to nudge the tab up a tad so that it stays in contact with the bulb's base.

When lightbulbs burn out, don't toss 'em in the trash. Instead, turn them into treasure for your Christmas tree. How you do that is your call. You can glue on baubles, bangles, and beads; paint the glass with Yuletide designs; or add scraps of fabric and ribbon to create characters ranging from snowmen and Santa Claus to penguins, puppy dogs, and pussycats. (You can find inspiration and detailed instructions in craft books and on scads of websites. Just search for "lightbulb Christmas ornaments.")

Lightbulb Changing: A Refresher Course

I know: You're thinking, "He's got to be kidding! Who doesn't know how to change a lightbulb?!" You're right—up to a point. But there *are* a few things that even experienced bulb changers often overlook, and they can result in serious trouble—or even tragedy. Whenever a bulb goes on the blink, keep these important guidelines in mind:

▶ Never use a bulb that has a higher wattage than that specified on the fixture (or lamp). Not only will the excess heat overload your home's wiring, but it may also burn anything it touches. **Note:** *Stop reading right now, check all the bulbs in your house, and replace them as necessary. If you're fresh out of the wattage grades that you need, keep those lights dark until you can go shopping for appropriate replacements.*

▶ Read—and heed—the package directions. For example, they may say that the bulb inside requires a ceramic fixture. Translation: The bulb will get too hot to be safely used in a socket that's made of plastic or other less durable material.

▶ Always kill the power to a fixture before you switch bulbs. This is important for two reasons: First, there is a chance that you could accidentally touch metal that's carrying electricity, and the resulting shock (while not fatal) will be extremely unpleasant. Second, every once in a while, power surges into a new bulb and bursts it wide open and you don't want to be holding on to it when that happens!

Do Your Bulbs Have Bees in Their Bonnets?

Are buzzing fluorescent lightbulbs driving you to drink (or at least increasing your consumption)? If so, send them flying and replace them with quieter versions. Just be sure to read the details on the packaging before you buy. The letter *A* on the box indicates that the bulb is a quiet soul. The letter *B*, on the other hand, tells you it's a real buzzer, so put it right back on the shelf.

Cranky Compacts

If you're a fan of compact fluorescent lights (CFLs), be aware that they do not perform well in all situations. They are most effective in places where they stay on for long durations. Turning them on and off frequently—either yourself or by way of a motion detector—will shorten their life. Also, CFL bulbs do not function very well or last very long in cold weather (attention, Snowbelt dwellers!).

Bear in mind, too, that CFLs contain mercury, so if you or someone in your household is prone to breaking lightbulbs, these so-called "green" lights probably are not your best choice. The mercury content also means that many communities have special disposal systems for CFLs—you can't just toss 'em in the trash. Requirements vary, so check with your town's waste-handling department about its guidelines.

AN OUNCE OF
PREVENTION

Switch Fluorescents Frequently

Even though fluorescent bulbs can produce light for a long time, the older they get, the more energy it takes to turn them on. This puts more and more stress on the ballast (the device inside the fixture that makes the bulbs light up) and causes it to wear out more quickly. How often you need to make a change depends (surprise!) on how much you use the light. As a general rule, if a fluorescent bulb stays on for eight hours a day, you should replace it every 12 to 18 months. In the case of a two-bulb fixture, make a clean sweep each time. Otherwise, the older bulb will create a drag on the new one and speed up its aging process.

FLUORESCENT LIGHT COVER CLEANER

The white plastic covers on tube-type fluorescent fixtures are made of a chemical mixture that makes the shades heat-resistant and flame-retardant. But age, heat, and prolonged exposure to light make the plastic turn yellow and dingy. This simple formula will restore that pristine whiteness.

6-10% hydrogen peroxide
Oxy-booster laundry detergent
Dishwashing liquid

Wearing rubber gloves and goggles, pour the hydrogen peroxide into a tub or basin to within 5 to 6 inches of the top. For every gallon of peroxide, mix in ¼ teaspoon of detergent. Immerse the cover in the solution, and let it soak in a sunny spot outdoors for six hours, until it turns as white as Frosty. Then refill the tub, add a squirt of dishwashing liquid, and wash the shade. Rinse it thoroughly, dry it with a lint-free cloth, and put it back on its fixture. Then stand back and enjoy your clear, white light!

LEDs: The Newest Kids in Town

Light-emitting diode (LED) lights are rapidly replacing CFLs as the bulbs of choice. They produce brighter light while consuming less energy than incandescent bulbs, and they can outlast any other type of bulb. And, unlike CFLs, these LED versions contain no dangerous chemicals, so you can dispose of them the same way you would incandescent or halogen bulbs.

Helpful Halogen Hints

Halogen lightbulbs burn brighter than their incandescent counterparts. And they last longer—that is, if you keep these guidelines in mind:

- **Keep 'em clean.** Any dirt or oil that gets on the glass can create hot spots, which will shorten the life of the bulb. So at the first sign of grime, turn off the power, and let the bulb cool down completely. Then gently wipe the surface with rubbing alcohol on a soft, lint-free cloth.

- **Don't touch!** Even when a halogen bulb is cool, never touch it with your bare hands. If you do, the oils from your skin can make the light flicker and die. Whenever you handle one of these sensitive characters, use a lint-free cloth or wear latex or cotton gloves.

Replacing a Ceiling Fixture

Lots of homeowners cringe at the mere thought of removing an old ceiling light fixture and hanging a new one. If you're one of those timid folks, take heart: It's actually a super-simple six-step process. Here's the drill:

STEP 1. Kill the juice to the circuit. Then remove the screws that hold the fixture to the ceiling, and check to make sure the power is off (see "This Is Only a Test" on page 48). Then disconnect the wires, and remove the old fixture and its metal mounting strap.

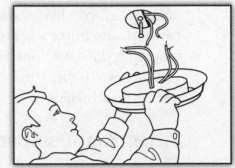

With the circuit turned off, disconnect the wires and remove the old fixture.

STEP 2. Fasten the new mounting strap to the outlet box using the screws that came with the new fixture. Then attach the grounding wire in the box to the grounding screw on the strap.

STEP 3. Have a helper hold the new fixture close to the box (using a broomstick as an arm extender if necessary) while you attach the wires in the box to the leads of the new wires and secure them with wire connectors.

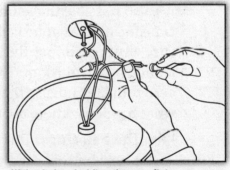

With a helper holding the new fixture, secure the new wires to the existing ones.

STEP 4. Gently push the wires into the outlet box, and screw the new fixture to the mounting strap.

STEP 5. Screw in the lightbulb(s), and attach whatever globe or other shade came with the kit.

STEP 6. Restore the power to the circuit, and switch on the light. That's all there is to it!

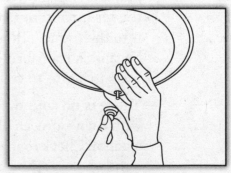

Once you've screwed in the bulbs, attach the globe.

DOORBELLS

Wiring's Out of Whack!

It's not often that faulty wiring makes a doorbell go mute. But it does happen. If you find that no current is flowing to your chimes, do yourself a favor: Skip the hassle—and expense—of having the system rewired, and buy a wireless version. It's a snap to install yourself, following the directions on the package, and once it's up and running, all you have to do is replace the batteries periodically and keep the outside button clean.

When Your Doorbell Goes Quiet...

There's a good chance that the problem is simply that weather and constant use have taken their toll on the outside button. But it's also possible that either the chime or transformer has gone belly-up. To find out for sure, unscrew or pry the button mechanism from the outside door. Then lay a screwdriver across the terminals. The next step depends on what happens. There are two possibilities:

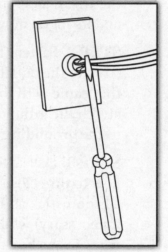

Test a doorbell by laying a screwdriver across the terminals.

▶ **The bell rings.** This means that you need a new button—and you're in luck because the installation process couldn't be simpler. Just attach the wires on the door frame to the terminal screws in the back of the new button and fasten it to the frame. (There's no need to cut off power at the circuit because a transformer reduces the power from the standard 120 volts to a safe 16 volts or so before the current reaches the bell.)

▶ **There is no sound.** Simply clean the plungers or clapper contacts with a cotton swab or a retired toothbrush dipped in rubbing alcohol. Check to make sure that all of the wire connections are tightly secured, and push the button. If the bell still doesn't ring, check the transformer (see "Timely Transformer Testing," at right).

Timely Transformer Testing

You'll likely find the transformer near your main electric panel. To test it, set a multimeter on "voltage," and put the probes on the screws that hold the thin doorbell wires. The reading determines the next step.

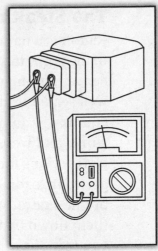

Test your transformer using a multimeter.

▶ **Less than 16 volts.** Call an electrician to replace the transformer. This job involves working with full 120-volt wires.

▶ **In the 6-volt vicinity.** Your transformer is functioning, but either your chimes or your wiring has gone bad. So remove the chimes' cover. Leaving the multimeter on the voltage setting, hold the probes to the wires while a helper pushes the doorbell. If the meter shows that current is flowing, it means that the chimes have died. So mount a new set on the wall, and attach the wires, following the guidelines for replacing a ceiling fixture (see page 57).

ALARMING MATTERS

4 Ways to Counteract CO Catastrophes

It's no secret that carbon monoxide is a killer, but the secret to preventing CO tragedies boils down to four simple measures:

• Properly vent and maintain all fuel-burning appliances.

• Have your furnace checked by a qualified heating contractor yearly.

• Use your devices properly—for example, never cook with a barbecue grill in any enclosed space, and don't try to heat your house with an oven that's designed for cooking.

• Last but not least, install and maintain CO alarms in your home. You can find them at virtually all home-improvement stores. Make sure the ones you buy conform to the latest Underwriters Laboratories (UL) standards, and follow the manufacturer's instructions for placement, operation, and battery replacement.

The Stealthiest Killer of All

Radon is a naturally occurring gas that comes from the breakdown of uranium in soil, rock, and water, and it's the leading cause of lung cancer among nonsmokers. What's more, any house—old or new, well sealed or drafty, with or without a basement, in any part of the country—can have radon trapped inside. Many home-improvement stores and websites sell DIY radon-testing kits, complete with simple instructions for setting up the measuring device and sending it away to get your reading. After that, your action plan depends on the numbers, but no matter what they are, a qualified contractor can help you get them down to a safer level. Your official state radon contact can point you to a pro in your area (see www.EPA.gov for those details).

The Ways and Means of Smoke Alarms

A smoke alarm that fails to go off when it should could result in tragedy. But one that goes off when there's nary a whiff of trouble can drive you nuts. Here's how to make sure that your vocal safety net performs as it should:

Site it right. Installing smoke alarms in bathrooms, kitchens, garages, or next to fireplaces can result in an almost continuous "concert."

Beware of quirky triggers. Both fresh paint and airborne dust can set off some smoke alarms, so you may want to disconnect the battery while you're painting a room or doing a major cleaning. (Just don't forget to replace it when you're finished cleaning or the paint has dried!)

Interpret the chirps. In most cases, a chirping sound indicates that the battery needs to be replaced—so perform that chore pronto. If that doesn't  produce peace and quiet, it means that the alarm has reached the end of its useful life and you need to install a new one.

Test regularly. Test the alarm once a month, and replace it ASAP if you even suspect that it's not performing at its peak.

Plumbing

There's no question that water is necessary for life. But it also ranks among Mother Nature's most destructive forces. So when we invite this potential monster into our homes and harness it to do our bidding, it's only natural that every now and then things can get out of hand. In some cases, when the ugly side of H_2O rears its head, your only recourse is to call a plumber. Fortunately, there are also plenty of times when quick action on your part can save the day or head off trouble.

SINKS & THEIR HARDWARE

Open Up Down There!

There's nothing like a clogged kitchen sink to muck up your plans. But whatever you do—even if you've got a dozen people showing up for dinner in half an hour—do *not* reach for a commercial drain cleaner. Those concoctions contain lye—and, as any plumber will tell you, over time, it'll eat its way through your pipes. And if you use a chemical-based cleaner that doesn't work, the plumber who rides to the rescue may add a charge for toxic-waste disposal to your bill. So do your pipes a favor, and try one of these three safer, gentler methods (in the order listed below):

> ▶ **Take the plunge.** Grab a plunger, then fill the sink with water to a depth that fully submerges the cup, and set it over the drain opening. Repeatedly push down and pull up until the water starts to flow down. If the fluid doesn't budge, it means the blockage is so far down that the plunger can't generate enough suction to dislodge it, so…

▶ **Flush it out.** Pour ½ cup of baking soda into the drain, wait a few minutes, and follow up with ½ cup of either white vinegar or lemon juice. Let it sit for 15 minutes. (The acid-alkaline combo will make a *lot* of noise, but don't be alarmed.) Rinse with hot or boiling water. If that doesn't work…

▶ **Blast it out.** Buy a pressurized drain opener, like CLR® Power Plumber®, and use it according to the directions on the can. One blast of the high-velocity air inside should drive out the wicked waste—especially after you've softened it up using the first two tricks above. But if the crud continues to cling for dear life to the walls of your pipe, bite the bullet and call a plumber.

Note: *Do not use the "Flush it out" method (above) if you've already tried a commercial de-clogger. The vinegar or lemon juice can react with the drain cleaner to create dangerous fumes.*

Bid a Safe Good-Bye to Grease…

And every other kind of cooking oil or fat. Over time, even small amounts of the stuff can build up in your drain lines—or your community sewer system—and lead to major trouble. So play it safe: Let your fat, grease, or oil cool down, and then pour it into a disposable container that has a tight-fitting lid, and toss it in the trash. Coffee cans are perfect when you've been cooking for a crowd. To corral smaller quantities of greasy gunk, reach for something like a cottage cheese container or a plastic peanut butter jar. But don't stop there! Go the extra mile and take these clog-prevention measures:

- Use paper towels to wipe out greasy pots and pans, then rinse them off or put them into the dishwasher.

- Scrape food scraps into the garbage can. Remember: Even salad dressing residue, globs of mayo, or a few uneaten French fries can form a small cog in a big clog.

- If you have a small amount of oil or greasy water, make it easier to handle by mixing it with a thicker material, like coffee grounds or paper towels before tossing it away.

Treasure down the Drain!

Don't cry over a spilled wedding ring—or any other trinket that's dropped into your drain. It's sitting snugly at the bottom of the U-shaped trap (called a P-trap) in your drainpipe, and your mission is simple. Grab a bucket, put it under the trap, and proceed in one of these two ways:

▶ If your trap has a plug on the bottom, simply unscrew it.

▶ If there is no plug, remove the whole trap by loosening the large nuts that are above and below it using a pipe wrench.

Empty the water into the bucket and fish out your treasure. Then give the trap a thorough rinsing and screw it back into place on the drainpipes.

WELL, WHADDYA KNOW!

The trouble that grease can cause in your drainpipes is only the tip of the "fatberg." That's the term wastewater managers have coined for the huge build-ups that form when kitchen fats mix with other chemicals in the sewer lines that take dirty household water to wastewater-treatment plants. Nearly half of the more than 36,000 sewer overflows occurring in the United States each year are caused by these blockages.

The granddaddy of all fatbergs appeared a few years ago in London. When residents complained that they couldn't flush their toilets, sewer inspectors quickly found the reason: The lines were blocked by a congealed mass of festering food fat. The glob was the size of a bus and weighed more than 15 tons. Clearing out the mess and repairing the damage took nearly six weeks. But it could have been much worse: If the berg had not been discovered when it was, raw sewage would have started spurting out of manholes, flooding streets, homes, and businesses.

Shut It Off!

I SPY A SHUT-OFF VALVE

In the event of any plumbing emergency, your first response should be to turn off the main water shutoff valve. So if you don't know where that is, stop reading right now and go find it! Here are some clues to guide you:

- In a cold-winter climate, the valve is in the basement or in a closet, where the main water-supply pipes come in.

- In warmer regions, the main valve is often outside near a hose hookup.

- In some places—especially in rural areas—shutoff valves are located inside the water meter boxes near the curb. If that's the case where you live, make sure you have a key so you can get into the box if necessary.

SHUT IT OFF AT THE SOURCE

Whenever a pipe or a water-using appliance springs a leak—or worse—you need to stop the water flow by closing the appropriate shutoff valve, either turn the knob clockwise, or if it has a lever-type handle, turn it so that it's perpendicular to the pipe. Here's where to find these essential controls:

Bathtub: Behind a panel in the faucet wall or in the basement.

Dishwasher: Under the kitchen sink or in the basement pipes below the appliance.

Sink: In the cabinet below the  unit. (There will be two shutoff valves: one for cold and one for hot.)

Toilet: On the wall under the flush tank.

Washing machine: Where the water hoses connect to the plumbing. (As with the sink, you'll find both hot and cold valves.)

Note: *Test all of your valves every three to four months to make sure they're in good working order.*

Fix a Chip in a Porcelain Sink

Porcelain sinks (and bathtubs) are what my Grandma Putt called "easy keepers"—but they are prone to chipping. Fortunately, those gashes are a snap to repair. First, pick up a two-component epoxy kit that matches the color of the porcelain. Then proceed as follows:

STEP 1. Clean the chipped area using a sponge and hot, soapy water.

STEP 2. Sand the damaged area with 400- to 600-grit "wet and dry" sandpaper to roughen up the surface and allow the epoxy to adhere tightly. Wipe away the resulting dust with a tack cloth.

STEP 3. Dampen a cotton swab with denatured alcohol, clean the sanded area, and let it dry completely.

STEP 4. Mix the epoxy ingredients per the instructions in the package. Mask the area, then apply as many thin coats as necessary, letting each one dry for the amount of time specified before you start again.

Thinly apply epoxy until the chip is filled.

STEP 5. Once the gap is filled, smooth out the epoxy with a flat-bladed scraper. Then remove the masking tape and, if necessary, make another pass with the scraper to ensure the epoxy is level with the surface.

Wait 24 hours before using the sink, and avoid scrubbing the area for at least a week.

Note: *If you can't find just the right shade of epoxy, buy a porcelain enamel paint that matches your sink. Gently sand the dried filler with 220-grit sandpaper, and brush on a thin coat of the paint. Continue sanding and painting, letting each coat dry, until the repaired area matches the surrounding surface. Just be sure you get enamel that's specially designed for use on porcelain—regular enamel won't cling much longer than the blink of an eye!*

Scrape the epoxy smooth.

Screech No More!

The fix for a screeching faucet couldn't be simpler. Just remove the handle and stem, and coat both sets of the metal threads with petroleum jelly. Screw the pieces back together, then step back and enjoy the sound of silence!

Drip, Drip, Drip—Dry Up!

If there's anything more annoying than a noisy faucet, it's the constant dripping sounds produced by a leak that keeps you up all night. Well, don't just lie there in torment—grab some string, wrap one end around the faucet, and run the other end into the drain. The water will run down the string and straight into Never Never Land.

When Drip, Drip, Drip Means Danger Ahead

In a standard washer-based (a.k.a. compression) faucet, a dripping faucet is usually caused by a deteriorating washer. Over time, those tiny drops will erode metal parts inside the faucet mechanism. Then, what could have been a quick and easy fix will escalate into a major project that could drain megabucks from your bank account. If the weepy wonder is a compression faucet, you can easily install a new washer yourself (see "2 Happy Campers," at right). But do yourself a favor: If you choose to have a plumber tackle the drip-stopping job—or if he's in your house doing any other work—have him replace the washers in all of your faucets, indoors and out while he's there. Chances are that those rubber rings are all about the same age, so any one of them could go belly-up at any time.

CALL A PRO

While both compression and cartridge faucets are fairly simple to repair, the inner workings of ball and ceramic disc types are much more complex. If you have either of these single-handled babies, and something goes awry, turn the fix-it task over to a plumber.

---

2 Happy Campers

If your leaky faucets are either compression or cartridge models, you're in luck: Both are highly user-friendly to the DIY crowd. But before you dive in, take two precautions to safeguard all the tiny parts: First, cover the drain opening so that nothing falls into it (the lid to a plastic storage container works well). Second, to simplify the reassembly process, line the parts up in the order in which you remove them. Here's the simple how-to routine:

Compression faucet

▶ Remove the screw from the top of the faucet handle and pull it off. (If there's a decorative cap, pry it off with a thin screwdriver or the point of a knife.)

▶ Use a crescent wrench to remove the packing nut, and pull up the stem assembly.

▶ Remove the screw that holds the washer in place, and install a duplicate. That should do the trick. If not, it indicates that the valve seat may need to be replaced, so call a plumber.

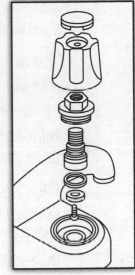

Compression faucet

Cartridge faucet

▶ If there is a plastic retainer ring, pry it off. Then unscrew the retainer pivot nut using pliers or an adjustable wrench.

▶ Lift off the spout sleeve, along with the spray diverter if there is one.

▶ Eyeball the O-rings on the faucet body, and if they're not in tip-top shape, replace them.

▶ Pry out the retainer clip using a small flat-edged screwdriver.

▶ Use pliers to pull out the old cartridge, and install a new one following the manufacturer's directions.

▶ Put the whole shebang back together.

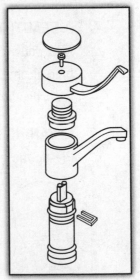

Cartridge faucet

Keep 'Em Clean

It's no secret that keeping your kitchen and bathroom fixtures spanking clean can lessen the likelihood that you'll want (or need) to replace them—and increase their appeal to would-be buyers if you decide to sell your house. Supermarket shelves are jam-packed with products that will help you accomplish that task. But you don't need to clutter your cupboards with all that stuff. This roundup of tip-top tricks will help you keep sinks, tubs, and showers looking their best for years to come.

A TRIO OF TOUGH CUSTOMERS

Here's how to banish three of the most unsightly—and challenging—bathroom and kitchen blemishes:

Burn marks (for instance, from curling irons or hot pots). Wet a fizzy antacid tablet (like Alka-Seltzer®), and rub it on the stain until it disappears.

Mildew on caulking around sinks or tubs. Simply wipe the area with a sponge dipped in rubbing alcohol. Or, if the foul fungi are stubborn, use a retired toothbrush to do the job.

Rust stains on any surface. Make a thin paste of lemon juice and borax. Spread it on the stains and scrub lightly with a scouring sponge.

A BEAUTIFUL BATHROOM FOLLOW-UP

After you've cleaned your bathroom fixtures, give them a rubdown with a little rubbing alcohol. It will kill germs, shine mirrors and chrome, and remove all traces of soap, deodorant, hair spray, and toothpaste.

CLEANING HELP FROM THE PRODUCE AISLE

Plastic-mesh produce bags (the kind that onions and potatoes come in) make
 perfect sink, tub, and shower scrubbers, no matter what kind of cleanser you're using. They won't scratch porcelain, tile, or marble surfaces, yet they're tough enough to clear off even the most stubborn grime, like mildew, soap scum, and greasy food residue.

ALL-PURPOSE SINK CLEANER

Whether your kitchen sink is made of stainless steel, porcelain, soapstone, or copper (or any other material under the sun), this simple formula will keep that hardworking surface looking its best: Mix 1/8 cup of baking soda with enough pure liquid soap to get a creamy consistency. Apply the mixture with a sponge or soft brush, and rinse with clear water.

Note: *Liquid castile soap is perfect for this job, but it's a snap to make your own. Just shred a bar of Fels-Naptha® or Octagon® soap, and dissolve it in about 1/4 cup of warm water. Also, of course, this magical mixture works like a charm for cleaning bathroom fixtures and any other surfaces in your house.*

TOIL-LESS TOILET CLEANING

It's probably safe to assume that cleaning a toilet bowl does not rank among your favorite pastimes. Well, nothing can make it as much fun as a three-ring circus, but any of these methods will get the job done as quickly, easily, and pleasantly as possible:

- For routine cleaning, simply drop a couple of Alka-Seltzer® tablets into the bowl. Wait 20 minutes, then brush and flush. No fizzy antacids on hand? Then sprinkle 1/4 cup of baking soda into the bowl, and drizzle 1/4 cup of vinegar over the soda. Then scrub with a long-handled brush.

- To remove unsightly mineral deposits, make a paste of 3 parts borax to 1 part white vinegar, slather it on the marks, and leave it for three to four hours. Then rinse with clear water.

- If you're going out of town for a few days, use this completely work-free method: Just before you head out the door, pour 1/4 cup of household bleach into your toilet bowl. When you get home, that porcelain will be as clean as a whistle—all you have to do is flush. (If any critters will be in the house during your absence, make sure you close the bathroom door tightly before you leave.)

Replacing a Bathroom Sink

If your old sink is showing serious signs of wear and tear, don't think that you need to have a pro replace it. Doing the job yourself will take some time, but it's a straightforward process. Here's all there is to it:

STEP 1. Measure the length, width, and depth of your current sink. Then trot down to your local plumbing-supply or home-improvement store, and choose a replacement with the same dimensions. If it's any larger, you'll have to modify the countertop to fit it, and that may not be easy. Also pick up a tube of silicone sealant, which you'll need to secure the new sink to the countertop. (Make sure it's 100 percent silicone caulk that's intended for kitchen and bathroom use.)

STEP 2. Remove everything from the cabinet under the sink—when you start dismantling the pipes under there, you'll need all the elbow room you can get.

STEP 3. Turn off the sink's water valves, and let the faucet(s) run until you're sure they're empty. Then unscrew and remove the faucet-spigot assembly.

STEP 4. Put a bucket under the P-trap, and then disconnect the drainpipe by unscrewing the nuts and scraping away the putty.

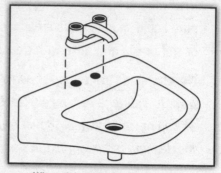

When the pipes are free of water, remove the faucets and spigot.

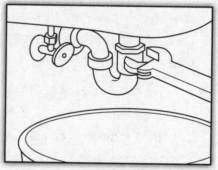

With a bucket placed under the P-trap, disconnect the drainpipe.

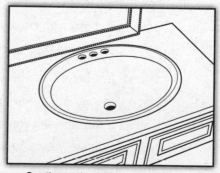

Gently set the sink into the opening in the countertop.

STEP 5. Remove the clips (if any) that attach the sink to the countertop. Then, using a putty knife, scrape out the sealant between the countertop and the rim of the sink. Lift the sink out, and set it aside.

STEP 6. Apply silicone sealant around the edges of the opening, following the directions on the tube. Gently set the new sink into place, and make sure it's sitting securely. If any sealant oozes out, wipe it away with a damp cloth.

STEP 7. Reconnect the P-trap. Then reinstall the faucet assembly, and seal all the edges with silicone caulk to prevent leaks.

STEP 8. Turn the supply valves back on, and let the water run. While it's running, test all of the connections and the edges of the sink for leaks. If there's any seepage, tighten up the connections or apply more sealant as needed. Otherwise, you're good to go.

DISHWASHERS & GARBAGE DISPOSALS

Withdraw Your Deposits

A lot of water runs through the average dishwasher, and the minerals in that fluid can make a mess of your dishwasher's heating element—and leave you with a hefty repair bill if you don't take action. So hop to it this way: Make a paste of white vinegar and baking soda, and wipe it generously onto the area. Rinse with full-strength vinegar, and your cleanup helper will be back in business.

When the Spray Arm Simply Sputters...

It's probably jammed with mineral deposits and food residue. To clean out the crud, first remove the dish racks, and then take out the screws that hold the arm in place. Lift it off, and lay it flat on a counter. Then poke a strand of thin wire into each hole. When you're through, give the arm a gentle shake to make sure nothing else is caught in there, and then scrub away the mineral deposits with a solution of vinegar and hot water.

Conquer Hose Woes

One of the most common dishwasher dilemmas is a leak caused by a crack or loose connection in the drainage hose that usually runs into the cabinet under the sink, where it connects to your garbage disposal. It's a little problem that can turn into big trouble if it floods your kitchen. Fortunately, it's an easy fix, but your game plan depends on the source of the leak. To find it, pull the access panel off the bottom of the dishwasher, and then lie down and shine a flashlight on the hose. If you see water dripping from the hose itself, you'll need to replace it. On the other hand, if the drip is coming from the spot where the hose connects to the dishwasher—and the hose opening is undamaged—simply resecuring the connection should save the day. In either case, here's what you need to do:

STEP 1. Kill the electrical circuit that serves the dishwasher, turn off the water valve (see "Shut It Off!" on page 64), and mop up any water on the floor.

STEP 2. Disconnect the drainage hose from the dishwasher (most likely it'll be held in place by either a ring-like clamp with a screw on the side or a spring-loaded compression clamp). Then eyeball the end of the hose. If it's in fine fettle, simply push it firmly back into place, reinstall the clamp, and proceed to Step 4.

STEP 3. If the hose is cracked, disconnect the end that goes into the garbage disposal. Take the hose to your local hardware store, and buy a matching model. Then slide the new hose into place and connect it to the dishwasher and the disposal.

AN OUNCE OF
PREVENTION

Wash Your Dishwasher

A couple of times a year, stand 1 cup of vinegar in the upper rack and 1 cup of vinegar in the lower rack, along with a full load of dishes. Run the machine as usual. The vinegar will be dispersed throughout the mechanism, removing any mineral deposits and soap residue. Think of this routine as the equivalent of your car's 15,000-mile checkup. It's just what your dishwasher needs to keep on truckin' for miles and miles (so to speak).

STEP 4. Turn the water and electricity back on and, keeping the access panel off, start the dishwasher and take it for a "test drive." As it's running, hunker down with your flashlight and check for any drips. If there are none, replace the panel and pat yourself on the back for a job well done!

It's Supposed to Get the Dishes Clean!

If you open your dishwasher to find soap residue, and still-dirty dishes as well, there's probably a simple reason—and an equally simple solution. The likely reason: The water isn't hot enough. Many machines won't work efficiently unless the water temperature is above 140°F. The simple two-part solution:

- ▶ If your dishwasher has a built-in water heater, raise the temperature to the correct level (check your owner's manual for the procedure).

- ▶ Always run hot water into the kitchen sink for a minute or so *before* you turn on your dishwasher.

Here's a trivia question for you: Who invented the dishwasher? No, it wasn't Thomas Edison. It was Josephine Cochrane of Shelbyville, Illinois, and she came up with the idea way back in the 1880s. Mrs. Cochrane, the wife of a politician, frequently gave formal dinner parties, and she was fed up with careless servants breaking her expensive china. So she fashioned a crude, but highly effective, machine that quickly became the talk of her little town. Before long, she was getting orders from hotels and restaurants throughout Illinois. She patented the device in 1886, and in 1893, it took top honors at the Chicago World's Fair for "the best mechanical construction, durability, and adaptation to its line of work."

The company she founded came out with a smaller machine, intended for home use in 1914, but there were very few takers. According to surveys, most women actually found dishwashing relaxing after a long day of more strenuous housework. It wasn't until the early 1950s that postwar prosperity and women's desire for more leisure time made dishwashers popular in American homes.

Keep Your Disposal Shipshape

Adopting this simple habit will ensure that your disposal's blades stay clean and odor-free: Fill a couple of ice cube trays with vinegar (any kind will do) and freeze them. Then every week or so, run three or four cubes through the disposal, and let the cold water flow for a minute or so. The grinding of ice on blades will remove any clinging food particles, and the vinegar will eliminate odors.

3 Steps to an Odor-Free Garbage Disposal

If your garbage disposal is starting to smell like an open trash can on a hot summer day, the reason is all but certain: Food residue has built up on the blades, and those tiny bits of food are rotting. Fortunately, you can solve that problem pronto, in three simple steps:

STEP 1. Turn on the cold water, toss in a handful of lemon or orange peels, and then run the disposal. After about 10 seconds, turn it off and let it sit for 15 minutes. The citric acid will soften the caked-on food and also attack the odiferous bacteria.

STEP 2. Turn the water and the disposal back on, and drop in three or four ice cubes. The flying ice shards will work like a sandblaster to get the blades spanking clean.

STEP 3. Tuck the stopper into the drain, and fill the sink about halfway with cold water. Then pull out the stopper and turn on the disposal. The water will send the smelly crud right down the drain.

Stay Out of Hot Water

That's what you'll be in if you're using hot water when you run your garbage disposal. Why? Because no matter how careful you are to avoid sending grease into the unit (see "Bid a Safe Good-Bye to Grease…" on page 62), some of the foods that you do grind up are bound to contain certain amounts of fat, and the hot water will melt it. Eventually, it will harden way down inside the mechanism. That spells a big blockage—and a big plumbing bill. So always run cold water when you're grinding up your dinner remains, and keep that chilly stream flowing for at least 60 seconds after you flick off the switch.

Cut the Clog

What if you've already run hot water down the disposal, and now all kinds of hardened who knows what is clogging it up? Fear not! Just mix up equal parts of baking soda, salt, and vinegar. Pour the concoction directly into the drain, and let it sit for 10 to 15 minutes. Then rinse with 2 cups of boiling water. That should clear things up.

Give the Jam a Jolt

If a soda-salt-vinegar bath doesn't free up the disposal's mechanism, try this routine:

- First, make sure the appliance is turned off. (You don't want to get a nasty surprise down there!) Then check to see if the GFCI switch got tripped. If it's off, reset it.
- If the switch is on, pull out the Allen wrench that came with your disposal (it should be hanging under the sink), and manually spin the motor. If that doesn't free it up, it's time to throw in your wrench and call a plumber.

REVEALED:
The Truth about "Feeding" Your Garbage Disposal

True or false? You should never put eggshells, potato peels, banana peels, celery, or coffee grounds down the disposal.

True *and* false! Whatever you do, folks, do not grind up banana peels or celery. If you do, their strings will foul up the works big-time! Avoid tater skins, too—the starch can gum up the blades. But don't hesitate to toss down eggshells. The warnings about them are just a bunch of old wives' tales. As for coffee grounds, they actually help keep the blades sharp and the inner parts turning freely. So, by all means, serve your disposal healthy helpings of used java!

SHOWERS & TUBS

2 Ways to Conquer Clogged Showerheads

When you step into the shower, turn on the faucet, and get a drowsy drizzle instead of a wake-up cascade, don't rush out and replace the head. Just clear out the mineral deposits that are blocking the water from getting through. You can do that in one of two ways and your shower will flow like Niagara Falls (well, more or less):

► Unscrew the head, and soak it for 10 to 15 minutes in a mixture of 1 quart of boiling water and ½ cup of white vinegar. (If your showerhead is plastic, use hot, not boiling, water.)

► Fill a plastic bag halfway up with white vinegar, and then slide the open end up over the head so that it's completely submerged. Secure the bag with duct tape, and leave it in place overnight. Then remove the bag and rinse the fixture with clear water. (This trick also works to clean the aerator on your kitchen spigot.)

Give Lip Service to a Shower Leak

Is H_2O seeping from the spot where your showerhead connects to the arm? If so, there's a quick fix in your purse—lip balm! Just unscrew the showerhead, wipe a generous layer of balm onto the threads, and screw the head back in place. End of drip!

Bathtub faucets come in the same four basic types that sink faucets do (compression, cartridge, ball, and disc), and they can spring the same kinds of leaks. In theory, the compression and cartridge versions are as easy to repair as their sink-bound counterparts (see "2 Happy Campers" on page 67). The problem is that getting to the working parts without damaging the wall and its tile covering can be mighty tricky. Plus, in the typical shower-tub combo, you have a diverter that directs water flow to either the tub spout or the showerhead. So don't even think of attacking tub-faucet leaks yourself—call an expert plumber.

CALL A PRO

Replace a Showerhead

DIY projects don't come any simpler than removing an old showerhead and installing either a spiffy new one or a handheld sprayer. In fact, it's as easy as 1, 2, (and maybe) 3.

STEP 1. To remove the existing showerhead, use an adjustable wrench to turn its collar counterclockwise. If the shower arm wants to twist right along with the head, wrap duct tape around the arm, and hold it in place with another wrench while you unscrew the head.

STEP 2. Wrap pipe-thread tape (a.k.a. plumber's tape, which is available in hardware and plumbing-supply stores) around the threads in the shower arm to fend off leaks. Install any washer that may have come with the new head. Then screw on the star attraction, and tighten it securely with an adjustable wrench.

STEP 3. If the new addition is a handheld sprayer, screw one end of the hose onto the handheld attachment and the other end onto the showerhead, following the manufacturer's instructions.

POWERFUL POTIONS

MOLD & MILDEW DEFENSE FORMULA

Damaging mold and mildew spores can spread like wildfire from your tub, shower door, or vinyl curtain liner to other surfaces in your home. This formula fends off trouble.

½ cup of rubbing alcohol
1 tbsp. of liquid laundry detergent with enzymes
3 cups of water

Mix the ingredients in a handheld spray bottle, and keep it on the side of the tub. Then, after your shower or bath, spray the solution on all wet surfaces.

Fill before You Caulk

Whenever you need to caulk a seam around a bathtub, fill the tub with water first. The reason: The extra weight will enlarge the space where the tub joins the wall, and you'll have to apply more caulk to fill it. That will make for a tougher, thicker seal that's less likely to crack down the road. Just one word of caution: Before you turn the water on, make sure you can easily reach around the tub on all sides. If you can't, you might want to put on a bathing suit and do this job from inside the tub!

A Zippy Way to Zap Hair-Jammed Drains

Hair, combined with shampoo, conditioner, and soap residue, can make an ugly mess of the drains in bathtubs and shower stalls—and sinks, too, especially when you add toothpaste gunk to the mix. But thanks to a handy gadget called Zip-It™, you can make quick work of that crud, with no nasty chemical de-cloggers and no formulas to mix up. The tool couldn't be simpler: It's a flat strip of plastic that's about two feet long, with sharp teeth sticking out from either side, all the way down. (It looks a little like a swordfish's beak.) You just grab hold of the handle at the top end, shove the toothed strip into the drain, and pull it back up. Your "catch" will be a disgusting mass of goopy hair and heaven knows what else—but your drain will be as free flowing as a mountain stream. Then you simply toss the tool and its trophy in the trash. (You can find Zip-It in most hardware and home-improvement stores.)

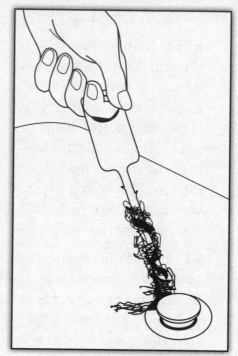

Zip-It™ zaps tough bathroom clogs.

Liquid Refreshment for Hair-Clogged Drains

If you'd rather not see the disgusting mess that's clogging your bathroom drains—or you simply don't have a Zip-It™ on hand (see "A Zippy Way to Zap Hair-Jammed Drains," above)—use this simple formula: Mix 1 cup each of salt and baking soda in ½ cup of white vinegar, and pour the mixture down the drain. Wait about 10 minutes, and then chase that cocktail with ½ gallon of boiling water. Then turn on the hot-water tap and let it run until the stream flows freely.

TOILETS

Stop the Flow!

An overflowing toilet may or may not indicate a serious plumbing problem—but regardless of the cause, you need to act fast to head off a flooded bathroom. Your mission is simple: Remove the top of the flush tank, grab the float, and pull it up to close the refill valve. That should buy you enough time to reach down and shut off the water.

This works because a toilet functions according to the law of gravity. By design, the tank contains just enough water to fill the bowl. When you flush, the water drops down into the bowl, pushing the waste through the drain. At the same time, the float drops, opening a valve that lets in sufficient water to refill the tank and bowl simultaneously. When the float rises far enough to shut off the water flow, the valve closes. Trouble strikes when water from the tank can't leave the bowl fast enough, and the refill supply spills over.

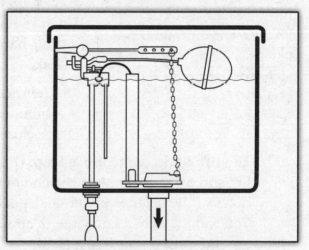

Gravity drives the inner workings of your toilet.

When a Toilet Trickle Has You in a Pickle...

The most likely cause is mineral deposits that have built up on the flapper valve and the valve seat. The quick fix: Shut off the water, flush the toilet to empty the tank, and scrub off the pesky crust with a plastic scouring pad dipped in white vinegar. (If your valve seat is made of brass, as older models are, use fine-grade steel wool.) When you're finished, turn the water back on and flush the toilet a few times to rinse out the residue.

If your toilet isn't flushing as forcefully as it used to, it could be that the little holes under the rim of the bowl have become clogged with mineral deposits. And the best tool to get those openings cleared out is a wire coat hanger. Just unbend the hook, and gently poke the end of it into each hole. Bingo—full-powered flushing action is back!

Find the Phantom Leak

A leaking toilet tank can waste hundreds of gallons of water each day—without your even knowing about it. Fortunately, there's an easy way to find out if this is happening in your bathroom. Flush the toilet, and wait for the tank to refill. Then drip a little food coloring into the tank. Wait 20 to 30 minutes. If the water in the toilet bowl turns color, call a plumber, who can repair the seal.

3 Reasons for a Faulty Flush

When you push the handle down and nothing happens, there are three possible reasons—and a trio of simple solutions:

• **The water got turned off.** Check the shutoff valve just under the tank. If it's closed, open it back up.

• **The lift chain came loose from the trip lever.** Remove the tank lid, and tuck the hook at the end of the chain into one of the holes in the lever. Which one depends on the length of the chain. You want it to hang down with about ½ inch of slack, so move it around until the fit is just right.

• **The handle is loose.** With the lid off (of course), hold onto the handle with one hand while you use a wrench to tighten the handle's locknut inside the tank. Just be aware that in this instance you need to forget the old expression "Right tight, left loose." Unlike just about every other gadget that's secured by turning, flush-tank handles are *tightened* by turning the locknut to the *left*. The reason is that if the nut were threaded in the usual way, the force caused by multiple flushes a day would quickly loosen the handle. But thanks to the nut's reverse threading, each flush actually strengthens its grip.

Puddle Got You in a Muddle?

When you find water pooling on the floor by your toilet, it's only natural to be concerned—but don't rush out and call a plumber. Depending on where the H_2O is, try one of these simple DIY maneuvers first:

▶ If the water is under the tank (and the tank isn't sweating), tighten the water-supply line connection on the bottom of the tank, as well as the bolts that fasten the tank to the base.

▶ When the seepage is coming from the base of the toilet, remove the caps on either side, and *very carefully* tighten the nuts on the flange bolts. Work on one side and then the other, tightening each nut just a little bit at a time. If you use too much pressure, or get one side snugger than the other, you could crack the toilet.

Still seeing water? Then now's the time to call a plumber.

Treat Your Tank Lid Tenderly

Whenever you remove the lid of your flush tank for any reason, resist the temptation to lay it across the toilet or set it on the bathroom counter. That topper may look as tough as nails, but it's actually quite fragile. If it's bumped off onto the floor, it's likely to break. Likewise, if you drop a tool on it, you're begging for a nice crop of shards. So before you start working inside the tank, carefully set the lid on a carpeted floor outside the bathroom or put it on a thick layer of bath towels as far removed as possible from the scene of action.

AN OUNCE OF
PREVENTION

Forget the "Flushable" Fib

Ladies, if you use tampons that are touted as "flushable," and you're taking the manufacturers at their word, I have some advice for you: Ignore that balderdash. Despite the claims you may read on the package, plumbers say that tampons are notorious for clogging the main drains that carry waste away from houses. The same goes for "flushable" baby wipes. So if anyone in your home uses either of these handy products, issue firm orders that they get tossed in the trash—not in the toilet bowl!

How to Replace a Toilet

Taking out an old toilet and installing a new one may sound intimidating, but it's actually one of the simpler plumbing jobs you can undertake. Here's the drill:

STEP 1. Turn off the water at the toilet's shutoff valve, then flush the toilet to remove most of the water from the tank and bowl. If necessary, use a plunger to force any remaining water from the bowl, and use a sponge to sop up any residue from the tank. Then disconnect the supply line from the base of the tank.

STEP 2. Remove the old toilet. (Because the average one weighs 120 pounds or more, you'll probably want to do this in two stages.) First, disconnect the bolts that hold the tank to the bowl, and hoist the tank off. Then pop off the caps at the base of the toilet, and remove the nuts and washers on the closet bolts that secure the bowl to the floor. Gently rock the bowl back and forth to free it from the wax ring at its base, and then lift it off. Immediately stuff a sturdy rag into the hole to keep sewer gases from escaping and to keep tools from falling into the abyss.

STEP 3. Pry up the existing wax ring, and inspect the flange underneath it. If the flange is damaged, a plumber will need to replace it before you proceed. But if it's in good shape, pull the rag out of the hole (whatever you do, don't forget this step!), and remove the closet bolts from the flange.

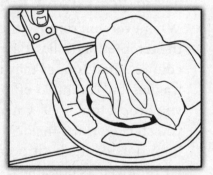

Once you've removed the old toilet, stuff a rag into the hole. Then pry up the wax ring.

STEP 4. Set the new wax ring into place, and hook the new bolts into their slots in the flange. (The ring and the bolts will come with your new toilet.)

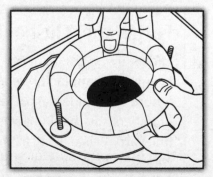

Install the wax ring and closet bolts that came with your new toilet.

STEP 5. Set the base of the toilet directly onto the wax ring, and slide a washer and nut over each bolt. Then tighten the bolts carefully to avoid cracking the toilet base.

STEP 6. Install the toilet seat and hardware according to the manufacturer's directions.

STEP 7. Connect the water supply, again following the manufacturer's instructions. Then turn the water back on, and let the tank fill up.

WATER HEATERS

Safety First

Any device that's full of hot water and that's powered by natural gas or electricity is a disaster waiting to happen. To make sure your domestic tranquility isn't shattered by your water heater, take these two precautions:

▶ **Give it a "seat belt."** Even a minor earthquake could topple the average water heater, which in turn is all but guaranteed to start a fire and cause extensive water damage. So secure your tank to some strong wall studs, using a strapping kit that's designed for the purpose (you can pick one up at your local hardware or plumbing-supply store). Or, if you prefer, wrap steel plumber's tape around the top and bottom of the tank and secure the tape to the studs.

▶ **Give it space.** Ideally, there should be nothing within a 3-foot radius of a water heater. In particular, beware of any materials (for instance, cardboard boxes) that can absorb moisture. They could cause the tank to corrode and, in a worst-case scenario, ultimately break open.

Get a Handle on the Handle

High up on the side of your water heater, you'll find a valve with a lever handle. It may look like just another plumbing device, but it's actually one of the most important pieces of safety equipment in your home: It keeps the water heater from blowing up if its thermostat conks out. So at least twice a year, put that lifesaver to the test. To do that, simply hold a bucket under the valve, push it open, and let it snap closed. It should give you a short blast of hot water. If it doesn't—or if the handle doesn't even snap back—have a plumber install a new one ASAP.

CALL A PRO

If your home was built before 1970, and it still has its original water pipes and/or water heater, there's a good chance that the insulation is made of asbestos. Clue: It'll resemble troweled-on plaster. Whatever you do, don't try to remove it! If you even touch the stuff, the tiny carcinogenic particles may float into the air. Left undisturbed, asbestos should pose no risk at all, but don't take any chances: Have a licensed and bonded asbestos abatement specialist look at it, and then either seal the stuff or remove it.

By Gum, It's Leaking!

When your water heater sprouts a small leak, don't panic. Just grab a stick of gum, chew it until all the sweetness is gone, and slap the wad over the hole. It won't be a permanent fix, but it should hang in there long enough for you to perform a more lasting repair job—or for a plumber to arrive on the scene.

Drain for Gain

Draining your water heater every few years will make it last longer and run more efficiently. That's because this chore gets rid of the crud that collects in the bottom of the tank and hinders its smooth operation. If the mere thought of performing this trick makes you cringe, don't fret—it's not as hard as it sounds. But *do* be careful because (of course) the water will be hot. Here's how to go about it:

STEP 1. Turn off the gas or electricity that powers the heater, as well as the cold-water supply pipe leading to the tank.

STEP 2. Attach a hose* to the drain valve near the bottom of the tank, and run the end of the hose into a basement floor drain or a kitchen or bathtub drain. If push comes to shove, use a bucket—although the process will take quite a while.

STEP 3. Open the drain valve and any hot-water faucet in your home. The water in the tank will drain out, carrying the sediment right along with it.

STEP 4. Close the drain valve, turn the power and the incoming water tap back on, and let the tank fill up.

Make sure you use a high-quality hose; some cheap, flimsy models get very soft when hot water runs through them and may leak.

There's No Hot Water!

When a gas water heater fails to deliver the goods, it's usually because the pilot light has gone out. So take a look-see and, if necessary, just relight it—or call your gas company and ask for help. In the case of an electric water heater, there's a good chance that the high-temperature cutoff valve has been tripped. Pressing the reset button should put the machine back in business. If it doesn't, the problem is a faulty thermostat—and replacing it is a job for a plumber.

WATER-SUPPLY & DRAINAGE PIPES

Seek the Leaks

It's easy to find and fix leaks that you can see, like the ones that cause a faucet to drip constantly. But don't assume that what you see is all you've got. Water leaks can occur in a whole lot of out-of-sight places. And the sooner you find them and fix them—or hire a plumber to do it—the less damage that insidious moisture will do to your home. To find those hidden seeps, turn off all of the running water in your house. Immediately check the reading on your water meter, and jot it down. Don't use any water for 30 minutes, and then read the meter again. If it shows that any water's been used, it means you have a leak lurking somewhere in the nether regions of your home. So call a plumber ASAP!

Many moons ago, I learned that one of the handiest fix-it helpers of all is an old garden hose. It's especially useful to have on hand when a plumbing pipe cracks. Just cut off a piece of the hose, slit it lengthwise, and slip it onto the wounded pipe. Secure the "bandage" with hose clips, C-clamps, or—in a pinch—duct tape or large binder clips. That should keep things under control until your plumber arrives.

2 Fast Leaky Pipe Fixes

So a pipe has sprung a leak, and you've called the plumber. Well, if that damaged conduit is in an accessible spot, don't just sit there twiddling your thumbs while you wait for help to show up. Instead, supply first aid in one of these ways:

- To fix a tiny leak, insert a toothpick into the hole, and break off the end of the toothpick so it's flush with the pipe. Then wrap several layers of waterproof tape around the pipe over the toothpick. (For a slightly larger hole, use a wooden matchstick.)

- Squeeze petroleum jelly into the hole or crack, and wrap waterproof tape around the pipe.

Comfort a Cranky Shutoff Valve

When a shutoff valve isn't used for a while, one of two things tends to happen: Either it simply won't budge, or it starts leaking when you turn it on. Here's how to solve both of those little problems:

▶ **Stubborn valve.** Put a few drops of lubricating oil around the stem next to the packing nut. Using a wrench or adjustable pliers, loosen the nut about one turn. Then retighten the nut partway with your hand. Wait three or four minutes for the oil to penetrate, and try turning the valve again. It should turn easily and smoothly.

▶ **Leaky valve.** Tighten the packing nut using adjustable pliers. If that doesn't do the trick, open and shut the valve a few times until the dripping stops.

It's a Wrap!

If you live in a cold-winter climate, you already know that you need to insulate your cold-water pipes to keep them from freezing when the temperature plummets. But your hot-water pipes benefit from protection, too, even if they're not as likely to freeze. That's because water loses heat as it travels from your water heater to your shower, bathtub, or sink. By covering the pipes with foam insulation, you'll save wear and tear on your water heater. As a bonus, you'll also cut back on the amount of gas or electricity needed to warm the water, thereby reducing your monthly utility bills. (Of course, just how much you'll save will vary, depending on the air temperature in the room and how much water you use.) Insulating water pipes is one of the easiest DIY fix-ups there is. Just follow this easy four-step plan of action:

STEP 1. Measure the length of the pipe you need to cover.

STEP 2. Run down to your local hardware store, and buy enough tubular foam insulation to do the job. (It comes with one side already presliced.)

STEP 3. If necessary, cut the long tubes into more workable lengths using a utility knife or long, sharp scissors.

STEP 4. Pop the pieces onto your pipes, and then stand back and admire your handiwork.

AN OUNCE OF
PREVENTION

Don't Blow It!

Some DIY "experts" recommend using a propane weeding torch or a butane welder's torch to thaw frozen pipes. Well, don't do it! Nor should you use a propane or kerosene heater or anything else that has an open flame. You could easily loosen welded joints or cause a buildup of steam to expand and burst the pipe. Whenever you're working with frozen pipes, your mantra should be "Slow and easy does it!"

Thawing Frozen Pipes

All you Sunbelt dwellers can skip this tip. But it's a crucial strategy for those of you who live in cold-winter territory—especially if you've recently moved to the snowy North. When you wake up one frigid morning, turn a faucet on, and nothing comes out, follow this warm-up plan:

▶ Check all of the faucets in your home. If one pipe is frozen, chances are that it's not performing a solo act.

▶ Before you attack the pipes with your thawing method of choice (see "4 Fabulous Ice-Melting Maneuvers," at left), turn on the faucets, and keep them open. That way, as the ice in the pipes begins to melt, the water will start to flow toward the spigots, thereby speeding up the melting process.

▶ Keep applying heat to the frozen pipe until full water pressure is restored—don't stop at the first sign of a sluggish stream.

▶ Always work from an open faucet toward the blockage so that steam can escape, and so that you'll know when you've melted the ice.

▶ If the frozen area is not accessible, or nothing that you do demolishes the ice dam, call a plumber—and be quick about it, because it's a sure bet that a whole lot of other frantic customers are in the same boat that you are.

4 Fabulous Ice-Melting Maneuvers

Thawing frozen pipes demands patience and a gentle source of heat. Only you can supply the former, but any of these comforting measures will deliver enough easygoing warmth to get the water flowing again:

• Move a hair dryer back and forth over the frozen zone.

• Wrap a heating pad around the stricken spot.

• Move a portable electric space heater close—but not too close—to the deep freeze.

• Soak towels in hot (not boiling!) water, and wrap them around the affected area.

Dodge Disaster: Your Frozen Pipe Prevention Plan

Most trouble is a whole lot easier (and less expensive) to prevent than it is to cope with after it hits you square in the face. And that old adage applies to burst water pipes more than it does to almost any other home catastrophe. These five simple strategies will help you keep those conduits intact when the temperature plummets:

- **Insulate exposed pipes.** This is especially important for those in unheated areas of your home, like the attic, crawl space, or garage. In moderately cold climates, inexpensive foam pipe insulation should do the trick (see "It's a Wrap!" on page 87). But if you live where winter is serious business, opt for thermostatically controlled heat tape (available at plumbing-supply stores).

- **Open your cabinet doors.** Kitchen and bathroom pipes can freeze in a hurry if, as is often the case, they abut exterior walls. By opening up the cabinet doors under your sink and bathroom vanity, you'll keep those danger zones warmer.

- **Keep your faucets open.** Contrary to what you may have heard, letting faucets drip is not a slam-dunk solution (in really frigid weather, even a roaring river will freeze). But it is true that letting the water flow very lightly will relieve the pressure inside the pipes and may prevent them from freezing—but if you live in a place with Arctic-like weather, all bets are off.

- **Leave the heat up.** Don't try to pinch pennies by lowering the temperature when you go out or (worse) turning off the heat in unused rooms. In cold weather, turning the thermostat down much below the upper 50s can be a recipe for disaster. And if you know that an unused room or closet has water pipes traveling through it, go one step further, and leave the door open so that heat can circulate from the rest of the house.

- **Turn the water off.** Whenever you leave home for more than a day—or even overnight during a wicked cold snap—shut off the water at the main valve. Then turn on all of your faucets, and let them flow until they stop. Even if any water remaining in the pipes freezes, it won't expand enough to cause a rupture.

SEPTIC SYSTEMS & WATER WELLS

Preserve Your Septic System!

A septic system that's well designed and well maintained can perform flawlessly for decades. On the other hand, if you don't give it proper care, it'll go down the drain (pun intended) fast—and replacing it is just about the most expensive home repair under the sun. For that reason, your most effective fix-it strategy is delivering heaping helpings of TLC, and that begins with conserving water. For example:

▶ Replace old showerheads, toilets, washing machines, and dishwashers with state-of-the-art, water-saving versions.

▶ Repair dripping faucets at the first sign of a wayward drop.

▶ Reduce your consumption. For example, take shorter showers, hold off washing clothes or running the dishwasher until you have a full load, and don't let the tap run for the whole time that you're brushing your teeth or shaving.

Fork Out for Preventive Maintenance

Have your septic system inspected every few years, and have the tank pumped out as often as necessary to remove accumulated sludge and scum. How frequently you need to schedule this cleaning depends on the size of the tank and the number of water users in your household. Your system's installer can provide guidance on that score.

Save the Friendly Bacteria!

A septic system can't function without friendly bacteria. So whatever you do, don't pour bacteria-killing toxins down the drain! The

CALL A PRO

If water backs up out of drains, or if there's a foul-smelling odor rising from the drainage field, it means that you've got serious trouble on your hands, so call your septic service provider immediately!

dastardly demons include commercial drain cleaners, bleaches, disinfectants, leftover prescription meds, chemical pesticides and fertilizers, and (surprise!) any product that's labeled "antibacterial."

Watch What's on Top

Never ever drive over or park on top of the drainage field. If you do, you'll deprive it of the oxygen it needs to function properly, and there's a good chance you'll also break, or even crush, some of the drain lines. For the same reason, only plant grass or shallow-rooted annual flowers over or near your septic tank and drain field. The underground parts of trees, shrubs, and deep-rooted perennials can damage the system.

Ditch the Disposal

Let's face it: A garbage disposal is a convenience, not a necessity. (In some places, like Manhattan for instance, the things are actually illegal.) But no matter where you live, if you depend on a septic system for your water supply, a garbage disposal can be a destructive menace. That's because the solid matter that the disposal sends down the drain can overload a septic tank's filtration system. As a result, food particles accumulate in the leach field, where they can form damaging—and potentially expensive—clogs. If you just can't bear to give up your garbage disposal, at least toss as much of your food waste as possible into a trash can or compost bin.

More, Please!

If you have a water well, and it's not delivering enough H_2O to meet your family's needs, you could drill a new one—but that'll cost you a pretty penny. Before you go that route, call a well installer and ask about having a secondary holding tank put in. Overnight and during low-use periods, the pump can work to fill this supplemental reservoir, which your household can then draw from while the main pump catches up with the action.

6 Ways to Keep Your Well Working Wonderfully

Repairing damage to a water well is *not* a DIY project. If anything goes wrong, a licensed well contractor will have to tackle the problem—and the price won't be cheap. But you can—and should—take these simple measures to ensure that clean, healthy water keeps flowing to your house:

- **Have your water tested** once a year for nitrates, bacteria, and other impurities. Your local health department can arrange a test, or provide you with a list of state-certified testing laboratories in your area.

- **Have a well contractor inspect the whole system** each year. The examination should cover the well itself, along with the pump, pipes, valves, pressure tank, and water flow.

- **Check the well cap and casing** at least several times a year. You want to make sure that the cap is tightly closed and there are no cracks or other openings that could let pollutants enter the well.

- **Make sure the ground slopes** away from the well, not toward it, or level with it. And whenever you mow in the area, be very careful not to ding the well casing.

- **Install anti-siphon valves** on all faucets that have hose connections. These devices prevent a common source of well-water contamination: unsanitary water being pulled back through garden hoses.

- **Avoid using hazardous chemicals,** such as paints, solvents, and gasoline, anywhere near the well. And swear off chemical pesticides and fertilizers altogether!

Don't Lose the Log!

Whatever you do, hang on to the well log that the contractor filed when your well was first drilled. That book contains the full scoop on the ground, the well's construction, and the mechanical apparatus that makes it work. All that information will come in mighty handy if anything goes awry, or if you ever want to have a new well drilled or the current one expanded (see "More, Please!," on page 91).

Heating & Cooling

The systems that heat and cool our 21st-century homes are complex and varied, to put it mildly. When things go wrong, in most cases your only recourse is to put out a fast SOS to your friendly neighborhood HVAC contractor. But some system glitches are easy enough to handle yourself—and you can head off many more by using the timely tips that are coming right up.

CENTRAL AIR-CONDITIONING

Keep It Free and Clear

Your first step on the road to a smoother-working and longer-lasting AC system begins with giving the outdoor condenser unit plenty of elbow room so that nothing interferes with the free flow of air. In particular:

- Don't plant anything but grass or an ultra-low groundcover within a 2-foot radius of the unit. And keep shrubs trimmed so that their branches don't invade the 24-inch no-go zone.

- Better yet, forget plants in that area altogether. Instead, cover the surrounding soil with bricks, paving stones, or gravel.

- Keep the grilles clear of falling leaves and twigs. (Pruning some branches from nearby trees could make this chore a lot easier!)

- To reduce the amount of dust that flies into the unit, add a thick layer of mulch to any nearby planting beds.

- On mowing day, bag your grass clippings, or at least send them flying away from the unit.

To Cover or Not to Cover?

True or false? When cooling season ends, you should put a cover over your outdoor condenser unit to protect it from the elements.

Absolutely false! That baby is designed to withstand just about anything Old Man Winter sends its way. In fact, a warm winter coat is likely to do more harm than good because it can trap moisture inside the unit and rust the metal casing.

Lighter Labor Leads to a Longer Life

You don't have to be a mechanical genius to know that the harder your air conditioner (or any other appliance) has to work, the faster the inside parts wear out. These simple ploys will ease the burden on your AC—and reduce your summertime electric bills at the same time:

- **Get shady.** Install white window shades, and keep them closed on sunny days. They'll reflect the sun's rays, so your house will stay cooler, and the AC won't have so much chillin' to do.

- **Give the thermostat some elbow room.** Always keep television sets, lamps, and any other electrical appliances away from your thermostat. The heat the devices generate will cause your cooling system to run longer and work harder than it needs to.

- **Open the damper.** We all know that in the winter months, when your fireplace is not in use, you should close the damper so that heat doesn't go up the chimney. Well, in the summertime, the exact opposite is true: You want to make sure that "door" is wide open so that hot air *will* go up the chimney, rather than linger indoors, adding to your AC's workload.

CALL A PRO

If, during your pre-season wake-up procedure—or at any other time—you see dark drip marks on the bottom of the case, it means that your unit is leaking oil or coolant, or both. So call an HVAC specialist immediately. Do not try to stop a leak by tightening a joint—that's likely to make the problem worse!

'Tis the Season (Almost)

The period when Old Man Winter fades away and spring starts moving in is a crucial time for your cooling system. Here are two things you need to remember:

• Whatever you do, don't ever run your central air-conditioning when the outside temperature is lower than 60°F. Doing so could cause serious damage to the compressor.

• Have an HVAC professional inspect, clean, and tune up the system after the temperature gets above 60°F, but before you really need to use the AC. You'll catch any problems in time to have them fixed before the hot, sticky weather sets in—and *before* the repair pros get so busy that you might have to wait for days before help arrives.

Quiet Your Cooler

It's annoying all right: You're trying to relax on your deck, and the danged AC condenser is rattling like an old jalopy barreling down a rocky road. Well, don't lose your cool. The commotion may be a snap to stop. Just turn off the power to the system (see Step 1 of "Your Pre-Season Problem-Prevention Plan" on page 96), and conduct this four-part search-and-repair mission:

• Unscrew and open up the unit's top grille, and clear out any debris that may be stuck in the fan. (You may need to enlist a helper to hold the grille open to avoid damaging the wires inside.)

• Tighten the bolts or screws that hold the blades in place.

• Make sure all the screws in the housing are good and tight.

• If the fan motor has oil ports, give them a dose of lubricant (see Step 5 of "Your Pre-Season Problem-Prevention Plan" on page 97).

If none of these ploys put the racket to rest, it's likely that the fan motor needs to be replaced, or at least serviced, by an HVAC professional. So get on the horn pronto!

Your Pre-Season Problem-Prevention Plan

Before the start of each cooling season, it's a good idea to give your outdoor condenser a little TLC to make sure it functions at peak performance when the temperatures start rising. Do the job on a day when the temperature is at least 60°F because that's the minimum temperature at which you can test the unit to make sure it's working. Also, enlist a pal to lend you a hand when you get to Step 3. Then proceed as follows:

STEP 1. Turn off the power to the system. There should be a switch, a pull lever, or a pull-out fuse block near the unit. If you don't see one, kill the AC's circuit at your home's main electric panel. Then rake up and remove leaves and any other debris that may have accumulated around the condenser over the winter.

STEP 2. Unscrew and remove the protective metal case (if any) that covers the unit. Then vacuum the fins using a soft brush. Go gently to avoid damaging the fragile metal. If you find any bent fins, straighten them using a blunt dinner knife or sturdy metal spatula.

Turn off the power, and remove any debris around the condenser.

STEP 3. Unscrew and lift up the top grille, to which the unit's fan and motor are usually attached. Have your helper hold this "lid" open to keep its wires and connections intact while you vacuum inside the unit.

STEP 4. With your pal still holding the grille up, cover any exposed parts inside the unit with plastic bags. Then spray the fins from the inside out, using a garden hose equipped with a trigger-controlled nozzle.

Spray the fins from the inside out.

STEP 5. Check the fan motor for lubrication ports.* If there are any, they'll be on top of the motor, just below the fan blades. Remove the plugs from the holes, and add lubricating oil, as specified in your owner's manual or on the oil can. Then spin the blades slowly by hand to disperse the oil within the fan. If your unit has a belt-driven compressor in the bottom (as older models often do), fill its lubrication ports, too. But remember: More oil is not better—use no more than 10 drops per port.

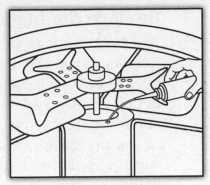

Add oil to the lubrication ports.

STEP 6. Close the grille, and put the outside case back on. In most cases, you can get the show on the road by simply restoring power to the unit, turning your indoor thermostat to cool, and selecting the temperature of your choice. But some compressors demand special treatment at start-up time, so unless you know for sure that your model can leap right out of the starting gate, follow the instructions in "Baby That Baby!" (see page 99).

Your owner's manual should specify the best type of lubricant to use on your particular machine. If it doesn't—or if you don't have your manual—jot down the make and model number, and take that note to a hardware or appliance-parts store and ask a knowledgeable clerk to recommend the appropriate type of electric motor oil. Whatever you do, don't even think of using penetrating oil or an all-purpose oil of any kind. Those products are not designed for long-term lubrication and can actually harm the bearings.

Evict All Trespassers!

Mice, fire ants, and (yes) even snakes can set up winter housekeeping inside hibernating AC condensers. So when you open up the top, check for any uninvited guests before you start your cleaning routine—and definitely make sure the interior population is zero before you screw the top back on the unit!

Replace the Insulation on Your AC Pipes

A central air conditioner works its cooling magic by transferring a gas from a condenser in the unit outside your house to evaporating coils indoors (usually located in the main supply duct above the furnace). In order for the system to function at peak efficiency, the pipe that carries the refrigerant must remain within a consistent temperature range—which it does when the pipe is properly insulated. But over time, the insulation can deteriorate, causing your AC to lose 10 degrees or more of its cooling power. Luckily, replacing that protective blanket is one of the simplest DIY jobs on the HVAC scene. Here's all you need to do:

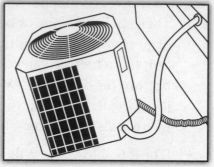

Your cooling conduit pipes run from your outdoor AC unit to evaporating coils in the blower system inside your house.

STEP 1. Track and inspect the pipe. The part outside, which connects to the AC unit, will be easy to spot. Likewise, it should be clearly visible where it connects to your home's blower system. You may also see the pipe running beneath the floor above the basement or crawl space.

STEP 2. Measure the length and diameter of the exposed areas, and buy enough foam pipe insulation to cover them (you can find it at home-improvement stores).

STEP 3. Carefully remove the remains of the old insulation using a razor-edged scraper. Then wipe the pipes with a cloth to remove any residue.

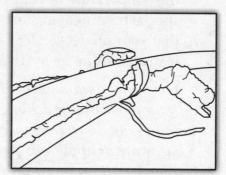

Scrape off the old insulation.

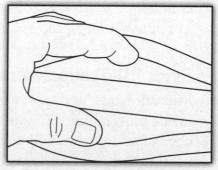

Foam pipe insulation comes pre-slit, with self-sealing edges.

STEP 4. Cut the new insulation into easy-to-manage lengths using a utility knife. Then slide the pre-slit side over the pipe, and push the foam into place. Once all the "sleeves" are on, remove the protective backing from the self-sealing edges of the slits, and press the edges together snugly. At locations where two lengths of foam join together, wrap the seams with electrical tape.

Baby That Baby!

Air-conditioner compressors are a lot more fragile than you might imagine, and some of them are spoiled brats that can hand you major problems if you don't start them up in exactly the right way. Unless you know for sure that your system has built-in controls to handle the start-up process seamlessly, follow these procedures:

▶ **At the start of the cooling season**—or whenever power to the unit has been off for more than four hours: Make sure the thermostat is set on "off." Turn on power to the system, and wait for 24 hours while the compressor's lubricant warms up. Then switch the thermostat back to "cool."

▶ **If a power outage occurs** while the AC is on: Switch the thermostat to "off," and after the power is restored, wait at least five minutes before turning it back on.

WELL, WHADDYA KNOW!

The world's first home air-conditioning system dates back to (believe it or not) 2000 BC. It was the brainchild of a wealthy Babylonian merchant, who had his servants spray water on the walls and floor of his bedroom in the evening. The ensuing evaporation, combined with lower temperatures outdoors, created blessed relief from the desert heat. Nearly 4,000 years later, in 1902, a young Cornell University graduate named Willis Carrier produced the world's first commercial cooling system for a Brooklyn printer. Within a few years, people in movie theaters, department stores, and office buildings throughout the country basked in the comfort of Carrier air-conditioning, but it took more than half a century before air conditioners became common-place in American homes.

ROOM AIR CONDITIONERS

Finesse the Filter

Just like whole-house AC, a room air conditioner delivers more chilling power and lasts longer when it has a spanking-clean filter. If your wall or window AC has a disposable filter, simply replace it with a new one every 30 days. To keep a foam or metal mesh version in tip-top shape, follow this procedure at least once a month:

- ▶ **Wash the filter** in a basin of warm water with a squirt or two of dishwashing liquid added to it.

- ▶ **Remove any accumulated odor** by gently dousing the filter with ½ teaspoon or so of baking soda per cup of water.

- ▶ **Rinse the filter** in cool, clear water, and let it dry completely before reinstalling it. Whatever you do, don't use the air conditioner until the clean filter is back in place!

Note: *In each case, the timing is approximate. If you have heavily shedding pets on the scene, or if you're cooling a room where dust flies frequently (like a workshop), you should clean or replace your filter more often. Conversely, if you spend a lot of time away from home, or you live in a mild climate that doesn't demand everyday cooling, you can go longer between changes. Just take a gander now and then, and let your eyes be your guide.*

Darn Those Drips!

When a window air conditioner starts dripping water into your house, the cause could be an ultra-dirty filter. But if you know that essential element is clean, those wayward drops indicate that the unit hasn't been installed properly. These machines are designed to tilt slightly toward the outside so that any condensation will drip off the far bottom edge and onto the ground. But if they're not sited just so when set into place, the water winds up on your floor. Fortunately, if the dripper is in a window that slides down against it, a dry floor is only three steps away. First, round up a helper who can lend a helping hand (literally). Then go at the job this way:

STEP 1. Remove any screws or brackets holding the window in place on top of the AC, and slide back the sliding extensions on the sides. Then raise the window about ½ inch, and have your assistant hold a hand on top of the frame to keep it from rising any higher.

STEP 2. Slide your hands under the inside edge of the air conditioner, and gently lift it up to meet the window. Make sure the machine is sloping toward the great outdoors. If it isn't, raise both the window and the unit a little more.

STEP 3. Put the extensions back into place, and reattach the hardware on top of the unit.

My, the Air Smells Musty!

When your room air conditioner starts sending out musty-smelling air rather than a sweet, comforting breeze, it may mean that algae have clogged up the drain tube. Your quick two-part fix-it plan:

• Working from the underside of the unit, poke a strand of thick wire or an unbent wire coat hanger into the tube, and move it around to clear out the debris.

• To keep a new crop of algae from from sprouting, shoot a teaspoon of ammonia into the hole, using an old syringe or dropper.

Quiet, Please!

When your window AC starts "talking" to you, the problem may be any of the same ones that cause noises in outdoor condensers (see "Quiet Your Cooler" on page 95). There are also five other possibilities:

▶ **The window frame and sash.** With the unit on, press the palm of your hand against the sash. If the noise stops or changes in pitch, insert thin wooden shims between the sash and the window frame.

▶ **The glass.** Again, make sure the AC is on, and press your palm against the glass. If that stops the vibration, either reputty or apply window insulation tape (available in hardware stores) between the frame and the edge of the glass.

▶ **The sill.** Some windowsills slope, which prevents the machine from sitting securely—so it's bound to bounce around and make noise. If that's the case, simply wedge a few shims in between the sill and the base of the unit.

▶ **Loose connections.** If the noise changes when you press both palms against the front panel, it means that the panel has too much room to roam inside. First, tighten the screws on the panel. If that doesn't work, use duct tape to seal the panel tightly to the unit's frame.

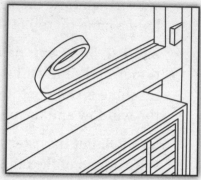

Stop a vibrating window glass by applying insulating tape, or tucking shims between the window sash and frame.

▶ **Loose inner workings.** Unplug the AC, and remove the chassis from its housing. Clean out any debris that may have found its way into the cabinet. Spin the fan blades by hand to check their condition. If a bent blade is striking the condenser fins, straighten the blade, as well as any dented fins. Give the chassis a shake to see if the condenser coil's pigtail wire is striking the fan's housing. If it is, insert a piece of adhesive-backed foam between them. **Note:** *Check your owner's manual for the exact procedure to follow in accessing the chassis; it varies, depending on the make and model.*

Tighten the screws to eliminate vibrations between the panel and the unit's frame.

If none of these tricks make the machine quiet down, call an HVAC pro for help. Or, depending on the age of the unit, it may be time to bite the bullet and buy a new air conditioner.

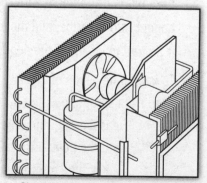

Check the fan and the pigtail that's attached to the condenser coil.

Store It and Score a Double Play

Both your window air conditioner and the sill it's sitting on will last longer if you remove the unit at the end of the cooling season and tuck it away in a dry, cozy place for the winter. (And, of course, you'll need to relocate the AC if you plan to install storm windows.) A utility room or closet is the ideal storage space. A basement will work, too—provided you stash the machine on a shelf, not on the concrete floor. Above all, avoid a shed, garage, or anyplace where wire-chewing rodents might roam. It's also important to follow this simple removal and storage-prep plan:

- **Unplug the air conditioner.** Then take off the front cover, and remove any padding or trim that encloses the unit.

- **Lift the machine up,** pull it out of the window, and set it on a solid work surface. (Get help for this step—these babies are heavy!)

- **Unscrew the wooden base** from the windowsill, and replace the original sash.

- **Clean the outside** of the unit with soapy water and a soft cloth. Then remove the case according to the instructions in your owner's manual, and vacuum the interior with a soft brush.

- **Straighten out** any bent fins, wash the drain pan, and remove any rust from it and the metal casing. Then let the unit dry thoroughly before you send it into hibernation.

Degrease Grates, Grilles, and Blades

Heating grates, air-conditioner grilles, and ceiling-fan blades all tend to attract more than their fair share of greasy dust. And that grime not only looks unsightly, but can also significantly reduce airflow from the device. Your one-stop cleaning solution: full-strength white vinegar. Simply wipe it onto the surfaces with a soft cotton cloth, and the gunk will come right off. To get inside tight spaces, dip a retired toothbrush into the vinegar, and scrub-a-dub-dub.

Dress It for Success

If you prefer to leave your window AC in place for the cold-weather months—or you have a wall-mounted version that needs to stay put—do yourself a favor: Buy an insulated cover that's specially designed to protect the unit and keep cold drafts from seeping into your house. Your owner's manual may specify a cover for your particular machine. If not, jot down the make and model, along with the dimensions of the unit, and take that to your local appliance or hardware store (or type it into your search engine if you prefer to shop online). Remember: The better this overcoat fits, the safer your air conditioner will be, and the warmer you'll be when the temperature drops.

CEILING FANS

What a Wobble!

When your formerly smooth-sailing ceiling fan suddenly starts to wobble, don't pass it off as a minor annoyance. In addition to grating on your nerves, the erratic dips and turns will wear out its moving parts faster than you can say, "Bob's your uncle!" Before you try any more complex measures, clean the blades because accumulated dirt can throw the blades out of balance. Granted, it doesn't happen often, but it can't hurt to try the simplest fix-it ploy first.

If dirt is not the culprit, the problem could be loose screws or a blade that's out of alignment. So first, tighten the screws in the blade mounts. Then use a yardstick to measure the distance from the edge of any blade to the ceiling, and jot down the figure. Repeat the procedure with all the other blades, at exactly the same point along the shaft. If any blade is out of alignment, gently bend the blade holder up or down until the blade lines up with its mates.

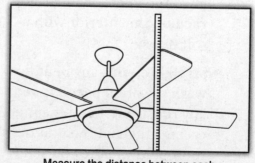

Measure the distance between each fan blade and the ceiling.

Run the fan at various speeds. If the danged contraption still teeter-totters, buy a fan-balancing kit at your local hardware store, and follow the procedure described in "A Perfect Balancing Act" (below).

A Perfect Balancing Act

Putting an out-of-kilter fan back in balance is a little time-consuming, but the process couldn't be simpler. Here's all there is to it:

STEP 1. Pull out the balancing clip that came with your kit, and slide it onto the trailing edge of any blade, halfway between the holder and the tip of the blade. Then turn the fan on to check the degree of teetering. Repeat the procedure with each blade, noting which one, when weighted down, most reduced the erratic spin.

Slide the balancing clip onto each blade until you find the one that is causing the problem.

STEP 2. Put the clip back on the faulty blade, and slide the clip away from the center in small increments. Move the clip, run the fan, then move the clip again until you've eliminated as much wobbling as possible.

STEP 3. Once you've found the best location for the clip, press an adhesive-backed balancing weight onto the center of the blade, parallel to the clip. Then remove the clip. Try the fan and add more weight if necessary.

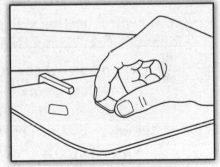

Press a balancing weight onto the center of the faulty blade.

Don't Scale the Heights

Tired of climbing up on a stepladder to keep the blades of your ceiling fan dust free? Then attach a dryer sheet to a paint roller with rubber bands, and screw an extension pole onto the roller handle. With your feet planted firmly on the floor, glide the roller over each fan blade. End of potentially unbalancing dust—with no risk of taking a tumble!

CALL A PRO

If balancing your fan's blades does not end your wobbly woes, call a licensed electrician, who can check for and possibly correct more serious problems, including installation errors. Just be aware that it may be time to bid good-bye to your old breeze-maker and get a new one.

Car Wax Deters Dust

If your ceiling fan has wooden blades, you're in luck: You have an ultra-simple way to help keep dust from building up. Simply remove the blades and give them a coat of paste car wax. Once the wax has dried, buff the surface, and reinstall the blades

Note: *Liquid car wax will also work, but use it very sparingly. An overdose can discolor the wood or damage its protective coating.*

HEAT-DELIVERY SYSTEMS

2 Secrets to Smooth Sailing

Your central heating system will work better and last longer if you follow these two important steps:

▶ **Get an annual checkup.** Have an HVAC pro conduct a thorough examination of your furnace or boiler and its delivery system before the cold weather sets in. This way, you'll catch and resolve any small problems before they turn into big ones—and before there's a waiting list a mile long for service calls. If you have an automatic fuel-delivery plan with your oil or liquid-gas supplier, the contract may include a free yearly inspection. **Note:** *If it doesn't, consider switching to a dealer that does offer such service.*

▶ **Go along on the "tour."** And ask questions. The more you know about all the levers, buttons, belts, and motors that make your system work, the better equipped you'll be to troubleshoot any problems—and to describe the details when you have to call.

Give It Air!

If you have either a gas- or an oil-fired heating system, you probably have metal duct pipes that carry outdoor air directly to the appliance's burner. Whatever you do, don't try to reduce drafts (and your heating bills) by plugging those outlets. Your furnace or boiler needs that air in order to accomplish complete combustion of its operating fuel. A lack of sufficient air leads to incomplete combustion—which generates potentially deadly carbon monoxide.

Turn It Off!

No matter what kind of fuel your system burns, it's crucial to kill the flow fast in the event of a fire or natural disaster of any kind. So make sure that every adult and older child in your household knows where to find the control valve and how to turn it off. Here's where to look:

- **Natural gas** enters your home at the meter, where you'll find a valve on the intake pipe. Use a wrench to turn the valve to a horizontal position so that it's at a right angle to the pipe.

- **Bottled gas.** You'll find either a lever or knob on top of the tank. Turn this control clockwise to close it.

- **Fuel oil.** The shutoff valve should be near the bottom of the tank, where the fuel line leads out of it. Turn the knob clockwise to stop the oil flow, or call your oil supplier.

AN OUNCE OF

PREVENTION

Lend a Helping Hand

Just like any other equipment, your central heating and cooling system needs a little help if it's going to operate at peak efficiency, season after season and year after year. In particular, remember these two guidelines:

• Keep the thermostat's fan switch on the "auto" setting. Leaving it turned to "on" not only makes the fan work harder and wear out more quickly, but it can also add $25 or more each month to your heating and cooling costs.

• Keep all registers, radiators, and return air vents free and clear. If any are blocked by furniture, draperies, or appliances, either move the stuff or lose it.

FORCED-AIR SYSTEMS

Be Good to the Blower

In a forced-air heating system—the most common type in modern American homes—the blower supplies the driving force. In order to keep running smoothly year after year, that heavy lifter requires an annual cleaning. On older furnaces, the blower motor also needs to be oiled every 12 months or so. (Newer models have permanently lubricated bearings.) Both of these chores should be part of your annual furnace inspection. But should you ever have to tackle either job yourself, turn off the furnace's power switch, open the blower compartment, and continue as follows:

▶ **Cleaning the blower.** Vacuum the fan blades and the blower housing using a soft brush. If your sweeper's attachment won't reach all the blades, wrap a soft cloth around the end of a ruler or a paint-stir stick.

▶ **Lubricating the motor.** First, check for oil ports on the exposed part of the motor. Remove the metal cap or rubber plug from each port, and add 2 or 3 drops of the lubricant recommended in your owner's manual (if there is none specified, or you don't have the manual, consult your HVAC contractor). Be careful not to overfill the ports—and whatever you do, never use all-purpose or penetrating oil, which can damage the bearings.

EMERGENCY RESPONSE:

I SMELL GAS!

The second you smell gas (the aroma resembles that of rotten eggs), close the main shutoff valve, and extinguish any open flames. Then evacuate the house, leaving the door wide open behind you. Do *not* touch any electrical switches, and don't use the telephone. Once you're away from the danger scene, call the gas company or the fire department from your cell phone or a neighbor's house. And don't even think of going back inside your place until the repair crew gives you a thumbs-up!

Is That Piglet I Hear?

If your forced-air furnace starts to squeal like an excited pig, or if the airflow seems weak, it's a good bet that the belt connecting the blower cage to the motor has come loose, or simply worn out. To make a positive diagnosis, turn off the furnace, remove the blower access panel, and aim a flashlight at the belt. Depending on what you see, you can resolve the problem in one of two ways:

- If the belt is frayed, cracked, or shiny, remove it, take it to a heating-supply or home-improvement store, and buy an identical replacement. In most cases, you can remove and reinstall a belt simply by pulling or pushing it over the lip of the motor pulley with one hand while turning the pulley with the other.

- To check the belt's tension, press down on it at the center of its span. It should give by about ½ inch; if there is more slack than that, you need to tighten it. On many blowers, you can turn an adjustment bolt on the base of the motor to tighten (or loosen) the belt. In other cases, you need to loosen the motor's mounting bolts and move the motor by hand.

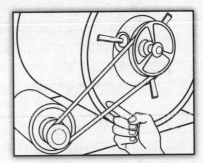

There should be about ½ inch of slack in the blower-connection belt.

Other Reasons for the Racket

A badly behaving belt isn't the only factor that can trigger blower noise or reduced airflow. Either of these two factors can also be at fault:

A jiggling motor. Tightening the bolts that hold the motor in place will solve that problem lickety-split.

Misaligned belt pulleys. This is a quick fix. Just loosen the setscrew on the motor pulley and align it with the blower pulley.

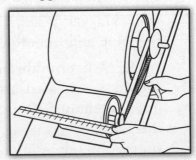

If the motor and blower pulleys don't line up, loosen the setscrew and move the motor pulley.

THE GAS BURNER BALANCING ACT

In order to operate at peak efficiency, a gas burner must maintain the right ratio of fuel to air. A quick glance at the flame will tell you how well that balance is holding up. Here's how to interpret the scene:

If the flame is...	It means that...
Yellow at the tip, with a hazy inner flame	The burner is not getting sufficient air.
Blue with a sharp outline and a hard-edged inner flame	The burner is getting too much air.
Mostly blue and soft-edged with a blue-green inner flame	The fuel-air balance is just right.

Note: *If the fuel-air balance is off in either direction, have an HVAC pro adjust the intake shutters on the burner tubes. Do not try this job yourself!*

Lose the Leaks

Leaky ductwork won't damage your forced-air system—but paying for the heated (or cooled) air that escapes can put a big dent in your bank account. So once a year, or if you suddenly notice an unexpected jump in your utility bill, check for leaks in all visible ducts. Most often, the trouble will crop up in the joints between duct sections. Make sure all seams are sealed good and tight. If the duct tape is worn, take it off. Then wipe the area clean with a cloth dipped in white vinegar. When it's dry, press professional-quality duct tape over the joint, and smooth it out to remove any air bubbles.

Ducts that run through unheated areas, like the basement or attic, should be insulated. You can have a heating contractor do the honors, but it's a simple DIY project: Just pick up batts of fiberglass insulation that are specially designed to fit ducts (you can find them in heating-supply and home-improvement stores), and follow the installation instructions on the packaging.

OIL BURNERS & TANKS

Cast a Cold Eye on the Flame

Gauging the job performance of an oil burner is the same as it is for the gas-fired versions (see "The Gas Burner Balancing Act," at left): Take a glance at the flame every once in a while. In this case, when you look through the observation window, you want to see a bright yellow flame with no trace of smoke. If that fire is sooty or dark orange in color—or if there is smoke spewing from the chimney outside—it means that the fuel-to-air balance is out of kilter. So have a heating pro adjust the burner.

Cleanliness Is Next to Coziness

If you have an oil-fired boiler or furnace, keeping its surroundings clean and tidy is an absolute must if you want to keep heat flowing efficiently through your home all winter long. To be specific:

- ▶ Make sure the floors and walls around the furnace remain free of dust, dirt, and grime.

- ▶ *Never* sweep dirt or debris under the burner unit.

- ▶ Once a week—or more often if necessary—use your vacuum cleaner's crevice tool to clear out the opening that lets air into the blower.

Any foreign material that finds its way inside the unit can hinder the blower's action or even cause the burner to fail.

Keep Your Tank in Tip-Top Shape

Whether your heating-oil tank resides in your basement or in the great outdoors, it demands consistent TLC if it's going to supply a steady flow of fuel to your furnace. Aboveground outdoor tanks are especially vulnerable because they're fully exposed to everything Mother Nature delivers in the way of rain, snow, hail, and wind. Your trouble-prevention plan begins with having an HVAC pro perform a thorough inspection before the start of each heating season. But your part of the deal never stops. Here's your DIY job description:

- Make sure the legs are stable and the tank is sitting on an even keel (even the slightest earth tremor can knock it off kilter).

- Keep the surrounding area free of debris so you can check the tank's underbelly for leaks. Also, make sure that both the tank and its supply lines are protected from damage, which could come in the form of anything from wayward bicycles, frolicking children, or careless construction workers to a cascade of falling ice.

- Be on constant watch for dents, as well as rust and oily stains that are dripping down the sides of the tank (what HVAC pros call "weepage"). If you spy any rust or weepage along the bottom of the tank, have the tank replaced pronto.

- Look for signs of spillage near the tank's fill and vent pipes. If you find any, call your HVAC contractor *immediately*.

- Outdoors, keep the tank's vent clear of snow and ice, as well as more solid blockers, such as fallen leaves and critter nests.

A Sneaky Underground Movement

An underground oil tank can leak like a sieve without leaving any telltale signs on the soil above. If your monthly utility bill shows an unexplained increase in fuel usage, it's all but guaranteed that you've got a leak on your hands, so call your HVAC pro now. If you delay, that seepage could cause environmental damage that'll cost you a boatload of time and money to remedy.

CALL A PRO

Whenever your oil burner needs any maintenance work at all, pick up the phone and call your service provider. If you attempt any DIY tricks, you're likely to void your service contract—and you could send your system belly-up to boot!

RADIATORS

The Myth of Metallic Paint

Common assumption: Painting your radiators with metallic paint will make them work more efficiently.

Reality: Metallic paint actually reduces heat transmission by as much as 9 percent or more. You say your radiators are covered with layers of the stuff? No problem! Taking it off is a snap. Here's all you need to do:

▸ Tap each radiator gently all over with a ball-peen hammer. The vibration will make most of the paint drop right off.

▸ Use a wire brush to remove any remaining patches.

▸ Brush the stripped metal with mineral oil to give it a sheen.

Note: *There is no need to disconnect the radiator before you start your efficiency-enhancement project, but do make sure the heat is turned off.*

Repaint with Care

You say you simply can't live with naked radiators? Then cover them with stove black, a traditional coating that's available in hardware stores and shops that specialize in fireplace and woodstove supplies. If you prefer the appearance of a bronze or silver radiator, heat-proof paint in a light brown or gray color will give you a similar look without compromising the heating unit's efficiency like metallic paint would do.

Shine More Heat on the Scene

To make a radiator or baseboard heater work more efficiently, wrap heavy-duty aluminum foil, shiny side up, around a piece of cardboard or thin wood, and tuck it behind the unit. The foil will do a terrific job of reflecting heat into the room, so it won't be absorbed into the wall.

Knock, Knock ...

Is no joke if your home is heated by radiators. And the cause is no mystery: In one-pipe steam-heating systems, steam flows from the boiler to the radiators, and the resulting condensation flows back to the boiler through the same pipe. If the radiator doesn't slope down toward the inlet valve, and the pipe doesn't slope down toward the boiler, water collects in the system, where it interferes with the flow of steam—raising a royal ruckus in the process. Only a plumber can tackle the pipe's position, but it's a snap to tilt the radiator into quiet mode. First, turn the heat off, and wait until the radiator has cooled down. The next step depends on the nature of the legs on the end of the unit opposite the inlet valve.

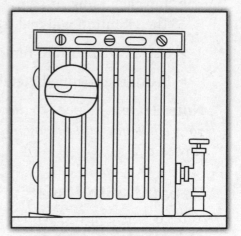

To stop a knocking noise, tilt the radiator toward the inlet valve.

- **Adjustable.** Turn the height-adjustment bolts with a wrench to raise the legs, increasing the angle of the incline.

- **Stationary.** Lift up the end of the radiator, and slide shims or wooden blocks under the legs. A height of ½ to ¾ of an inch should do the trick.

Bleed for Comfort

If the heat in your home isn't circulating well, the bottom of your radiator is warm while the top portion is cold—or the whole thing is cool to the touch—it's almost guaranteed that there's air trapped inside. Setting it free so that your system can function efficiently entails a technique called "bleeding," which you do by opening what's called (surprise!) the bleeder valve. On some models, you can use a flat-end screwdriver; other types require a special key, which you can pick up for peanuts at your local hardware store. Then follow this four-step process with every radiator in your home, beginning with the ones on the top floor:

STEP 1. Turn off the heat, and make sure the intake valve is closed. Then hold a cup or thick towel under the bleeder valve at the top of the unit. (You may want to wear gloves to protect your hands from the hot water that will sputter out.)

STEP 2. Insert the key or screwdriver into the valve, and turn it counterclockwise. You will hear a hissing sound, but don't be alarmed—that's the normal sound of air escaping.

STEP 3. Keep the valve open until water starts to come out, and then close the valve. Then move on to the rest of your radiator "herd."

STEP 4. If you have a sealed heating system, check the pressure and add water if necessary. Then turn the heat back on.

As a preventive measure, bleed your system at the start of each heating season.

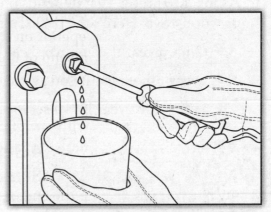

Bleed radiators once a year, or whenever heat is circulating poorly.

It's Spitting at Me!

If your radiator's air vent is spewing out water, or the unit has simply fallen off in the heat-production department, there may be a simple two-word remedy: white vinegar. To put V-power to work, unscrew the air vent, and soak it in hot vinegar for 30 minutes to dissolve any rust or stuck debris. Rinse the vent with cold water for a minute or so, and then blow through it. If your expended air did not come out the other end of the valve, repeat the soak-and-rinse procedure, followed by the breath test. Once the air is flowing freely, wrap plumber's tape (a.k.a. thread seal or PTFE tape) around the threaded end of the vent, and screw it back in place. Make sure the vent opening is facing upward. Then start your heating system and cast your eye on the air vent. If it releases steam but fails to close afterward—or if no steam comes out—it's time to replace the vent.

FIREPLACES & WOODSTOVES

Only You Can Prevent Chimney Fires . . .

And the way to do it is to have a professional chimney cleaner inspect the structure every year for creosote buildup and overall soundness. It also needs to be cleaned periodically. The same pro who performs the inspection can handle that job, or you can do the honors yourself (see "4 Steps to a Santa-Worthy Chimney," below). As for the timing, that depends on how often you use your fireplace or woodstove. Here's the basic rule of thumb:

▶ Once a year if you burn three or more fires a week

▶ Every other year if you average two fires a week

▶ Every third year if you set logs ablaze only once in a while.

Cleaning up soot from your fireplace or woodstove is no picnic—but two types of potential trash can make the job a whole lot easier: Sprinkle used, moist tea leaves or still-moist coffee grounds over the soot. Either one—or a combination of both—will prevent the noxious particles from flying into the air when you sweep the stuff up.

4 Steps to a Santa-Worthy Chimney

Cleaning a chimney is one of the messiest jobs on the planet, but it's a straightforward procedure.* Here's one way to go about it:

STEP 1. Chop down (or buy) a small fir or pine tree that's just a little wider than your chimney, and round up a rope that's long enough to reach from the top of the chimney to your hearth, with about 3 feet to spare on either end. Also, enlist a willing helper.

STEP 2. Set the tree on the hearth. Then climb up onto the roof, lower one end of the rope into the chimney, and have your pal tie it tightly to the trunk of the tree.

STEP 3. From your perch on the rooftop, haul the tree up through the chimney. Drop the free end of the rope down the flue, so your accomplice can grab it and pull the tree back down.

STEP 4. Repeat the process once or twice (depending on how dirty the shaft was to begin with), and Santa will enjoy a clean descent on Christmas Eve!

* Before you start, cover the hearth and everything in the vicinity with sturdy drop cloths!

A Clean Chimney: It's in the Bag

If you don't have access to a little evergreen tree, fill a burlap sack with rough, bulky material, such as old tire chains or hardware cloth. Just make sure that the filled bag is wide enough to scrape the sides of the chimney. Then proceed according to the directions in "4 Steps to a Santa-Worthy Chimney" (at left), with you pulling the bag up through the chimney and your helper pulling it back down—or vice versa.

Say "Sayonara, Soot!"

Soot that builds up in your chimney can cause it to draw less efficiently, or even start a fire. Fortunately, you have two simple ways to banish the buildup:

POWERFUL POTIONS

SOOT-REMOVAL FORMULA

When nasty soot builds up on your hearth or the sides of your fireplace, take it off with this mighty mix.

Dishwashing liquid
Hot water
Pumice powder*
Ammonia

Mix the first three ingredients together to form a dough-like consistency. Then add ammonia a little at a time until you've got a thick, spreadable paste. Wipe the mixture onto the brick with a brush or cloth, and let it dry thoroughly (normally 10 to 15 minutes). Then scrub the paste—and the soot—away using a wet, stiff brush.

* Available in pharmacies, hardware stores, and online.

- Before you light the fire, toss a handful of salt on the logs. It'll help loosen any soot that's clinging to the chimney.

- Whenever you peel potatoes, spread the skins out on paper towels and let them dry thoroughly. Then burn them in your fireplace or woodstove. They'll produce a powerful heat that sends soot soaring up and out of the chimney. (In the summertime, when you're not building indoor fires, store your dried spud skins in glass canning jars and put 'em on soot-prevention duty when the chilly weather returns.)

Abolish the Antenna

If you still have a TV antenna strapped to your chimney, take it down *now*. (No matter how long you leave it up there, it's not going to bring in new *I Love Lucy* episodes.) Why the rush? Two reasons:

- The strapping puts stress on the mortar, causing the bricks to loosen.

- In a strong wind, the strapping and the antenna join forces to push the chimney sideways, which further loosens the bricks.

The Chimney Crown Affair

Your chimney's crowning glory is its crown—the concrete slab that surrounds the flue and protects the brickwork below. It's essential that you check the crown periodically. If you find large cracks or

Seal the Deal

Brick is sturdy stuff, but over the years, rain can roughen the surface of your chimney (or any other outdoor brick), and it begins to absorb water. In cold temperatures, that moisture expands, and the bricks start to crumble. So stop trouble in its tracks by coating your chimney with a clear masonry sealer. Just make sure you get a brand specifically made for use on brick and concrete. A general masonry sealer won't do the job.

other damage, you'll need to have a pro replace the slab. But you can easily fix any small dings yourself. Use concrete mortar to patch up surface cracks. To fill a gap in the joint between the flue and the crown, pick up a tube of caulk that's rated for use on exterior concrete and load it into your caulking gun. Run a thick bead of the stuff around the whole circumference of the flue, pushing the caulk down to completely fill the opening. Then use your finger or the edge of a narrow piece of piping to round off the filler and smooth it out.

Cap It!

When rain falls into your chimney, it mixes with creosote to produce an acid that can severely damage the flue. An open chimney also issues a y'all-come invitation to birds and other critters to settle down and raise their families in this cozy nesting place. The ultra-simple solution to both problems: a metal flue cap. Just measure the top of your chimney, and buy a cap to fit it. You can find one (along with expert guidance) at a local masonry-supply or chimney-service shop. Then slip the cap over the top of your chimney, tighten the screws, and say a loud, clear

Install a chimney cap to prevent damage from rain and nesting critters.

"No trespassing!" If you'd rather not climb up on your roof, a roofing or chimney-service professional will be delighted to do the job.

Warm Up Your Woodstove

A cast-iron woodstove can last for several generations—if you remember one crucial fact: These babies are brittle, and they can easily crack if they heat up suddenly. So never start a roaring fire in a new stove or one that's been idle for a while in cold weather. Instead, break it in gradually by building a small fire and then adding more fuel after the stove's body has warmed up.

Ice Is Not Nice

A sudden jolt of heat isn't the only thing that can crack a cast-iron stove. Ice or snow can also deliver a thermal shock that splits the metal. So always exercise caution in two ways:

▶ Never burn a piece of wood that has ice or snow on it.

▶ Never try to thaw ice-covered wood by leaning it against the stove. Instead, keep all your logs (or even small branches) well away from the stove until the wood is warm and dry.

Look After the Liner

The firebox liner in your woodstove performs two critical functions: It increases the stove's mass so that it delivers heat more evenly, and it protects the outer walls from damage from high heat and heaving logs. Depending on the age, make, and model of your stove, the liner could be made of cast iron, firebrick, precast masonry, ceramic tile, or metal. Before the start of each heating season, check carefully for cracks or dings. If you find any, consult your owner's manual or call a woodstove dealer for the best way to respond. A simple patch-up job—by you or a pro—may be all that's required to put the stove back in business. Or you may need to replace the liner.

A Dollar for Your Door?

A woodstove with a loose door deals you a double whammy: less heat and more soot. To test for tightness, let the stove cool down thoroughly, and then hold a dollar bill against the side of the opening so that about half of it is inside. Then close the door and try to pull the buck out. If it won't budge, you've got a good seal, at least in that spot—but it's a good idea to try the test in several different areas. If the bill slides right out at any point, it means the door is too loose to function efficiently, and you'll need to do one of two things: Adjust the door, following the instructions in your owner's manual, or replace the gasket (see "Replace Your Stove Gasket," at right).

Replace Your Stove Gasket

If you've adjusted your woodstove door, and it still isn't tight enough to hold on to a dollar bill—or if your stove has a nonadjustable entry hatch—you need a new gasket. If your owner's manual provides gasket specifications, simply mosey on down to the closest woodstove dealer, and pick up the right model. Otherwise, remove the old gasket* and take it to the shop with you. While you're there, also buy a tube of silicone gasket cement. When you get home, follow this simple four-step replacement process:

> **STEP 1.** Clean out the gasket channel using a flat-end screwdriver, followed by coarse-grade steel wool.

> **STEP 2.** Cut the gasket material to a length that's ½ inch or so longer than the perimeter of the door (so you can tuck the ends in next to each other).

> **STEP 3.** Apply a bead of cement all the way around the channel, and press the gasket into it. Let it dry for the length of time noted on the cement tube.

> **STEP 4.** Replace the door if you removed it earlier, and repeat the dollar bill test. The new seal should pass with flying colors; if it doesn't, call your stove dealer for advice—you may need to have a pro examine and repair your unit.

* Remove the stove door, too, if that makes the job easier for you.

CALL A PRO

When you're using your fireplace or woodstove and you smell smoke inside your home, or you see smoke seeping through cracks in your chimney, douse the fire and call a registered chimney sweep immediately. A leaking flue can release toxic fumes into your home or cause a fire—or both. The problem occurs most often in houses that were built before the 1940s, when protective liners came into common use. But any liner—whether it's made from flue tile or firebrick—can develop cracks. Such a defect, of course, is one reason why an annual inspection is crucial.

Cabinets & Countertops

The cabinets and countertops in your kitchen and bathrooms see hard use, day in and day out. For the most part, they're also on full display to everyone who visits your home. So it's only natural that you want to keep these hardworking surfaces looking their best. The tips, tricks, and tonics in this chapter will help you do just that!

KITCHEN CABINETS

Say Good-Bye to Grease

Every time you cook with oil, fat, or grease of any kind, tiny bits of the stuff escape into the air and settle on your cabinets. In a surprisingly short time, an oily coating builds up on the surface, where it acts like a magnet for dust, hair, and other airborne gunk. There are potent commercial cleansers that can clear the crud off your cabinets, but they can easily damage the delicate surface. The simple—and safe—solution: Fill a 1-gallon bucket almost halfway with water. Then add ½ gallon of white vinegar and 1 cup of baking soda, and stir well to blend the ingredients thoroughly. Dip a sponge in the solution, and scrub your cabinets, moving with the grain of the wood. Rinse with a soft, clean cloth moistened with warm water. Then dry the surface with another soft, clean cloth. Whatever you do, never let your cabinets air-dry; the water can leach into the wood and ruin the finish.

Handle with Care?

The areas around door handles and drawer pulls are especially prone to accumulating greasy grime—simply because they're constantly being touched. Here's a powerful, but gentle, way to ditch that dirt:

► Make a paste of baking soda and water, and wipe it onto the greasy area with a clean sponge, going with the grain of the wood. Then rinse with clear water on a soft cloth, and cast an eagle eye on the surface.

► If traces of grease remain, dampen a second clean sponge with white vinegar, and wipe the spots away. Then rinse, and dry thoroughly using an old towel.

► To rout grease and dirt from handles and other hardware, scrub them with a toothbrush dipped in the baking soda paste, then rinse and towel-dry.

Nix the Nicks

Got a few nicks and scratches on your wooden cabinets? No problem! You can heal that wound in a snap using either shoe polish or a crayon. Either glide the crayon over the spot, or wipe the polish onto the mark with a soft, clean cloth. Then buff with a fresh cloth.

Note: *Either of these quick fixes will work just as well to cover up dings in wooden bathroom vanities.*

About!—Face!

Make that reface. Most kitchen cabinets start to look worn, dingy, and dated long before the frames, shelves, and drawers even begin to show signs of age. That's the bad news. The good news is that for a fraction of the price you'd pay for new cabinets, you can replace the doors and drawer fronts while leaving the cabinet frames, shelves, and drawers intact. Home-improvement stores and numerous websites sell DIY refacing kits that include everything you need for the job, including hardware. All you need to do is provide precise measurements and choose the style and color you want, along with new drawer and door handles. (Be sure to order extra, undrilled door fronts to cover any exposed cabinet ends.) When your order comes in, perform your marvelous makeover in these six simple steps:

STEP 1. Remove the old doors and drawer fronts.

STEP 2. Clean the cabinet faces and sides with trisodium phosphate (TSP) to remove all traces of grease or oil. Let the surfaces dry, and lightly sand them with 150-grit sandpaper. Then wipe them with a tack cloth to remove any residue.

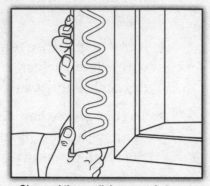

Glue and then nail door panels to any exposed cabinet ends.

STEP 3. Either paint the face frame or apply self-stick veneer that matches your new doors and drawer fronts (see "Reface the Frames," at right).

STEP 4. Apply carpenter's glue to each end panel, press it into place, and secure it with finishing nails. Use a nail set to sink the heads, and fill the holes with color-matched wood filler.

STEP 5. Attach the hinges to the new doors. Then have a helper hold each door in place while you attach the hinges to the cabinet.

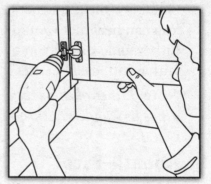

Attach the new doors to the cabinet frames.

STEP 6. Screw the new front panels onto the drawers from the inside. If the drawer had a separate facing attached to a four-sided box, simply screw on the new one. But if the original version had a panel fastened to a three-sided box, use a handsaw to cut off the top, sides, and bottom of the front so that it's flush with the box. Screw the new front to the back end. Then remove the drawer-slide hardware, turn it around to face the other way, and reattach it.

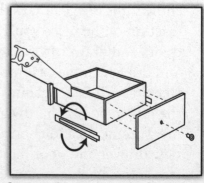

Screw on the new drawer fronts, trimming the front of the original drawer if necessary.

Reface the Frames

When it comes to revamping the face frames of your cabinets, you have two options:

▶ **Pre-finished wood veneer.** Most of the companies that make replacement doors and drawer fronts also make matching wood veneer that's coated with extra-strength pressure sensitive adhesive (PSA). It comes in a roll that usually contains enough material to cover about 15 cabinets (depending on their size, of course). All you do is measure the upright and horizontal parts (stiles and rails, respectively), cut the veneer to the right-size strips, peel off the backing paper, and apply the pieces to the wood.

That sounds like a simple DIY project—and, in theory, it is. But, in reality, achieving top-quality results is a delicate, time-consuming, labor-intensive process that entails cutting angles, matching up seams, and pressing out bumps and air bubbles. And if the work isn't done just so, any imperfections will stand out like a flock of sheep on a putting green. My advice: Unless you've got an ultra-steady hand, a keen eye for

When you take off old cabinet doors, don't dump 'em in the trash—at least not all of them. Turn them into one-of-a-kind, useful works of art—or give them to someone who will. The best choices depend on the size and contours of the doors in question. You can find ideas and instructions in craft books and online (type in "uses for old cabinet doors"). Here's a trio of easy DIY projects:

Chess- and checkerboard. Spray-paint the molding in your choice of color, then carefully measure and mark off the squares. Either paint them or affix paper squares using a spray adhesive.

Message board. Just cover the wood inside the raised frame with either blackboard paint or magnetic whiteboard paint (both available in most paint, hardware, and home-improvement stores).

Serving tray. Paint, strip, or decoupage the surface, and attach a decorative handle at either end.

detail, and a *lot* of patience, turn this part of the job over to a pro—or go with option number two:

▶ **Paint.** Many refacing firms also offer paint that matches the colors of their drawer- and door-front collections. All you have to do is prep the surfaces as you would for any other paint job, then grab your brush, and let 'er rip.

3 Keys to a Happy Paint Job

Whether you choose to tackle the whole nine yards yourself, or paint just the frames and farm out the doors and drawer fronts, the road to success (with less stress) begins with this three-point prep plan:

• **Consult an expert.** Remove one of your doors and take it to your local paint shop. The experienced, knowledgeable pros on duty will be happy to recommend the best primer, paint, and tools for the surface at hand, as well as the most effective pre-treatment techniques. For example, unless you need to smooth out rough spots or fill gouges, you may be able to skip the sanding step entirely. A liquid de-glosser and/or a maximum-adhesion primer could do the trick nicely.

Painting your cabinets can give you the look of a whole new kitchen for even less than a refacing job will cost—and with a literally unlimited range of color options. You can do the whole project yourself, but my advice is this: Confine your brush-on efforts to the exterior frames, and send the doors and drawer fronts to a professional who can spray-paint them off-site. The result will be a spit-and-polish, good-as-new appearance that you'd be hard-pressed to deliver at home. Plus, you'll be spared not only a messy, time-consuming job, but also the hassle of navigating around seemingly acres of drying wood for days on end. Your friendly neighborhood paint dealer will be happy to recommend a top-notch paint shop or cabinetmaker.

CALL A PRO

- **Make a map.** Before you detach a single element, draw a map of your whole cabinetry layout, and assign a number to each cupboard and drawer. Then, as you remove each door and drawer front, write the appropriate number on the back. Why bother? Because, even though panels of the same basic dimensions may appear to be identical, any holes drilled for hinges or other hardware could vary by just enough to make after-painting matchups a nightmare.

- **Stash the hardware.** As you take off each door and drawer front, put all of its hardware into a plastic bag (minus pieces that you need to clean or replace), and tuck it inside the cabinet or drawer. That way, when it's time to put everything back together again, all the parts will be at your fingertips.

Move 'Em On

If you decide to replace rather than revamp your cabinets, don't get rid of them. Instead, put them to work in other parts of your home. If they're still in good shape, paint them, and add new handles if you like. Then use them to store stationery supplies in your home office, towels and toiletries in a bathroom, soaps and stain removers in the laundry room, or toys and books in a child's bedroom. Even if the cupboards are not much to look at—or if you have all the storage facilities you need—you can still put those castoffs to good use. Just haul 'em to your garage, workshop, or shed, and fill 'em with tools or gardening supplies.

Don't Give Your Hardware the Heave-Ho!

At least not before you ponder these two facts of modern life:

▶ Depending on its age and material, there's a good chance that your current supply is better made by far than comparable new versions. The older the fixtures are, the sturdier they're likely to be.

▶ At today's prices, replacing dozens of pulls, handles, and hinges of even decent quality will cost you a pretty penny.

So unless you simply can't live with the look of your old cabinet appendages—or your kitchen is so tiny that you can easily afford to splurge on new top-of-the-line models—consider sprucing up and reinstalling those venerable veterans.

Soak 'Em Back to Life

If your hardware is simply showing signs of wear, tear, and grime provided over the years by human hands, a good, hot bath may be all it needs to reawaken its former vitality. To give it a rejuvenating makeover, fill a sink or bucket with hot water and a few squirts of dishwashing liquid (enough to make a nice crop of suds). Add ½ cup of white vinegar, and swirl the solution around with your hand. Drop the dingy pieces into the drink, and let them soak overnight. Then pull 'em out, one by one, and scrub them with a soft toothbrush. Rinse with clear water, dry with a soft towel, and they should look as good as new.

Good Riddance to Bad Rust

Rusty patches demand a little more intensive treatment than a simple soak-and-scrub routine—but bidding them bye-bye is still quick and easy. Depending on the kind of metal and the ingredients you have on hand, here's all you need to do:

- To "de-rustify" chrome, use this old auto detailers' trick: Rub the surface with a balled up piece of wet aluminum foil. The aluminum will combine with the rust (a.k.a. iron oxide) to form a slimy brown layer of aluminum oxide. Wipe it off with a soft, clean cloth, and bingo—clean, shiny chrome!

- For other metals, slice a potato in two, sprinkle the cut surface with either salt or baking soda, and scrub the rust patches away.

- Fresh out of spuds? Then mix 2 tablespoons of salt with 2 tablespoons of lemon juice or white vinegar to make a paste. Rub the stuff on the rusty spots with a soft, dry cloth. Then rinse with clear water, and dry thoroughly.

Ta-Ta, Tarnish

Tarnish will take off with either of these kitchen-counter capers:

▶ To spruce up uncoated brass, dip a soft, clean cloth in hot vinegar, then sea salt or kosher salt, and rub the tarnish away.

▶ Both brass and copper will lose their tarnish if you rub the surface with a paste made from equal parts of salt, flour, and white vinegar.

POWERFUL POTIONS

WOOD CABINET POLISH

Once you've refaced your wooden cabinets—or gotten your old ones spanking clean—keep them sparkling with this fabulous formula:

½ cup of linseed oil
½ cup of malt vinegar
1 ½ tsp. of lemon juice

Mix the oil and vinegar in a small jar or bowl, and stir in the lemon juice. Then apply the polish with a soft, clean cloth, adding a little elbow grease, and your cabinets will be the talk of the town (or at least your house).

Silence Is Golden

When your kitchen cabinets (or bathroom vanity doors) forget that they are meant to be seen and not heard, the best way to say "Hush!" depends on where the noise is coming from. Here are the options:

• **Banging doors.** The obvious solution is to attach inexpensive commercial door bumpers to the "loudmouth's" corners. But for instant relief, reach into your first-aid kit—or your bathroom medicine cabinet—and grab a box of adhesive bandages. The small circular or square types work best for this purpose, but in a pinch, you can trim the sticky ends on the larger strips. Whichever kind you use, it will probably take a double layer to deliver peace and quiet.

• **Squeaky hinges.** Squirt mineral oil into the joints. A silicone spray will also work, but don't use a petroleum-based product like WD-40® because petroleum distillates are dust magnets. Avoid vegetable oil, which can turn rancid and sticky over time.

Inside Operations

To my way of thinking, if anyone gave out a Household Space-Waster Award, standard kitchen cabinets—with their set number of immovable shelves—would win it hands down. Of course, you can take advantage of some of that wasted vertical space by stacking up your mugs, bowls, and plates—but if the tower topples, you can wind up with a lot of pottery shards on your hands. A safer option is to add more shelves. You have four good choices:

▶ **Solid shelves.** These are like the ones that came with your cabinets. Whether you make them yourself, or buy extras from a local cabinet supplier, solid shelves provide good, stable storage space. Bear in mind, though, that each shelf will take up close to an inch of space itself, and the less room there is between shelves, the harder it is to reach to the back.

▶ **Wire stacking shelves.** These are lightweight, inexpensive, and easy to arrange in just about any configuration. Most of them are a little shallower than standard kitchen cabinets, so you can wind up with some room to spare at the front or back, but that's a small price to pay for the extra vertical space they give you. You can find wire shelves in home-improvement stores and online.

▶ **Wire shelves that hang down from the ones above them.** They simply slide onto the shelf and add 4 to 6 inches of space, giving you a perfect place to store flat, lightweight drawer cloggers, such as napkins, paper plates, and boxes of plastic wrap, aluminum foil, and wax paper.

▶ **Wire-mesh shelves that run on rollers.** These are tailor-made for base cabinets. If you need something from the middle or back, you just pull on the handle until your target is easy to reach. Their rectangular shape makes the most efficient use of the area, and raised sides keep the contents from falling overboard when you slide the unit out. You can find these dandy devices in home-improvement stores, organizing stores, and online. **Note:** *In most cases, you will have to remove the shelves from your cabinets to make room for the roll-out unit.*

VANITIES & MEDICINE CABINETS

Replacing a Bathroom Vanity

Nothing adds more oomph (or resale value) to a bathroom than getting rid of an old, out-of-style vanity. And, like many DIY projects—at least the ones we're covering in this book—installing a new one is a whole lot easier than it may sound. You can easily handle a small vanity yourself, but for a larger model, enlist a helper. Here's the basic 10-step process:

STEP 1. Turn off the water. Then set a bucket under the P-trap and disconnect the supply lines (see "Replacing a Bathroom Sink" on page 70).

STEP 2. Using a utility knife, cut away the caulk between the vanity and the wall—on the sides as well as the top. Carefully lift off the countertop, and take it out of the bathroom.

STEP 3. Remove the screws that hold the cabinet to the wall. Then pull the unit away and cart it off, being careful not to ding any walls in the process.

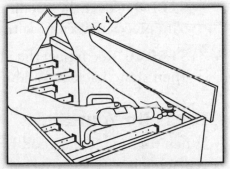

Remove the screws and pull the old vanity away from the wall.

STEP 4. Use a stud finder to locate the wall studs, and mark each one in a spot that's a little higher than the top of the new vanity (so you can find the dots when you slide the new unit into place).

STEP 5. Set the cabinet in place, and mark the locations for water and drain lines. Then use a spade bit and a hole-saw attachment to make the holes.

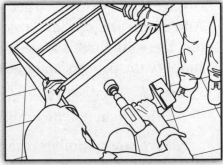

Use a spade bit and a hole-saw attachment to make holes for water and drain lines.

STEP 6. Set the cabinet in place over the pipes. Then use a level and shims to make sure the unit sits flush against the wall, and secure it to the wall studs with screws.

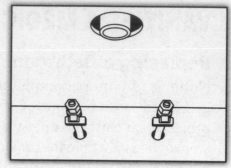

Set the cabinet in place over the pipes.

STEP 7. Once the vanity is on its site—and before you add the countertop—install new faucets (if you choose), following the manufacturer's directions.

STEP 8. Run a bead of tub-and-tile caulk around the top perimeter of the cabinet, and gently set the countertop in place. Then apply another thin bead between the countertop's edges and the wall, using your clean fingertip or a damp cloth to smooth the surface.

STEP 9. Cover the opening at the base and any other gaps using the trim pieces that came with the vanity.

STEP 10. Reconnect the plumbing, and turn the water back on. Then stand back and admire your masterpiece!

Dress Up Your Sink

When it's time to bid good-bye to your old bathroom vanity, consider replacing it with a converted dresser or buffet. (Coat the wood with marine-grade varnish to protect it from possible water damage.) Besides adding a personal touch to your bathroom, it'll give you more storage space than you'd get with most standard bathroom vanities. And unless you opt for an elegant antique, it should cost a lot less, too. Here are three simple tricks to help you (or your hired carpenter) simplify the process and maximize your storage space:

- Choose a vessel-type sink bowl that sits on top of the dresser, rather than one that must be recessed into the surface.

- Have your plumber recess the pipes into the wall.

- Use a wall-mounted spigot and faucets.

Note: *To minimize the cost, check your attic or basement, and scout out local yard sales, flea markets, and thrift shops for both dressers and sinks. Any good-sized, nonporous bowl or planting pot can serve as a sink. You (or your plumber) can easily drill a hole in the bottom to accommodate the drain and pipe.*

An old dresser makes a one-of-a-kind vanity.

Spray Away the Overspray

Hair spray that misses its mark can make a royal mess of vanities, mirrors, medicine cabinets, and bathroom walls. But even layers of built-up residue are no match for this potent formula: Just mix 1 part liquid fabric softener to 2 parts water in a handheld spray bottle. Spritz the messy surface, and then wipe the gunk away with a soft, dry cloth. That's all there is to it!

And the Misnomer-of-the-Year Award Goes To . . .

Your bathroom medicine cabinet. Why? Because the one thing that you should try not to store on those convenient, narrow shelves is medication of any kind. They (and cosmetics, too) fare better in cooler, drier conditions than the average bathroom offers up. So do yourself a favor, and take your meds and makeup to your bedroom, or to a cool, dry pantry shelf.

Can the Can Rings

Tired of scrubbing away the ugly rust rings left on your vanity and bathtub by metal cans of shaving cream and hair spray? If so, then stop the stains before they start with this simple trick: As soon as you bring the cans home from the store, coat the bottoms with clear nail polish. End of problem!

COUNTERTOPS

Three for the Show

Various countertop materials require slightly different treatments to keep them at their peak of form and function. But every one of them, from bargain-basement plastic laminate to ultra-pricey granite, is a sitting duck for these three hazards:

► **Heavy objects.** A sudden jolt from a hefty pot, tool, or small appliance can chip, dent, or crack every standard countertop material you can name. Your obvious damage-prevention plan: Be careful!

► **High heat.** While some surfaces can tolerate more heat than others, none of them are entirely heat-proof. So never set a hot pan or casserole directly on the counter; always cushion the blow with a trivet or sturdy, insulating pad.

► **Sharp edges.** Likewise, even the sturdiest surfaces are vulnerable to scratches, scrapes, nicks, and gouges. So do all of your chopping, dicing, and slicing on cutting boards (yes, even if you have butcher block counters). And when you need to remove any dried-on food, use a plastic scraper—not a metal spatula.

Mind Your Metal

Stainless steel countertops rank high on the low-maintenance list—which is why they're the number one choice in professional kitchens. The chic, sleek material lives up to its name: It cannot be stained by cleansers, food, or any other spilled substances. For routine cleaning, all you need to do is wipe it with mild dishwashing liquid, a commercial household cleanser, or my All-Purpose Counter Cleaner (see page 136). But stainless steel does have one minor drawback: It scratches easily. On the plus side, it's simple to remove the marks. How you go about it depends on the severity of the damage:

• **Minor scratches.** Simply brush 'em out with a nonabrasive household cleaning pad (like 3M Scotch-Brite® or a generic version), using a random circular motion.

- **Deep scratches.** Rub the marks with fine sandpaper (grade 180 to 220), and buff with a Scotch-Brite pad. If your countertops are mirror-polished stainless, go at the scratches with an automotive compound and a machine-polishing pad.

Boost Your Butcher Block's Defenses

Some folks would have you believe that unless you treat a butcher block countertop with a polyurethane sealer, its care and upkeep will be a full-time job and then some. Hogwash! If you've never sealed your butcher block, or you've just gotten new, unsealed versions for your counters or kitchen island, it's a cinch to establish—and maintain—a first-class moisture and stain barrier. Just use the four-step process below two or three times a week for the first month. After that, repeat the procedure every one to three months, depending on the type and amount of use the surface gets and the humidity in your home. (As you might expect, the more moisture there is in the air, the less frequently you'll have to offer up oily refreshments.) Here's your action plan:

STEP 1. Wipe the countertop with a clean, damp (not wet!) cloth to remove any dust or debris, and let the wood air-dry.

STEP 2. Dribble mineral oil* over the surface (⅓ cup should be plenty for an area measuring about 36 by 72 inches).

STEP 3. Rub the oil into the wood, using a soft cotton cloth.** Follow the grain of the wood, and don't overlook the vertical edges.

STEP 4. If you must use the countertop immediately, wipe the excess oil with a clean, dry cloth. Otherwise, let the oil soak in for 24 hours.

* Hardware and home-improvement stores sell mineral oil that's made for wooden countertops. But you can buy the stuff in the laxative aisle of your supermarket for a lot less. It works as well—and it's food-safe too.

** Don't wash these rags in your washing machine—they'll make an oily mess of the drum. Instead, you might want to keep them in a sealed plastic bag and use them again and again. Mineral oil never turns rancid.

TLC, Big B Style

Once you've got your butcher block on a regular oiling schedule—or if you've opted to seal the wood—keep it clean by wiping it as needed with a mild soap-and-water solution, then rinsing with a slightly damp cloth and rubbing the surface dry. Whatever you do, never use commercial cleaners or (heaven forbid!) furniture polish.

If a stain appears, simply sand the mark away with fine sandpaper, and apply a mineral oil "bandage." The area will be a little lighter at first, but with time and routine oil jobs, the tone will soon even out.

POWERFUL POTIONS

ALL-PURPOSE COUNTER CLEANER

This simple formula combines the power of baking soda and vinegar with the antiseptic properties of witch hazel and tea tree extract or tincture. The result: A super-strength, antibacterial cleanser that needs no rinsing. One warning: Don't use this cleaner on granite countertops—the acidic vinegar will damage the surface.

½ **cup of baking soda**
½ **cup of white vinegar**
¼ **cup of witch hazel**
1 **tsp. of tea tree extract or tincture***
½ **cup of water**

Mix the ingredients in a handheld spray bottle, and use the mixture to clean your kitchen countertops and backsplashes, as well as your appliances, inside and out.

* *Available in health-food stores and the health-food section of many supermarkets.*

Lovely Laminate

Plastic laminate—sold under numerous brand names, including Wilsonart®, Nevamar®, and (of course) Formica®—has been a staple in American households for more than half a century. It's the least expensive of all common countertop materials, comes in a gazillion colors and patterns, and for the most part it's a cinch to maintain. Why the qualifier? Because, just like any other kitchen surface, laminate can pick up its fair share of workplace injuries. Here's how to deliver first aid fast:

▶ **Light scratches.** Find a matching crayon, and color the nick away.

▶ **Deeper scratches and dings.** Pick up some

special scratch-repair paste from your hardware store. If you can't find a color that matches your countertop, you can blend two or more colors to get the right shade. Clean the damaged area with rubbing alcohol, fill the chip or scratch with the repair paste, smooth it out, and scrape off any excess with a putty knife. Let the paste cure for 24 hours, and your counter will be as good as new.

▶ **Scorch marks.** Buff 'em out with either car wax or a half-and-half mixture of baking soda and white (not gel) toothpaste. Whatever you do, don't use an abrasive cleanser; it'll probably remove the finish.

Great Grimy-Grout Cleaner

Even folks who love ceramic-tile counters admit that they have one glaring flaw: While sealing the grout will prevent stains, nothing can keep those gutters from collecting whatever your kitchen—or bathroom—can dish out in the way of dirt, crumbs, and other debris. But there is a DIY "miracle" spray that will get even the grimiest grout as clean as a whistle. To make it, mix together 3 cups of rubbing alcohol, 2 cups of household bleach, ½ cup of liquid floor cleaner, and 1 quart of water in a bucket. Pour the solution into a handheld spray bottle, use it as you would any spray cleaner, and rinse thoroughly with clear water. Store the leftover mixture in a

Going Under Puts You on Top

On top of kitchen-counter maintenance, that is. If you decide to replace your kitchen countertops (or your entire cabinetry), do yourself a laborsaving favor and go with an under-mounted sink instead of the standard drop-in variety. The reason: With a drop-in sink, the rim that sits on the counter's surface can collect a swamp's worth of yucky brown gunk that's the very dickens to eradicate. But when the basin is mounted under the countertop, there's no place for dirt to collect, and that translates into a lot less work for you—and zero chance of damaging the surface as you clean around a grime-gathering perimeter.

tightly sealed container, well out of reach of children and pets.

Note: *To repair or replace chipped, cracked, or broken tiles, follow the same procedure described in "Go for Broke" (see page 28).*

The Corian Conundrum

Widespread assumption: Because DuPont™ Corian® and similar solid surface countertop materials are the same color all the way through, you can easily sand away any scratches.

The whole truth: The Internet is chock-full of DIY instructions for eliminating Corian scratches by using various grades of sandpaper, sanding disks, scouring powders, and abrasive pads. Most of them work some of the time, but few, if any, work all of the time. And even in the best-case scenario, any spot repair is guaranteed to show. To do a first-class job, you have to sand the entire countertop with an orbital palm sander and four or five grades of progressively finer sandpaper. Unless you're highly skilled at refinishing work, it's a good bet that you'll wind up with a counter full of swirl marks that'll look worse than the scratches you started with. Plus, the sanding process will fill the air with tiny particles of polyester resin that can penetrate a standard dust mask—it takes a respirator to keep them out of your lungs. Your best bet: Turn this job over to a pro. Any shop that sells solid surface countertops should be able to recommend a good one.

Be Good to Your Granite

Granite countertops have been all the rage for a number of years now, despite the fact that they cost an arm and a leg. They're also a lot more delicate than their weight and appearance would imply. Here are some general guidelines for heading off trouble:

- Never—and I mean *never*—use any acidic cleaner on granite, including DIY formulas that contain vinegar or lemon juice. And when you serve citrus fruits or beverages, don't let them touch the countertop because they'll make permanent stains.

- For routine cleaning, wipe the countertop with denatured alcohol or cheap vodka. If you prefer a commercial cleanser, use one that's specially made for granite, not a general all-purpose product.

- When a spill occurs, immediately blot the liquid up with a paper towel. Don't wipe—you'll only spread trouble. Then flush the area with water and mild soap, rinse several times with clear water, and dry with a soft, clean cloth. If a stain lingers, go at it using one of the remedies in "Spots, Begone!" (below).

- If you spot water marks, especially on black granite, it's almost a sure bet that they're not water spots at all, but remnants of a mistakenly applied sealer. Simply spray denatured alcohol onto the area, and rub with a soft, clean cloth using circular motions. Repeat several times, using fresh cloths, and work quickly because the alcohol evaporates fast.

- Buff away surface scratches using dry 0000 steel wool. Deeper scratches and nicks should be tackled by a pro.

Spots, Begone!

Don't cry over stained granite—but do act fast, employing one of these remedies:

▶ **Ink** (including felt-tip markers). Wipe light-colored stone with bleach or hydrogen peroxide (not both!). For dark stone, use lacquer thinner or acetone.

▶ **Oil-based stains.** Make a thick paste of baking soda and water, and with a plastic or wooden spatula, spread it over the stain to a thickness of ½ inch. Cover the paste with plastic wrap, and leave it for 24 to 48 hours. Then wipe it away with clear water, and dry with a soft, clean cloth.

▶ **Organic stains** (such as coffee, tea, tobacco, or food). Wipe with 12% hydrogen peroxide and a few drops of ammonia. If that doesn't work, use the paste described above, but substitute 12% hydrogen peroxide for the water.

▶ **Rust.** Make a paste of commercial rust remover and diatomaceous earth (available in hardware stores and garden centers), and use it as described for oil-based stains above. But be forewarned: Rust stains are extremely difficult to remove from granite.

Caring for Quartz

Engineered quartz is the latest trend in upscale countertops. Unlike granite, it's not a naturally occurring stone. It's made from ground quartz combined with polyester resins to bind it and pigments to give it color. As a result, it's stronger than granite and much less picky about cleaning routines. For normal cleanup, wipe the countertop with a soft, damp cloth or paper towel. When a little more oomph is called for, use any mild, nonabrasive cleanser that contains no bleach, which can strip color from the surface. Also be aware that some highly acidic foods and juices can discolor the stone, so wipe up any spills ASAP.

PART 2

OUTSIDE YOUR HOME

In Part 1, I shared some of my best advice for solving and preventing trouble inside your house. Well, the problems that befall the surfaces and systems within those walls can't hold a candle to the curveballs Mother Nature can—and routinely does—throw at your home's exterior. Just think about it: Day in and day out, your walls, roof, and outdoor structures are wide open to blistering sun, biting cold, blasting rain, and bashing wind. While there may be nothing you can do to prevent wild and woolly weather from coming your way, there is plenty you can do to reduce the toll it takes on your house and yard. That's what this section is all about. I'll offer up my time-tested tips and science's high-tech tricks for repairing and maintaining everything from windows to walkways, shingles to sheds, doors to decks, and—your home's first line of defense—its exterior walls.

Exterior Walls

If you've got no walls, you've got no house. It's as simple as that. This is the chapter where *Fix It Fast and Make It Last* ceases to be simply a smart, money-saving concept and becomes an absolute necessity. Of course, there are some chores that you'll need to hand off to an experienced pro. But there are also a whole lot of fix-it feats and problem-prevention ploys that you can easily handle yourself. So read on for some dynamic DIY strategies.

WOOD SIDING

Let the Sun Shine In

Without a doubt, the biggest enemy of wood siding is moisture—and the biggest enemy of moisture is Ol' Sol himself. If those warm rays can't reach the walls of your house and air can't circulate, dampness will build up, making the paint peel and the wood rot. The simple trouble-prevention plan: Keep all foundation shrubs trimmed back so that no greenery touches your house. And when you install any new shrubs—or even densely planted perennial beds—make sure the plants will be at least 18 inches away from the walls once they reach maturity. (Otherwise, you'll have an almost full-time clipping job on your hands!)

Don't Let Trees Trash Your Wood Siding

Or any other part of your house. Just like any other plant material, trees (especially dense evergreens) that grow too close to your walls can lead to major siding damage. But that's just for starters. An ill-chosen tree can also send its roots through your foundation, fill your gutters with fallen leaves, and clobber your roof with storm-tossed branches. If trees or large shrubs are within striking distance of your house, get 'em outta there now! And whenever you're shopping for new woody plants, make a photocopy of the list below. Take it with you to the nursery, and check it against the label on every plant that strikes your fancy. It can help you avoid a mountain of trouble (and possibly save you big bundles of bucks) down the road!

5 Must-Know Tree and Shrub Facts:

▶ How tall will it grow?

▶ How far will it spread when it reaches maturity?

▶ What shape and form does it have (spreading, weeping, or upright)?

▶ Do the roots run deep or stay close to the surface?

▶ How dense will the shade be five years from now?

Clean Wood Is Happy Wood

Or to put it in more objective terms, it's far less susceptible to rot and mildew, the two most destructive wood woes. Depending on how soiled your siding is, you can offer up a healthy dose of cheer in one of these three ways:

• For routine cleaning, simply spray the siding with a garden hose. Then use a long-handled brush to clean off any dirty patches and—this is especially important—to scrub under the edges of clapboards or shingles, where dirt and debris build up. Repeat this process once a year, in spring or summer.

• If it's been a while since your house had a shower—or if you live in a climate where mildew is a problem—scrub the siding with Healthy Siding Solution (see page 144), and rinse it with a garden hose.

• Every few years—and especially before painting your home's exterior—rent some power-washing gear, and let 'er rip!

HEALTHY SIDING SOLUTION

This double-barreled formula will get off the grimiest dirt and prevent mildew from building up on your home's wooden siding.

1 qt. of chlorine bleach

⅓ cup of household detergent (like Spic and Span®— either powder or liquid)

3 qts. of warm water

Mix the ingredients together in a bucket and scrub. Then rinse with clear water from your garden hose.

Stop Rot in Its Tracks

The way some folks carry on, you'd think that wood rot is a genuine horror-movie monster just waiting to attack your house and send it crumbling to the ground. Not so—although you do need to keep an eagle eye out for any damage and repair it quickly. About once a year, stroll around the perimeter of your house and look for loose caulking or patches of rotted wood. If you find any, use a knife or chisel to dig out the rot or old caulk. Then fill the hole with a two-part epoxy wood filler; just follow the directions on the package. Several brands are available in hardware and home-improvement stores, but one of the best is made by Bondo®, the same company that makes auto-body filler. It sets up hard enough for sanding in 15 minutes and can be stained or painted in 25 minutes.

Note: *If the damaged section is more than 3 or 4 inches across, cut a piece of slightly thinner wood that's a little smaller than the hole. Apply a thin layer of filler to the bottom of the opening, and press the wooden "bandage" into it. Then fill in around the edges and over the top of the piece with more filler.*

Batten Down a Bulging Board

A bulge in your wood siding may look ominous, but it's usually harmless—and it's as easy as pie to fix. All you need to do is screw it down with a long wood screw, following this procedure:

▶ Locate a stud that's close to the bulge. (Clue: You'll see a pattern of seams and/or nail heads between boards.)

- Drill a pilot hole for the screw, then drill a countersink (a larger, shallow hole) at the surface to fit the head of the screw.

- Drive the screw through the board and the sheathing and into the stud.

- Fill the countersink with exterior-grade wood filler, let it dry, and sand it smooth.

- Prime and paint the spot, and you're good to go!

Keep Splits from Spreading

If you spot a split in your clapboard (a.k.a. lap) siding, it's important to fix it as soon as possible before the damage can spread and become a much bigger problem. But don't be intimidated! It's a simple three-step process:

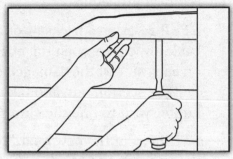
Remove the split section.

STEP 1. Use a chisel or strong putty knife to carefully pry up the split section and remove it.

STEP 2. Apply waterproof wood glue to all edges of the piece.

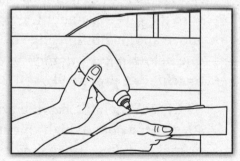
Apply waterproof glue to the wood.

STEP 3. Set the broken piece back into place, and secure it with galvanized siding nails. Sink them slightly using a nail set, and cover the holes with wood filler. Once the filler dries, sand the surface smooth and cover it with paint.

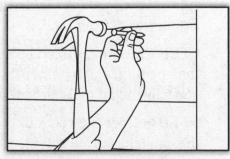
Nail the glued piece in place.

Replacing Damaged Clapboards

When any piece of clapboard is too far gone to make a fix-it job possible, replace it following this six-step process:

STEP 1. Drive wedges up under the damaged board to pull it out from the siding below. Pull out the nails with pliers or a claw hammer or, if that's not possible, use a hacksaw to cut them off flush with the sheathing. To free up the top, hammer wedges under the board that overlaps the damaged one and follow the same nail-removal procedure.

STEP 2. Using a hacksaw or a backsaw, cut through the board on each side of the damaged area. Pull the section out, and take it to a lumberyard to find the closest match.

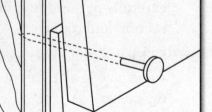

Cut out and remove the damaged section.

STEP 3. Cut the new board to fit the opening and give it a "test drive." If it doesn't slide right into place, with its top edge under the board above and its bottom edge over the one below, plane or sand the edges to achieve a precise fit.

STEP 4. When the newbie fits just so, give it a coat of high-quality primer, making sure to cover both sides and all edges, as well as the sides of the opening where the old siding was cut out.

Slide the new, primed board into its slot and nail it into place.

STEP 5. Set the primed board into the opening, and hammer it with 16d galvanized nails, driven through both top and bottom edges.

STEP 6. Coat the edges of the patch with acrylic latex caulk. When the caulk has dried sufficiently (check the package directions for timing), paint the "bandage" to match the rest of your house.

Shake a Shingle

The replacement process for shakes and shingles is essentially the same as it is for clapboard, but here are a few tips to make the job easier and the results better:

- If the victims are made of natural, unstained redwood or cedar, take your replacements from an inconspicuous part of the house, and use the new versions in that spot. This way, your patch-up job won't stand out like a rosebush in a cornfield.

- If the damaged shingle (or shake) won't come out easily, split it into several pieces using a hammer and chisel and remove the chunks one by one.

- Unless your new shingle comes pre-drilled (as some do), drill pilot holes to keep the wood from splitting when you nail it in place. Be sure to use corrosion-resistant box or casing nails. In concealed spots, hot-dipped galvanized steel will work. In exposed areas at corners and under eaves and windows, go with stainless steel, brass, or aluminum nails, which are less likely to stain the wood.

Note: *Shingles and shakes are the same thing. The only difference between the two is that shingles are smooth-cut on both sides, while shakes are left in their natural, rough state on one side.*

PAINTING YOUR HOUSE

6 Pointers for Practically Perfect Painting

As every owner of a wood-frame house knows, it takes more than a garden hose, or even occasional power washing, to keep those walls at their peak of form and function. Every so often, the house all but speaks up and shouts, "Paint me—*now!*" And there's no doubt about it: Even a vinyl-clad, aluminum-clad, or stucco house takes on a whole new lease on life when it's sporting a fresh coat of paint. Whether you choose to do the job yourself or farm it out to a pro, this handy handful of tips will help you achieve the best possible results:

- **Time it right.** Plan this (or any other outdoor painting project) for a period of several warm, dry days. The temperature of the paint, the surface of your house, and the air should all be between 50°F and 90°F and the humidity should be below 85 percent.

- **Don't scrimp.** Resist the temptation to buy bargain-basement paint. Premium-quality brands hold up better and longer than their low-priced counterparts, and they're more likely to give you the coverage you need in just one coat.

- **Round up.** The label on a paint can will generally tell you that 1 gallon will cover about 400 square feet of surface. But that number refers to wood, aluminum, vinyl, and other smooth surfaces. Anytime you're painting uneven or rough material, such as concrete, brick, or stucco, add at least 20 percent to your paint quantity.

- **Consider the current coating.** It's fine to apply latex over oil-based (a.k.a. alkyd) paint. But don't do the reverse—you'll be asking for trouble because oil-based paint doesn't adhere well to latex (see "What Went on Here?," at right).

- **Give it a good foundation.** A paint job can only be as good as the primer coat you put under it. For the full scoop, see "Prime Time," at right.

- **Brush, don't spray!** Exterior walls need the protection of a thick coat of brushed- or rolled-on paint. To get paint to come out of a sprayer, you have to thin the stuff so much that your walls wind up wearing more thinner than paint. Sprayed-on paint doesn't adhere well to the surface. Within a year, you could find yourself forking out cash for a new paint job.

Just Testing

Having trouble deciding on a trim color? Forget those tiny chip samples that just get lost when they're up against house siding. Instead, get yourself some large pieces of cardboard—like the sides of a large-screen TV box—and paint them with your potential trim color. Now prop up the board in a window frame, step back, and see how you like the combo. It's a great way to evaluate different colors without having the headache of repainting over and over again.

Get a High-Tech Matchup

Make sure you get your paint from a store that does its color blends by computer (as most paint and hardware stores do these days) and keeps all the details under your name in its database. That way, if you need another gallon to finish the job, or you decide to paint something else the same color, you can just run back to the shop and buy the identical shade with no guesswork required.

What Went on Here?

If you don't know whether the paint on your house is latex or oil-based, give it this simple test: Moisten a rag with rubbing alcohol and wipe it over the surface. Then look at the rag. If it's picked up color from the wall, you've got latex paint. If no color rubs off, the paint is oil-based.

Shop with the Best

If you're tackling a paint job yourself, and you're new to the game—or it's been a while since you've picked up a brush—buy your materials from a dealer that caters to professional painters. The folks who work in these shops are experienced pros themselves, and they stay on top of cutting-edge products and techniques. Along with top-quality supplies, you'll get advice that could save you loads of time, effort, and money. Before you leave home, jot down the dimensions of the surfaces you'll be painting, as well as their composition, what kind of paint or stain (if any) is on them now, and what condition it's in. The more information you can supply to the staff—and the more questions you ask—the more likely you are to turn out a paint job that's the toast of your town!

Prime Time

A good primer, properly applied, makes all the difference between a long-lasting paint job and one that gets flaky before its time. Before you (or your helpers) pick up a brush, keep these pointers in mind:

• Use the same brand of primer and top-coat paint. Although all paint products of the same type are pretty much alike, each manufacturer adds its own set of ingredients to ensure such performance factors as good surface adherence, mildew resistance, and shelf life. If you mix brands, some of those chemical additives could clash, making your paint job age prematurely.

- If you'll be applying latex over old coats of oil-based paint, use an oil-based primer that's especially made to work with latex paint. (And make sure you wash and prepare the surface thoroughly.)

- Try to paint your top coat within 48 hours of applying the primer. Definitely make sure you wait no longer than two weeks to finish your paint job. After about 14 days, compounds that form on the primer's surface will prevent the top coat from bonding well.

- Follow the square-foot guidelines on the label. Don't try to squeeze more coverage out of the gallon. If you do, the coat will be too thin, and the top coat may not stick.

- If you're painting anything metal, such as drainpipes or metal window frames, use a rust-inhibiting primer for the first coat. Then follow up with any good exterior paint or enamel.

- Cover stains, including wood knots, dark paint, old water marks, or mildew, with a stain-blocking primer. Different types are formulated to cover different kinds of stains, so read the label carefully to make sure you've got the right blocker for the job.

VINYL & ALUMINUM SIDING

Clean Up Its Act

If your aluminum or vinyl siding is in good shape, then all it needs is an annual cleaning. First, give it a nice strong spray from a garden hose. Hit any spots with a scrub brush and a solution of ¼ cup of laundry detergent and 2 gallons of water. Whatever you do, don't use abrasive cleansers on aluminum siding—they could easily damage the finish. Mild abrasives are fine on vinyl siding because the color isn't just surface-deep as it is with aluminum.

Attack Age Spots

If it's been a few years since you gave your siding a shower, it may be sporting dirt splotches or mildew that needs to be scrubbed away. A solution made from ¼ cup of powdered, bleach-free laundry detergent dissolved in 2 gallons of water should do the job nicely. Just work it onto the siding with a stiff brush, and rinse it clean with a garden hose. If you need more potent cleaning power, pick up some trisodium phosphate (TSP) at your local hardware store, and use it according to the directions on the package.

7 Essential Prep Steps for Super Siding Cleaning

Before you clean your siding—whether you're using a scrub bucket and garden hose or full-fledged power-washing gear—follow this get-ready routine:

▶ Turn off the power to any outside lights that might get wet.

▶ Sweep away any cobwebs or spiderwebs—once they're wet, they're the very dickens to spray off.

▶ Cart off any hanging flower baskets, patio furniture, or other movable objects that may be in the way of the spray.

▶ Cover any plants that could be dripped on by cleaning solution.

▶ Send your pets inside, and close all your doors and windows.

POWERFUL POTIONS

SUPER SIDING SOLUTION

For really stubborn spots on aluminum or vinyl siding, use this remarkable recipe.

1 qt. of chlorine bleach
⅔ cup of TSP
⅓ cup of laundry detergent
3 qts. of water

Mix the ingredients together in a bucket, dip a stiff brush into the solution, and scrub your dirty siding. Immediately rinse it clean with a shower from your garden hose.

▶ To play it extra-safe, when you turn on the hose or pressure washer, direct the spray away from doors, windows, and other openings.

▶ Issue an all points bulletin to your family so that no one comes around a corner and gets a surprise shower!

Bottoms Up

Whenever you clean your siding with anything other than plain water, start at the bottom and work your way up. Why? Because, like any other substances, liquid cleansers must obey the law of gravity—so they run down. If you start the job at the top or the middle, you'll wind up with stubborn streaks where the cleaning solution has run through the still-dirty part—and those drip paths will be mighty hard to remove.

Powerful Power-Washing Pointers

When it's time to power wash your siding—whether it's made of vinyl, aluminum, or wood—keep these two timely tips in mind:

• Try to schedule your cleanup for a weekday—you're likely to get a better deal on the equipment rental price. If the minimum period is a full day, and it won't take you that long to finish your job, see if you can find a neighbor who'd like to go halfsies with you on the time and the cost.

• When you're wielding the washing wand, always aim downward to avoid spraying water under the siding panels or shingles.

Heal Power-Washing Wounds

Power-washing equipment does a fine job of cleaning aluminum siding, but sometimes all that pressure makes the surface coating buckle and peel. If that happens to you, don't despair—you can patch up the bald spots in no time. All you need is 600-grit sandpaper (from the body-finishing section of an auto parts store), exterior spray paint that's the same color as your siding, and a transparent sealer such as Plasti Dip spray (available in most hardware stores). Then proceed with this three-step first-aid routine:

▶ Sand the damaged area so that it blends smoothly with the surrounding siding, and wipe away any dust.

▶ Spray on the paint, and let it dry for the length of time specified on the can.

▶ Apply the Plasti Dip according to the instructions on the package.

Bingo—your siding's as good as new!

Deal with Dents and Scratches

Repairing minor dings in aluminum siding is easy. Here's all there is to it:

• **Dents.** All manner of misguided missiles, from storm-blown tree limbs to wayward baseballs, can dent aluminum siding. The

AN OUNCE OF PREVENTION

Faded Glory

Unlike aluminum siding, vinyl will never flake or chip because the color goes all the way through the material. However, exposure to the sun's ultraviolet rays does cause vinyl to fade. If you decide to perk up your walls with a paint job, be sure to choose a lighter tone than the original shade—never darker. That's because a new, deeper color will absorb more radiant energy, which may cause the siding to warp and buckle in a manner that can't be repaired. And then you'd have to replace the whole kit and caboodle.

simple solution: Mosey on down to your local auto parts store and pick up a body filler such as Bondo®. Follow the instructions on the product label, then sand and paint the spot as described in "Heal Power-Washing Wounds" (see page 153).

- **Scratches.** Simply sand the "owie," apply a metal primer, and let it dry. Then brush on a little acrylic latex paint in a matching color.

Crack Goes the Siding!

Just as aluminum siding can be dented easily, the vinyl version is vulnerable to cracking. Your ultra-simple repair routine depends on the size of the wound. Here are the options:

▶ To repair a shallow split, gently pry up one side using a wooden toothpick, matchstick, or mini pry bar. Insert a little bit of PVC cement into the opening, and press it closed.

▶ For a larger crack or hole, pick up a vinyl-siding repair kit at a hardware or home-improvement store. Remove the wounded panel, and wipe the back with PVC cleaner. Apply PVC cement following the directions on the package, and press on the patch, finished side down. Then snap the doctored-up siding back in place (see "Replacing Vinyl or Aluminum Siding," below).

Note: *Whenever possible, always do any vinyl-siding repairs in the late spring or summer, when the weather is toasty warm. If you try to work with vinyl in the winter, it'll be very brittle and more likely to crack.*

Replacing Vinyl or Aluminum Siding

When you're faced with a badly damaged panel, the easy-as-pie replacement process begins with a trip to your local lumberyard or home-improvement store. Pick up a replacement panel, along with a package of aluminum siding nails and an inexpensive gadget called a zip tool that's specially made for unlocking these metal or plastic strips. Then launch into this five-step process:

STEP 1. To release the damaged panel from the one above it, hook the curved end of your zip tool under the bottom edge of the upper panel, and slide it along the seam, pulling down on the tool as you go.

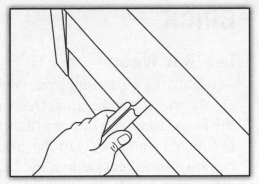

Use a zip tool to detach the damaged siding strip from the one above it.

STEP 2. Insert shims to prop up the top panel. Then use a claw hammer or pry bar cushioned on a piece of wood to pull out the nails holding the damaged strip.

STEP 3. If necessary, cut the replacement panel with tin snips, using the original strip as a guide. Then set the new one in place, locking its bottom edge over the top of the panel below it. If an end abuts any trim at a window or corner, leave a ¼-inch space to allow for expansion.

STEP 4. Nail the top of the new panel in place, driving each nail just a tad to one side of the old hole in the slot. Make sure you don't pound the nails flush. It's crucial to leave a $\frac{1}{16}$- to $\frac{1}{8}$-inch space under the head so the siding can expand and contract with changes in the weather. Vinyl siding especially will become wavy if it's fastened on too tightly.

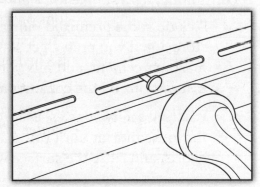

Drive a nail through each slot, letting the nail head stick up $\frac{1}{16}$ to $\frac{1}{8}$ inch above the surface.

STEP 5. Lock the top panel to the replacement strip by pressing against the seam. Use the zip tool to pull down while you push in if that makes the process easier.

BRICK

Let 'Em Weep

Arguably the most important components of any brick veneer wall are the metal flashing near the bottom that directs water away from the foundation and the tiny drains called weep holes that carry the redirected water safely to the ground. The flashing and weep hole combo also appears above and below windows and doors. If those little holes get blocked, you'll be in deep trouble because the trapped moisture will rot doors, windows, and sheathing—and that can translate into thousands of dollars in repair bills. The ultra-simple way to keep your home dry and your bank account solvent: Several times a year, clean out every single weep hole with a pipe cleaner or a straightened-out wire coat hanger.

You Have a Point There!

Eventually, the mortar in every brick wall begins to crack and crumble. While the replacement (a.k.a. repointing) process is time-consuming, it's a simple fix. Here's the gist of it:

- Pick up some premixed mortar at a brickyard or building-supply store. Or, if you prefer, get some builder's sand and type N masonry cement, and mix your own "paste" following the instructions on the cement package.

- Wearing safety goggles, use a cold chisel and hammer to remove the loose mortar until you reach a solid layer. Brush out the debris, and rinse the surface with a garden hose.

- Put a glob of mortar on a board or the back of a trowel, then roll some of it into a sausage shape, and press it into the joint with your fingers. Or, if you prefer, use a tool called a tuck pointer that you can pick up at the same place you got the mortar.

- Let the mortar dry until it shows a print when you gently press it with your thumb. Then smooth out the joint and shape it to match the adjacent ones. You can use your tuck pointer for this

Virtually all modern "brick" buildings are made of a one-brick veneer layer applied to a wooden framework that supports the structure. That's why the average do-it-yourselfer can safely and easily replace a few damaged bricks (see "New Bricks for Old," below). But if your walls need more than four contiguous bricks swapped out, or if you have an older home whose walls are solid brick—and therefore load-bearing—don't even think of attempting the job yourself, or even farming it out to your local handyman. Have an experienced professional mason do the honors. Otherwise, you could find yourself in deep—and expensive—trouble.

CALL A PRO

job, or improvise with an old spoon, a wooden craft stick, or a piece of metal tubing.

• Once the mortar is almost dry, remove any excess with a wire brush.

New Bricks for Old

You might think that replacing a broken brick is a job that only an experienced bricklayer can tackle. Not so! In fact, it's a whole lot easier than it sounds. Here's all there is to it:

STEP 1. Find a replacement. Even basic red bricks can vary enormously in color, so if at all possible, take a chunk of the old one to the brickyard, along with the dimensions of the brick face.

STEP 2. Wearing goggles and leather gloves, break up the damaged brick and remove it piece by piece. If you're removing several bricks, start at the top and work down. You can simply go at them with a cold chisel and heavy hammer, but the job will go faster if you first score the old surface with a power drill and masonry cutting wheel. Whichever method you use, be very careful not to damage any adjacent bricks.

STEP 3. Clean out the cavity, and dampen (but don't drench!) it and the new brick.

STEP 4. Spread a roughly 1-inch-thick layer of mortar on the bottom and both sides of the opening and on the top and both sides of the brick.

Slide the new brick into the opening.

STEP 5. With the brick resting on a board or large trowel, hold it up to the opening, and slide it in. Tap it into place until it's flush with the existing bricks. Add more mortar if necessary to fill all the joints, and shape them to match the other seams.

STEP 6. Keep the repaired section damp for three days. Give it regular, light mistings from a garden hose, and cover the area with a plastic sheet to help retain moisture.

Paint at Your Peril

While you certainly *can* paint brick, you'll save yourself a passel of time and money if you leave it in its natural state. That's because painting exterior brick changes it from a relatively maintenance-free surface to one that you'll have to repaint every five to seven years— or more often, depending on your climate and the severity of the weather in any given year. Plus, if you decide to remove the paint at some point down the road, it'll cost you a bundle, and the results may be far from perfect. In other words, don't do it!

Undo Unintended Paint Jobs

You say you didn't mean to paint your bricks, but your brush went astray as you were touching up some wood trim? Not to worry! One of these ploys will get the stuff off:

▶ **Wet paint.** Immediately blot up as much as you can with paper towels. If the paint is latex, wipe the residue with a wet rag. For oil-based paints, soak the rag with paint thinner rather than water.

▶ **Dried paint.** Scrape off as much as you can, and use commercial paint remover to finish the job.

Banish Mold and Mildew

To foil foul fungi, use one of these two tactics:

- Scrub the surface with full-strength white vinegar and a stiff nylon brush. (Don't use a wire brush; metal particles could get trapped in the brick, leaving you with rust stains.)

- If you'd prefer a less labor-intensive approach, make a half-and-half mixture of chlorine bleach and water, and pour it into a handheld spray bottle. Thoroughly spritz the area, leave it on for 60 minutes, and then rinse it off.

Rout Out Rust

When you've already got stubborn rust stains on your bricks—perhaps because someone else scrubbed them with a wire brush a while back—get some oxalic acid crystals at a hardware or home-improvement store. Dissolve 1 pound of the crystals per gallon of water, and apply the solution to the spots with a rag or paintbrush. Let it sit for three hours, then scrub with a stiff nylon brush and rinse thoroughly.

Become an Ivy League Dropout

Ivy-covered walls may look distinguished, but your brick (or stucco) walls will last a lot longer if they're not sporting any stuck-on vegetation. But don't just pull the greenery away. If it's clinging to the wall by means of rootlets, or "holdfasts," they could take any weak mortar or bricks right along with them.

Instead, cut the foliage away a few square feet at a time, leaving the rootlets in place until they've dried out, but not so long that they turn hard. One to two weeks should do the trick, but check back every few days. Then, when the time's right, mix up a solution of laundry detergent and water, and scrub the suckers away with a stiff nylon brush.

Note: *You don't need to forgo vines* *altogether. Just train them on a trellis that's about 6 inches from the wall.*

STUCCO

Do a Crackerjack Job on Cracks

Once a year, you should check for cracks in your stucco walls. Ignore hairline versions. They're generally harmless, and any repair job is likely to be a bigger eyesore than the minor blemish. If you find larger cracks, though, hop on the fix-it bandwagon pronto, following this three-step routine:

STEP 1. Clean out the crack using a stiff brush. Then use a chisel to undercut the edges so the opening is wider at the base than it is on the surface—thereby providing better adhesion.

STEP 2. Cover the crack with a wide strip of masking tape. Then slice through it with a utility knife to expose the area that needs to be filled.

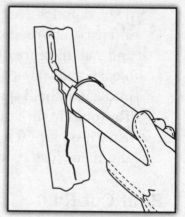

STEP 3. Pack the "trench" with either stucco caulk or premixed stucco compound* (both available in building-supply and home-improvement stores). Then smooth the surface with a putty knife, and remove the tape before the filler hardens.

Fill the crack with caulk or premixed stucco compound.

To fill cracks up to ⅛ inch across, use caulk; for wider ones, go with stucco compound.

Home, Home in the Crack

When you live in a stucco house, it's crucial to repair cracks as soon as you spot them. That's because in addition to letting moisture into the wall, those openings are prime real estate for house-hunting bugs. And when suppertime rolls around, woodpeckers and other insect-eating birds will zero right in on the nests—further damaging your wall as they enjoy their fine-dining experience.

Big Trouble Ahead?

A long vertical crack could be perfectly harmless—or it could indicate that your foundation is settling, which could cause significant damage to your home. To find out how serious the problem is, use epoxy to affix a strip of duct tape across the crack, and keep a close eye on it over the next couple of months. If at any time you notice that the tape has split or twisted, it means that the stucco is shifting, so call a professional home inspector immediately to assess the degree of risk involved and what, if anything, is necessary to dodge potential disaster.

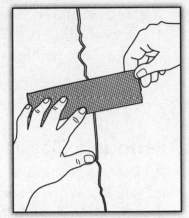

Detect shifting stucco using duct tape.

Perfect Patching

A damaged area in stucco measuring more than 2 square feet demands professional attention. But anything smaller than that is an easy DIY fix. Here's how to go about it:

▶ Wearing safety goggles, remove the damaged material with a wire brush. Then use a hammer and cold chisel to undercut the edges (see Step 1 in "Do a Crackerjack Job on Cracks," at left). Clean out the debris, and dampen the area with a wet sponge.

▶ Use a trowel to fill the opening with premixed stucco compound, overfilling it a tad. Let it dry for the amount of time specified on the product label (usually about 15 minutes). Then smooth the surface and scrape off any excess compound.

Call a mason or a stucco specialist immediately if you notice a white flaky or crumbly crust forming on your walls. This indicates that salts inside the stucco are being leached out by moisture coming from inside the structure—and that could mean you've got a major problem on your hands.

CALL A PRO

- ▶ Feather the edges to blend with the surrounding surface. Use a trowel, stiff brush, or whisk broom to give the patch a texture as close as possible to that of the surrounding wall.

- ▶ To ensure that the stucco sets up properly, wet it with a fine spray from a garden hose each morning and evening for three days.

Perform a Classic Facelift

Whitewash is a traditional coating for stucco homes, and for good reason: It stays neat and fresh-looking for decades. Over time, though, it can start to look dull, dingy, and age-stained. To restore its youthful good looks, make a batch of whitewash by mixing white portland cement with water to get a pancake-batter consistency. Give the stucco a thorough dousing with a garden hose, and then apply the mixture with a whisk broom or masonry brush.

If you'd prefer a more colorful coat, you can tint the whitewash by adding masonry dye. Just be aware that you'll have to paint each wall in a single session using the same batch of color wash because it's all but impossible to match the shade exactly on the second go-round. But that doesn't mean you have to paint the whole house in one fell swoop—you can easily come close enough with the color that the slight variations won't be noticeable on separate walls.

Hello, New Paint!

Unlike brick, stucco does accept paint extremely well, and it's a quick and easy way to spruce up a cracked, faded surface. Just follow these basic guidelines:

- **Fill any cracks** (see "Do a Crackerjack Job on Cracks" on page 160).

- **Clean the surface thoroughly.** If you use a power washer, be sure to hold the wand at least 3 feet away from the wall to avoid damaging the stucco.

- **Give it two coats of exterior acrylic latex paint.** Choose a top-quality brand, apply it with a thick-napped roller, and use a masonry brush for joints and crevices. To make sure the first coat fully penetrates the stucco, roll and brush in multiple directions, pressing on the roller if necessary.

Note: *If your stucco is prone to cracking, consider using elastomeric paint, which is specially formulated to eliminate that problem. There are numerous brands on the market. The good ones are all far more durable than top-rated acrylic latex paints, even under the most severe weather conditions.*

INSULATION

Is There a Blanket in There?

All across the country, local building codes now require homes to have insulated exterior walls. But if your house was built before 1965, and your utility bills are sky-high, a lack of insulation may be the culprit. There are two easy ways to find out for sure:

- ▶ **Check an electrical box.** Take the cover plate off an outlet on an exterior wall. (Kill the juice to the circuit first!) Then peek into the opening. If there is any insulation, you'll see its edges around the box.

- ▶ **Look in a closet.** Cut a small hole in a closet or other inconspicuous spot that abuts an exterior wall.

If your inspection turns up no sign of insulation—especially if you live in a cold or very hot climate—you could consider having a contractor install the blown-in version (it is not a DIY project). On the other hand, you may be able to raise your comfort level and lower your bills for a lot less money by adding more insulation to your attic (see page 210 for the lowdown on that process).

NASA Strikes Again

Thanks to spin-off technology from our space program, you can now insulate your house simply by brushing on a coat or two of paint. The secret lies in vacuum-filled ceramic particles that minimize the path of hot-air transfer through ceilings, walls, and roofs. This amazing stuff works on just about every kind of surface under the sun, including wood, stone, stucco, concrete, wallboard, metal, and even dried-out asphalt shingles. Several ceramic-based products claim to have this insulating power, but the only one NASA recommends is made by Hy-Tech Thermal Solutions. Learn more about this nifty new product at www.hytechthermalsolutions.com.

Plug the Leaks

Even if your walls are insulated, you could be losing a lot of heated—or cooled—air through the openings around electrical outlets. So head to your local hardware store and buy foam insulating gaskets for all of the receptacles and light switches on your exterior walls. Then remove each cover plate, press the gasket onto the back, and screw the plate back in place. Then let the savings begin!

The Surprising Truth about Asbestos

Common assumption: If there is any asbestos in your home, you need to get it outta there yesterday!

- ▶ **The facts:** Asbestos can cause major health problems, but the damage only occurs when you inhale the fibers over an extended period of time, usually after working for years in factories and other places where the tiny, sharp particles filled the air all day long. If you have an older house that has asbestos insulation, getting rid of it could actually cause a lot more harm than good. That's because the removal process would release the fibers into the air.

- ▶ **The bottom line:** If you know that asbestos is in your home, have a reputable contractor perform a thorough inspection and take whatever mitigating steps are deemed necessary. But don't insist that the stuff be removed—and whatever you do, don't DIY!

Doors & Windows

We expect our doors and windows to connect us with the outside world and, at the same time, keep us safe and sound from the wildest weather Mother Nature sends our way. When these heroic structures fall in battle, they're mighty expensive to replace. But with regular helpings of TLC and Johnny-on-the-spot attention to any problems that crop up, your doors and windows can perform their duties for a lifetime—and then some!

HINGED DOORS

3 Fast and Funky Fixes for a Sticking Door

Exterior doors are prone to sticking in their frames for two simple reasons: First, by necessity, doors have a very narrow window of opportunity in which to swing. Second, doors are nearly always installed when they and the door frames are dry, so when heavy rain pours down or summer's humidity sets in, both the door and the frame expand to fill the narrow gap that was there to begin with. You may think the best solution is to remove the door and plane (or sand) down the edges. But that's a big hassle and, more importantly, once the moisture level drops, you'll have an oversized space between the door and the frame. So before you launch any complex maneuvers, try one of these tricks:

▶ **Soft-soap it.** Rub a bar of soap over the top and side edges of the door. This just may give it enough lubrication to open and close smoothly.

An ultra-simple way to ID the sticking spots on a door frame is to insert an old playing card into the space between the closed door and the jamb, and slide the card from top to bottom. Then direct your DIY action to any areas where the card doesn't pass freely.

▶ **Whack it.** First, figure out where the door and frame are sticking and in which direction the frame would have to move to expand the gap between the two. Then hold a piece of scrap wood against that part of the frame, and give the wood a few good whacks with a hammer or rubber mallet. The frame should shift just enough to let the door move more freely.

▶ **Trim the paint.** If your door has been painted many times over the years, the built-up layers may be causing the problem. So scrape or sand the paint off the sides and top of the door, as well as the inside of the frame. And the next time you paint, give those surfaces just a single, thin coat.

Tighten Up Loose Screws

When a door drags on the floor or rubs near the top, it's all but certain that the screws have worked themselves loose—as door screws invariably do over time. The quick fix: Tighten all the hinge screws in the door and the jamb. Get 'em in good and firm—but be sure to use a screwdriver, not a drill, because that's likely to overtighten them, thereby stripping the screw holes or destroying the heads.

Simple Stripped-Hole Solutions

If you've already got stripped screw holes, your best mitigation measure depends on the scene of the "crime." Here's the rundown:

- **The doorjamb.** Replace the original screws with 3-inch versions, which will run through the jamb and into the framing behind it.

- **A solid door.** Drill a pilot hole with a ⅛-inch bit, and drive in a screw that's 1 inch longer than the original one.

- **A hollow-core door.** Dip a wooden golf tee in carpenter's glue, tap the tee into the hole, and use a utility knife to cut it off flush with the door. When the glue dries, drive in the original screw or a new one of the same size. Got no golf tees on hand? Then use wood splinters, toothpicks, or matchsticks instead. They'll accomplish the same hole-filling purpose.

Give the Door a Shove

Sometimes, driving a long screw through the jamb and into the wall framing is all it takes to pull the door away from its sticking point. Here's the DIY procedure:

► Close the door to find out where it's rubbing and, therefore, which hinge(s) you need to attack. If the door rubs the side jamb near the top (the most common spot), your "patient" is the upper hinge. If it rubs at the overhead jamb or the lower side jamb, focus on the bottom hinge. If the door rubs the whole way along the side jamb, all three hinges need attention.

► Remove the hinge's middle screw, and use a drill to drive in a new 3-inch screw until it's snug against the hinge's surface. Then give the screw another quarter turn, and close the door. If it still sticks, continue tightening and checking until it moves freely. But keep a close eye on the door trim. If any gaps begin to appear at the joints, it means that the jamb is tight against the framing and you'll need to focus on the other side (see "Jiggle the Jamb" on page 168).

Floor It!

If all the hinge screws are good and tight (see "Tighten Up Loose Screws," at left) and your door still rubs against the floor or threshold, this simple trick should solve the problem: Pinpoint the area where the bottom is rubbing, and tape a sheet of coarse sandpaper over the spot. Then open and close the door over the gritty patch until it's back in the swing of things.

Jiggle the Jamb

This space-making ploy works on the same principle as the hinge-adjustment trick (see "Give the Door a Shove" on page 167), except that it expands the area on the latch side of the jamb, rather than the hinge side. Near the center of each area where the door is rubbing, drill a ⅛-inch pilot hole and then drill a countersink to accommodate the head. Drive the screw into the wood, and tighten it gradually. Cover the screw head with wood filler, then sand it and paint or stain the spot to match the surrounding wood.

Note: *Depending on the length of the scraping area, you may need to use two or more screws.*

Jeepers Creepers...

Use your peepers—before you open the door to anyone. Most homeowners have become savvy about using extra-sturdy dead bolts and reliable window locks to deter criminals. But a whole lot of equally smart bad guys have learned that if they simply ring the doorbell, the resident will open the door—expecting to see a friendly neighbor, or maybe a Girl Scout selling cookies. So don't take any chances: Unless you have a window that lets you see who's standing on your doorstep, run down to your local hardware store and pick up a wide-angle peephole. Then install it this way:

- With a tape measure, find the center of your door. Then mark the spot where you want to install the peephole, choosing a height that's convenient for all the members of your household.

- Drill a hole. Most peepholes require a ½-inch "home." Use a standard bit for a metal, fiberglass, or composite door. For a wooden door, go with a brad point bit to ensure a splinter-free hole that requires no sanding. In each case, run the drill at full speed while pressing lightly.

- Insert the two-part peephole. Push the lens into the hole from the inside and the sleeve from the outside. Then screw 'em together. That's all there is to it!

Installing a Dead-Bolt Lock

One of the simplest ways to make your home more secure is to outfit all of your exterior doors with heavy-duty dead-bolt locks. You could call in a professional locksmith, but with a few simple tools, you can do the job in less than an hour—at about a third of the price a pro would charge you. So hop on down to your local home-improvement or hardware store and buy a dead-bolt lock (see "4 Dead-On Dead-Bolt Shopping Tips," on page 170). Then follow this simple seven-step process:

STEP 1. Pull out the template that came with the lock, and tape it to the inside of the door so that the center of the dead bolt will be 6 inches above the center of the doorknob. (The template shows you where to drill the two large holes to accommodate the lock's cylinder and bolt.)

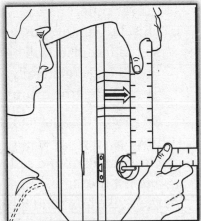

Tape the drilling template to the inside of the door.

STEP 2. Brace the door with clamps to keep it stationary. Then, from the inside, drill the cylinder hole with a 2 ⅛-inch hole saw, using the same setback* as the doorknob. When the saw's pilot bit penetrates the opposite side of the door, remove the scrap wood protector (shown in the illustration) and finish drilling the hole from the exterior side. (To cut through a steel door, use a bimetal hole saw set.)

The distance from the edge of the door to the center of the hole, which will be either 2 ⅜ inches or 2 ¾ inches.

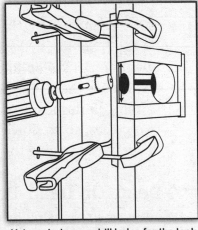

Using a hole saw, drill holes for the lock cylinder and bolt.

STEP 3. Drill the bolt hole in the center of the door's edge, using a 1-inch hole saw or spade bit. In both cases, make sure you keep your drill square and level.

STEP 4. Insert the bolt latch set into the door, and trace the profile of the rectangular faceplate onto the door's edge. Cut the vertical edges with a utility knife, and use a sharp 1-inch chisel to remove just enough wood so the faceplate will be flush with the door's edge (generally about ³⁄₁₆ inch). Then install the cylinder and bolt.

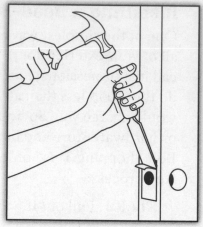

Carefully chisel out space for the faceplate.

STEP 5. Coat the end of the bolt with lipstick or water-based paint. Then close the door and slide the bolt snugly against the jamb. This indicates where the strike box should be. Then trace the profile of the strike plate on the jamb.

STEP 6. Drill overlapping 1-inch holes for the strike box. Then chisel out the recess for the strike box and plate.

STEP 7. Set the strike box into its opening. Drill pilot holes for the screws,

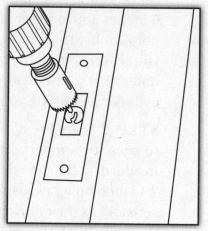

Use lipstick to mark the spot for the strike box on the jamb.

and secure the strike box and plate to the jamb and the 2-by-4 framing underneath. Generally, there is a hollow space between the two pieces, so go slowly and gently to avoid driving the screws too deep and damaging the jamb.

4 Dead-On Dead-Bolt Shopping Tips

Whether you're installing a new dead bolt or replacing your current one, keep these pointers in mind as you make your choices at the hardware store:

▶ **Consider the cylinder.** In most cases, a single-cylinder lock (that is, one that is keyed only on the outdoor side) is your best bet. That way, you can lock the door from the inside by simply flicking the lever. On the other hand, if you have a window that's close to your dead bolt, choose a double-cylinder lock. Otherwise, a burglar could simply break the glass, reach in, and unlock the door. Just make sure that you keep a key in a designated spot indoors, and that everyone in your household leaves it there!

▶ **Buy strength.** Dead bolts carry sturdiness ratings of 1 through 3, with Grade 1 being the strongest. They cost only a little more than Grade 3 versions, so don't pinch pennies when your security is at stake.

▶ **Get a strike box.** These are sold separately from the dead-bolt kits, but it's well worth your while to buy and install one. That's because it strengthens the dead bolt by spreading the impact of a would-be intruder's blow over a wider area and also by extending the strike area to the structural door frame, not confining it to the jamb.

When you re-key door locks or install new ones, you can wind up with a lot of inoperative keys on your hands. But think twice before you toss 'em in the trash. Here's a sampling of productive new careers for those little metal marvels:

Boot and shoe cleaner. The tip of a key is the perfect size and shape for digging out caked-on mud or snow from the treads of shoes or work boots.

Jewelry. String lengths of chain through the key holes to make funky necklaces.

On-the-go screwdriver. Just file down the end and attach the key to your key chain, and tuck it in your pocket or purse.

Plumb bob. When you need a vertical reference line for a job such as tiling a wall or hanging wallpaper, tie a key to a string and hang it up. The key will lie flush against the wall, making it easier to check your work as you go along.

Weights. Sew keys into the hems of draperies, tablecloths, or any other fabric that needs to stay put.

▶ **Opt for a rectangular faceplate.** With most dead bolts, you can choose between a round faceplate, which requires no chiseling, and a rectangular version, for which you must chisel out a resting place. Unless you have a steel door (which can't be chiseled), don't be tempted by the prospect of faster installation! A recessed faceplate makes for a stronger lock.

SLIDING DOORS & WINDOWS

Track It Down

When a sliding door or window starts to stick, a likely cause is dirt that has built up in the track. So grab a flat-head screwdriver to scrape the crud loose, and then vacuum it up. Just be sure to take your time, and work carefully so you don't gouge or otherwise damage the track or the frame.

Roll 'Em!

If a good cleaning doesn't make your door slide smoothly, it means one of two things: Either the rollers under the door are ready for the junk heap, or they simply need to be adjusted. So try this ploy first:

• Locate the two adjusting screws on the face and edge of the door, and pry off the trim caps that cover them.

• If one side of the door is lower than the other, raise it by turning the screw clockwise until the door looks even on its track. Then give it a trial slide. If it still sticks, turn both screws a quarter turn to raise the whole door, and check the movement again. If the going is still bumpy, it means that the door needs to be removed so the rollers can be examined and then either cleaned or replaced. It's a good idea to let a strong, experienced professional handle this process because a sliding glass door is extremely heavy and surprisingly delicate. In other words, it's a real bear to handle without breaking the glass, injuring yourself, or damaging walls—or anything else it bumps up against.

Keep 'Em on the Fast Track

Once you've got your door gliding right along (see "Track It Down" and "Roll 'Em!," at left), use this three-part routine to fend off any future hang-ups:

- Every time you vacuum, use the brush attachment to give your door and window tracks a once-over.

- Every few weeks or so, clean the track with a cloth dampened with denatured alcohol.

- After you've cleaned the track, rub a bar of soap or paraffin wax along the channel, using long, even strokes.

Get It Outta There!

Sliding windows operate a little differently from sliding doors. In this case, tracks along the top and bottom of the window frame guide either one or both sashes over a ridge in the bottom channel. There may or may not be glides or rollers on the bottom of the sash(es) that ride on top of the ridge. When you need to remove the sashes, whether to clean them extra thoroughly, replace the glass, or examine the rollers, here's how to go about it:

▶ **Sliding sash.** Slide it to the center of the frame. Then take hold of the sash on both sides, push it up into the top track, and when it clears the lip of the frame, swing the bottom edge out toward you. If the window refuses to budge, tighten the screws in the upper track. This will push the track upward, expanding the opening.

▶ **Stationary sash.** Unscrew the brackets that hold it to the frame at the top and bottom corners, as well as the bumper in the center of the lower track that keeps the sash from moving. Cut and scrape away any caulk or paint that may be sealing the outside edges. Then slide the sash to the center of the frame, lift it up, and pull it out as you did its movable partner.

DOUBLE-HUNG WINDOWS

Don't Wrestle with Your Windows

If you're forever jerking and shoving to make a window slide up or down, I have four words of advice for you: Stop it right now! Brute force puts undue wear and tear on a window and shortens its life span. So make the going easier with this ultra-simple two-part ploy:

- **Rub both of the channels** with fine steel wool, and then vacuum away the dust and debris.

- **Spritz the channels** with silicone lubricant (available in hardware stores). In a pinch, you could rub the space with paraffin or candle wax, but the silicone spray will work better and last longer.

A Little Tap'll Do Ya

Correction: Make that a whole bunch of little taps. When you find that you can't open a double-hung window for love nor money—and there are no locks or other security devices keeping it in place—chances are there's been an overzealous painter at work. Here's how to cut through the paint that's got your window stuck shut:

▶ Grab a putty knife and a hammer, and put on protective goggles (so you don't wind up with sharp little paint chips in your eyes).

▶ Set the blade of the putty knife against the paint-filled space between the window frame and the molding, and tap very gently to break the seal—and only the seal.

▶ Work your way down each side and across the bottom, moving the putty knife in small, overlapping increments so you leave no crust unbroken.

Once you're done tapping, your window should slide up and down smoothly. If any dried-on paint still prevents free and easy movement, sand or scrape the spots away.

Paint Properly to Prevent Stuck Windows

Before you start, clean the glass and let it dry thoroughly (see "Window Washing 101: What the Pros Know" on page 180). And when you buy your paint and primer, pick up a 1½- to 2-inch sash brush. Its angled bristles give you a fine, accurate line. Then follow these steps:

- Prep and prime the surface according to the paint manufacturer's directions.

- Raise the bottom sash and lower the top one as much as you can, until they've almost switched places.

- Paint all the exposed parts of the top sash (which is now on the bottom). Carry a thin line onto the glass to seal the glazing.

- Close the window almost all the way, and paint the rest of the top sash and the entire bottom sash. Don't get any paint in the space between the sash and the stops (the little pieces of wood that hold the sashes in place).

- Paint the window casing, sill, and apron. Then, before the paint dries, slide both sashes up and down several times until you see a clear opening between them and the stops.

- When the paint has dried, hold a broad putty knife against the glass, parallel to the newly painted frame. Then use a razor-blade scraper to remove any paint on the outside of your "fence." Don't worry that you'll scratch the glass—as long as you've cleaned it before you started, there won't be any dirt to cause trouble.

WELL, WHADDYA KNOW!

Have you ever wondered where we got the word *window*? You haven't? Well, I'm going to tell you anyway. By necessity, the early Scandinavians built their houses to be simple and snug. Because doors had to be kept closed as much as possible during the long, frigid winters, smoke and stale air were sent out and fresh air brought in by way of a hole, or "eye," in the roof. Because the wind often whistled across that opening, folks called it *vindr auga*, meaning the "wind's eye." British builders borrowed the term and tweaked it to become *window*.

Replacing a Broken Windowpane

A broken windowpane is a pain, but provided it's the single-thickness version, replacing it is fairly simple. Here's how to go about it:

STEP 1. Measure the opening, and have a piece of glass cut to order, subtracting ⅛ inch from both dimensions.

STEP 2. Wearing goggles and work gloves, pull out the broken glass. With a hammer and putty knife, chip out the glazing compound from the edges of the frame. Use pliers to pull out the metal glazier's points.

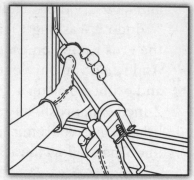

Apply glazing compound to all sides of the opening.

STEP 3. Seal the exposed wood with linseed oil. When it's thoroughly soaked into the wood, apply glazing compound to the channel all the way around the opening. Then position the new glass in the frame, and press it firmly.

STEP 4. Press new glazier's points against the glass and into the muntins with a screwdriver. Use at least two points per side, spacing them 4 to 6 inches apart. Don't use the old holes!

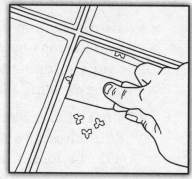

Press new glazier's points into the muntins at 4- to 6-inch intervals.

STEP 5. Apply more glazing compound over the edges of the glass. Holding a putty knife at an angle, draw it across the compound. Work out from the corners and press firmly against the muntins so that the compound is not visible from inside the house. After every few strokes, dip the putty knife in linseed oil to keep it from sticking to the compound. Let the compound cure for about a week before painting over it.

Spread glazing compound over the edges of the glass, and let it cure before painting.

CASEMENT WINDOWS

Comfort Cranky Cranks

The key to long life for modern casement windows—and their close cousins, awning and multi-louvered jalousie windows—lies in one word: lubrication. The minute you find that a crank is getting stiff and hard to turn, loosen the setscrew, remove the handle, and pop off the cover. Then spritz silicone spray onto all the pivot points on the crank arm, the top and bottom guide arms, and the gears if you see any. Bingo—your window will be back in the swing of things!

Note: *If you don't spot any gears, it means that they've been encased and permanently lubricated, so just spray the pivot points.*

Get a Handle on Crank Problems

When a window crank is loose or simply not turning as smoothly as it should be, the solution could be as simple as tightening the setscrew near the base of the handle. If that doesn't do the trick, remove the handle and eyeball the teeth inside it. If they're rounded rather than sharp, it's replacement time in the old corral. Chances are you won't find an exact duplicate, but hardware and home-improvement stores sell generic kits that work with most casement mechanisms. To find the closest match for your window, take the old handle with you on shopping day.

Note: *If all of your cranked windows are the same age and get just about the same amount of use, you might want to change all of them at once because it's likely that their handles' teeth are about to lose their grip, too.*

Close 'Em Up!

In order to keep all crank-operated windows in good health, it is absolutely essential to keep them closed whenever it's raining or snowing. Otherwise, the moisture will corrode the operator block and crank handle and put them out of business before their time.

Replacing a Worn-Out Crank Operator

When the gears on the crank operator shaft cease to turn easily—or at all—then it's time to replace the operator. Fortunately, it's a quick and easy fix. Here's the five-step process:

STEP 1. Order a new operator from a company selling window-replacement parts. (If you can't find the make or model number, just peruse online catalogs to find a a match.)

STEP 2. Open the window until the crank arm bushing is aligned with the guide track notch on the window sash. In most cases, you can simply push down on the arm to pop the bushing out of the track. But some types need to be pried off with a flat-head screwdriver or unscrewed from a channel on the bottom of the sash.

STEP 3. If the operator has a guide arm (a.k.a. split-arm operator), unhook that, too.

STEP 4. If the operator cover is removable, use a utility knife to cut through any paint or stain that may be sealing it to the window jamb. Then take out the screws on top of the casement cover and gently pry it off.*

STEP 5. Remove the crank operator, then set the new one in place and screw it to the jamb using the existing screw holes.

* If the cover is not removable, you'll find the operator screws on the outside of the window frame.

Beyond Crank Trouble

If your casement window's glass is broken, or if condensation has formed between the panes, you'll have to replace either the glass or the entire window. If the sash is not damaged, you may be able to order only new glass and have it installed in the existing frame. What's more, the cost may be covered under your warranty. To find out for sure, call your window manufacturer. And be prepared to provide the sash dimensions and the other information that's etched into a corner of the glass or stamped onto the hardware (the location varies from one window maker to another).

A GLASS ACT

Save That Pane!

When a windowpane suffers a minor injury, don't rush out and replace it—there may be plenty of life left in that glass. Here's how to offer up first-class first aid:

▶ **Crack.** Put a drop or two of super glue in the center of the crack. The glue will spread along the length of the crack and, quite possibly, make it vanish. (Even if the crack doesn't disappear, the glue will seal the opening.) Just make sure you close the window gently in the future—cracked panes, glued or not, will break more easily if the window is slammed.

▶ **Shallow scratch.** Using a soft, clean cloth, vigorously rub extra-whitening toothpaste (not gel!) onto the scratch for a minute or two. Then wipe the glass clean with a second cloth.

▶ **Small hole.** If, say, a tiny stone or poorly aimed BB gun has left such a hole, drop a small bead of clear nail polish into the opening using the applicator brush. Let it dry, and then add a little more polish. Keep up the drop-and-dry process until the hole is filled. (Don't try this trick on automotive glass because that's a different "critter" altogether and needs to be doctored by a pro.)

The Window-Washing Old Wives' Tale

True or false? The most effective way to wash windows is to spritz the glass with a spray cleaner and then go at it with a fistful of paper towels or scrunched-up newspaper and plenty of elbow grease.

A resounding false! According to professional window cleaners, all that rubbing simply moves the dirt around from one place to another. What's even worse is that rubbing also gives the glass a static charge that attracts dust and grime like a magnet. Almost as soon as you're finished, the window looks dirty again. For a truly effective way to shine up your windows—and prevent scratches caused by rubbed-in dirt—see "Window Washing 101: What the Pros Know" (on page 180).

Window Washing 101: What the Pros Know

Professional window washers recommend cleaning exterior windows at least twice a year* using the right tools and this five-step routine:

STEP 1. Make a cleaning solution by mixing 1 teaspoon of dishwashing liquid per 2 gallons of hot water. Don't use more soap than that! It won't be any more effective, and it'll leave soapy residue behind. If you prefer a vinegar-based formula—which works especially well if your glass is greasy—use my Heavy-Duty Window Cleaner (below).

STEP 2. Remove loose dirt or cobwebs with a soft-bristled brush.

STEP 3. Dip a natural sponge or a strip applicator (a squeegee look-alike with a soft, woolly fabric strip on the business end) into the cleaning solution, wring out the excess, and wash the glass. Use a nylon scrubbing pad to attack stubborn spots, such as bird droppings or tree pitch.

STEP 4. Pull a squeegee over the soapy pane in whatever direction you prefer (straight down, horizontally, or in a reverse-S pattern). Overlap passes, and at the end of each stroke, wipe the blade clean with a lint-free cloth.

STEP 5. Dry the panes and frames with a fresh lint-free cloth.

* Always try to wash windows on a cloudy or overcast day. Otherwise, the sun will make the cleaning solution dry prematurely, causing unsightly streaks.

POWERFUL POTIONS

HEAVY-DUTY WINDOW CLEANER

When your windows are extra grimy or greasy, this formula will bring back the sparkle and let the sun shine through!

¼ cup of white vinegar

2 tbsp. of rubbing alcohol or pulp-free lemon juice

3 cups of warm water

Mix the ingredients together in a bucket—multiplying the recipe as needed—and go to town (see "Window Washing 101: What the Pros Know," above).

Mitigate Mineral Madness

Unfortunately, over time, hard-water runoff from masonry or rain falling through metal window screens can leave your windows with mineral stains that normal washing cannot erase. But there is a simple way to get rid of the ugly spots. After a regular washing, wet the glass and then go at the stains with either fine (000) steel wool or an oxalic acid-based cleansing powder, such Zud® or Bar Keepers Friend®. Pour the powder onto a wet cotton towel and mix it around to make a paste. Then rub the stains away, rinse with clear water, and squeegee the glass twice to remove the residue. Do not, under any circumstances, use regular brands of scouring powder. They won't remove the spots, and they'll leave you with scratched glass to boot.

Horse Sense for Stained Glass

Stained-glass windows can (and routinely do) last for centuries, but only if they get the kind of TLC they need. If you're lucky enough to have one of these treasures—whether old or new—in your home, follow these guidelines to give it a long, happy life:

- Use a very soft brush to remove surface dust—either by hand or with a vacuum cleaner. Do not apply any pressure to the glass.

- Clean individual pieces of glass with a soft cotton cloth and a pH-neutral cleaning solution mixed with distilled water. There are commercial formulas made specially for stained glass, but don't waste your money. Horse shampoos work just as well and cost a lot less. (Because a horse's skin is more sensitive than ours, these products are formulated to be pH neutral.)

If a stained-glass window shows any sign of a bulge, if it rattles in the wind, or if the cames develop a coating that resembles powdered sugar, get professional help. Most stained-glass studios offer free on-site estimates. To find a good one near you, contact the Stained Glass Association of America at www.stainedglass.org.

CALL A PRO

- Do not, under any circumstances, use a commercial window cleaner or any product (store-bought or DIY) that contains ammonia, vinegar, or another acidic substance. Likewise, avoid all abrasives and scrubbing pads.

- Never try to clean or polish the cames (the lead or zinc frames around the glass pieces).

Note: *You can buy horse shampoo from tack shops, most feed stores, and online retailers that carry equestrian supplies.*

STORM DOORS, WINDOWS & SCREENS

Poke 'Em Till They Weep

Aluminum and vinyl storm windows have weep holes on the bottom edge of the frame so that rainwater will drain to the outside. If those gaps are blocked, moisture will build up and eventually rot the wooden sill. So periodically take an inspection tour, and check for jam-ups of dirt, leaves, or other gunk. If you find any, clear out the crud with a nail, a pipe cleaner, or a wire coat hanger.

That's the Spirit!

Your aluminum windows and storm doors are in fine shape, except for one thing: A coat of corrosion has built up on the surfaces. Don't rush out and replace the things! With a little TLC, they'll look as good as new. Just remove the danged deposits by rubbing them with steel wool dipped in mineral spirits.

Fill the Pits

You say your problem isn't corrosion—it's oxidation pits on unpainted aluminum doors and windows? Fret not! Just wad up a ball of aluminum foil and rub it back and forth across the pitted areas. This won't make the damage disappear completely, but little bits of the foil will catch in the pits and make your doors and windows look better, at least for the short haul.

Safe Storage for Storm Windows

Like all sheet glass, storm windows fare best when they're stored on edge, in as upright a position as possible. Here's an easy way to give your storms a snug, safe home for their summer recess:

Two pallets and a couple of boards make a safe storage rack for storm windows.

• Scavenge or buy two wooden pallets, and use them to form the top and bottom of a sort of window "garage," with solid boards for the sides. Make sure the slots in the pallets line up precisely!

• Nail 1-by-4 or 2-by-6 strips along the top and bottom on both ends to keep the box off the floor.

• Settle the container in a dry place that's well removed from potentially damaging action (for instance, from misguided tools or frolicking pets). Then slide your windows into the slots.

Close It Quicker

If you've adjusted your storm door's closing mechanism to its maximum speed, but it's still shutting more slowly than you'd like, try this trick: Simply unscrew the closer bracket on the door frame and move it farther away from the door. This will increase the angle between the tube and the door and reduce its closing time.

Prevent Storm-Tossed Storm Doors

In high winds, it's not uncommon for a storm door to blow right off its hinges. The solution: Install a chain retainer (available in hardware and home-improvement stores) to keep it in place. Attach one end to the overhead doorjamb, then open the door as far as you want it to go, and stretch the chain out to that position. Mark the spot, and then screw the retainer to the door frame. Barring a hurricane-level gale, your door should stay safe at home!

SUPER-STRENGTH SCREEN CLEANER

Whether you wash your screens in winter or spring, this superpowered spray will get the metal clean and the openings free and clear.

1 qt. of ammonia
2 tbsp. of borax
2 squirts of dishwashing liquid
3 qts. of warm water

Mix all of the ingredients together in a bucket, and pour the solution into a handheld spray bottle. Then use it to give all of your screens a yearly shower, following the directions in "Clean-Screen Routine," (at right).

Clean-Screen Routine

Window and door screens are magnets for every kind of airborne gunk under the sun. Over time, the built-up grime not only interferes with airflow into your house, but also weakens the wire mesh, which (of course) leads to early screen death. So make sure you give all of your screens an annual shower. If you take them down for the winter, clean them thoroughly before you store them away. Otherwise, do the job in the spring, just before open-window weather gets under way. Regardless of the timing, here's the drill:

► Remove the screens from their duty posts, and lean them up against a fence, wall, or tree.

► Vacuum them with a soft brush. Then hose them off with a fine spray, and spritz both sides with my Super-Strength Screen Cleaner (above).

► Wait five minutes or so for the cleaner to loosen up the crud, and then gently scrub the mesh and frames with a soft-bristle brush. Rinse thoroughly, and check to make sure you've left no spots unbrushed.

► Prop the clean screens up vertically in a sheltered spot (in the sun, if possible) and let them air-dry.

Simple Surgery for Stricken Screens

When a screen suffers a large tear or major gouge near the edge, your only option may be to replace it, but smaller wounds are easy fixes. In either case, though, act fast before a little problem turns into a big, buggy one. For the replacement routine, see "Replacing a Damaged Screen" (below). And here's how to deal with minor dings:

- **Tiny holes.** For holes less than an inch or so across, straighten out the ends of the torn strands, and then spread either epoxy glue or clear nail polish over the spot. Before the covering is completely dry, use a pin or a toothpick to poke through the clogged openings.

- **Larger holes or tears.** Pick up a roll of adhesive-backed screen repair tape at a hardware or home-improvement store, or order it online. Then, following the directions on the package, apply it to the trouble spot.

Replacing a Damaged Screen

Few DIY projects are easier than replacing a screen in a metal frame. Here's the ultra-simple four-step process:

STEP 1. Use an awl or a nail to pry up the end of the spline (the round vinyl or rubber strip that holds the screening in place). Then remove the screen and measure the frame's opening. Take the measurements and a piece of the old spline to a hardware store, and buy these supplies: a spline that's identical to the original, a piece of screening that extends 2 inches beyond the frame on all sides, and an inexpensive tool called a spline roller.

Before you store your screens for the off-season, wrap them in protective overcoats and "button" them up with tape to keep out dust. Retired sheets or shower curtains, plastic sheeting or bubble wrap, or brown wrapping paper will all work just fine. Whatever you do, though, avoid newspapers because the ink may rub off on the wire mesh. And in that case, dust will be the least of your worries!

STEP 2. Set the frame on a flat surface, lay the new wire mesh on top, and press it into the frame's groove using the *convex* end of the spline roller. Keep the screen taut by pulling it on the opposite side (or having a helper do the honors). Roll the spline into the groove using the *concave* end of the roller.*

STEP 3. As you roll your way to each corner, cut a slit in the screening at a 45-degree angle to the joint. This will keep the screen from buckling. Press the spline into the corner with a screwdriver, and continue with the roller around the rest of the frame.

STEP 4. Once the spline is in place, cut off the excess screen with a sharp utility knife angled away from the spline, being careful not to slice the mesh (or your fingers).

If you're working with fiberglass screen, roll the mesh and the spline into the groove at the same time using the roller's concave end.

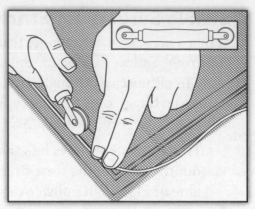

Use a spline roller to press the spline and screen into the groove in the frame.

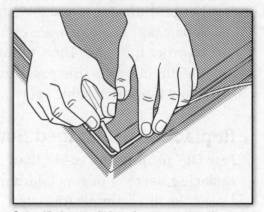

Cut a 45-degree slit into the screen at each corner, and press the spline in with a screwdriver.

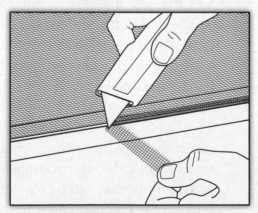

Use a sharp utility knife to cut away the excess screening.

GARAGE DOORS

Keep It Moving

A garage door will freeze up fast if you don't keep its moving parts well lubricated. So every six months, spray the hinges, door tracks, pulleys, latches, springs, and chain drive with a lubricant that's especially made for garage doors. Your owner's manual may recommend a specific product, but one excellent brand is 3-IN-ONE® Garage Door Lube (available in hardware and home-improvement stores).

Give It a Test Drive

Once a month, put these two crucial safety features to the test:

▶ **Auto-reverse.** Hit the wall button (or your remote opener) to raise the door, and set an empty cardboard box on the floor directly below it. Then close the door. It should reverse its course instantly as it comes close to touching the box. If it doesn't, increase the mechanism's close limit following the instructions in your owner's manual.

▶ **Balance.** Disconnect the opener by pulling the release cord or lever. Then open the door manually about halfway. It should hold its position, with perhaps a slight movement up or down. If the door either falls or rides back up, have a garage door pro adjust the spring tension.

Slow Going

When your garage door has gotten sluggish, the problem lies in one of two places: the electric opener or the tracks. To pinpoint the culprit, disconnect the opener and raise the door manually. If it goes up just fine, you'll know the opener is on the blink, so call a pro for help. On the other hand, if the door won't open smoothly, it means the rollers are sticking in the tracks. A good shot of lubricant may do the trick—or you may need to focus on damaged rollers or tracks that are misaligned (see "Get Back on Track" on page 188).

Get Back on Track

Unlike most garage door woes, roller and track glitches are usually easy tweaks. Here's the lowdown on both fronts:

- **Replace damaged rollers.** Simply remove the victim from its bracket, take it to a garage door dealer or home-improvement store, and buy a matching replacement. Then bolt the new roller back in place. A word of caution: Do not, under any circumstances, remove the roller bracket. If that's broken, call a pro.

- **Realign roller tracks.** Measure the space between the tracks at several spots to determine where they're out of sync. Then loosen the mounting bolt in that area, and use a hammer and small wood block to tap the track into its proper place. Finally, tighten the bolt back up.

WEATHER STRIPPING & CAULKING

2 Wacky Ways to Locate Leaks

If you suspect that outside air is entering your home (maybe because your furnace and air conditioner seem to be working overtime), but you don't know where the leaks are, try one of these two tests:

- ▶ **The incense exam.** On a breezy day, light a stick of incense and pass it alongside doors, windows, and any other places where outdoor air might sneak in. When the smoke moves horizontally, you've found a chink in your home's "armor."

► **The skin test.** No incense on hand? Then wet the back of your hand and move it along the perimeter of exterior windows and doors. You'll feel any cool (or hot) air as it blows through the opening.

Ins and Outs

Not sure where leaking air is coming from? Here's the simple rule of thumb: Moisture on the storm window indicates that warm air is leaking out from indoors. Condensation on the interior window means that cold air is sneaking past the storm sash.

Helpful Hints for Highly Effective Weather Stripping

To make the most of your weather-stripping efforts, keep these two pointers in mind:

• **Act early.** Self-stick types do not adhere well when temps drop below 50°F. Plus, you'll lose bucketfuls of heat if you apply any kind of weather stripping when chilly winds are blowing.

• **Prep the surface.** To make sure that self-stick stripping really sticks, wipe the surfaces with a de-glosser (available in paint stores) or rub them with trisodium phosphate (TSP). Then rinse thoroughly with a clean, wet cloth and dry the frame with a towel.

AN OUNCE OF
PREVENTION

Seal with Caution

While it is true that caulking or weather-stripping any gaps in door and window frames can save you big bucks on utility bills, don't get carried away. If you seal up your house so tightly that little or no air can get in or out, you'll be asking for a whole other set of problems. To be specific, you'll ensure that noxious fumes given off by building materials, furnishings, high-tech equipment, and cleaning products won't be able to escape. Neither will the dampness and tiny organisms that create mold. Remember the hoopla about "sick building syndrome" a number of years back? Well, this is what caused it. The result was an epidemic of environmentally triggered illnesses and allergies, in homes as well as schools, hospitals, and office buildings.

Outsmart a Warped Window

It's all but impossible to make weather stripping work on a wood-framed double-hung window that's warped on the bottom. But that doesn't mean you need to let the air blow in—or replace the window. Instead, fend off the chilly wind this way:

▶ Open the bottom sash, and squirt a band of caulk on the sill. Cover the caulk with plastic wrap, lower the window, and lock the window shut.

▶ Let the caulk dry for the length of time specified on the package. Then raise the window, remove the plastic wrap, and enjoy your custom sealing job.

Weather-Stripping a Door

For a door, nail-on vinyl or butyl rubber tubing is far more effective than felt or foam weather stripping, but the installation process is basically the same for all types—and it's a piece of cake. Here's all there is to it:

Whether you use felt, foam, vinyl, or rubber to weather-strip your windows and doors, don't let the leftovers go to waste. They can lend a hand in scads of ways around the old homestead. Here's just a handful of examples:

Get a grip. For a more secure, comfortable hold on wooden tool handles, wrap them with self-stick foam, overlapping it about half a width as you go.

Stand up. Give your outdoor winter footgear better traction by gluing strips of flat weather stripping onto the heel, toe, and middle sections of waterproof boots or shoes.

Communicate. Fasten a horizontal strip of thick foam or felt weather stripping to a wall, and use it to tack up notes.

Ensure quieter closings. Attach $1/2$-inch squares of stripping (any kind will work) to the inside corners of cabinet or screen doors to keep them from banging shut.

Slide! Secure felt-strip runners to the bottoms of storage boxes, bins, and baskets to make them glide more easily across wooden shelves.

Rehab • Revamp • Revive

STEP 1. Thoroughly clean the doorjamb. Then measure the top and sides at the inside stop, and cut lengths of stripping to fit.

STEP 2. Starting on the hinge side, nail the strip to the jamb with the tubular side flush against the stop.*

STEP 3. Nail the strips to the top and latch sides, with the tubular side extending over the edge just far enough to touch the door when it's closed.

STEP 4. With the door closed, attach a sweep to the inside of the door so that it touches the threshold. If necessary, cut the sweep to fit, using a hacksaw on the metal part and a utility knife on the vinyl gasket.

Needless to say (I hope!), if you've chosen to use stick-on felt or foam weather stripping, you'll follow the same installation steps outlined above. But you'll be pressing, not nailing, it in place.

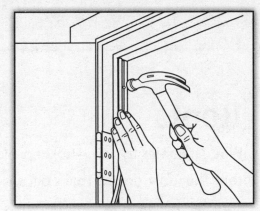

Cut lengths of stripping to fit, then nail it to the hinge side first.

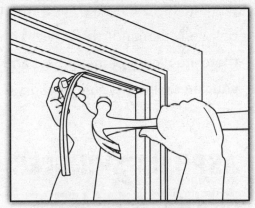

At the top and latch sides, the tubular side should just touch the door when it's closed.

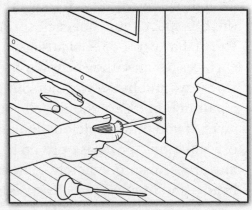

Screw a sweep to the bottom so that it touches the door's threshold.

Roofs

When it comes to home upkeep, maintaining a shipshape roof literally tops the must-do list. That's because even the tiniest ding or worn spot can let water seep under the shingles. And from there, if left untreated for even a short time, the elixir of life can do enormous damage to your home—and your bank account! Major roofing work definitely demands the services of an experienced professional. But there are plenty of minor fixes and routine maintenance chores that you can easily take care of yourself.

ASPHALT SHINGLES

Give It a Look-See

The first step in ensuring good health and a long life for your asphalt-shingled roof—or any other kind—is to keep a close eye on it. Inspect your roof each spring and fall and after every severe storm. Pay extra-special attention to south- and west-facing surfaces because they bear the brunt of damage from both the sun's rays and heavy weather. Simply surveying the scene through a pair of binoculars should tell you whether anything has gone awry. If you find suspicious-looking spots, climb up for a closer examination—or have a pro do it. Either way, it's best to deal with any problems immediately, before raindrops start falling on your head—and money starts flying out of your bank account!

Rooftop Snow May Look Pretty . . .

But when the beautiful flakes start to melt, they turn into a trickle . . . then a flowing stream that can create ice dams and lead to roof leaks faster than you can say "Frosty the Snowman." So if you live in snow country, get yourself a snow rake with the longest possible handle. Then, after every major snowfall, haul it out and rake off the accumulated white flakes. Just be ultra-careful not to hit any overhead power lines!

Unfortunately, if your home has more than a single story, your elongated rake probably won't be able to reach the top floor. But even if you're happy as a clam climbing aloft in good weather, *don't even think* of going up on your roof when it's covered with snow—call a pro to tackle the job. And be quick about it because it's a sure bet that a lot of other folks will need shoveling services, too.

I think it's safe to say that we're all grateful for the roofs over our heads. But have you ever thought about the evolution of this essential architectural feature? Here's a brief timeline:

40,000 BC. The earliest-known roofing material—the skin of woolly mammoths—is first put to use in Siberia.

5000–1800 BC. The hunter-gatherers weave the first thatched roofs throughout what is now Great Britain and Europe.

100 BC. Ancient Greeks and Romans introduce *imbrex* and *tegula*, overlapping, watertight roofing tiles generally made of fired clay, but also from marble, bronze, and gilt.

1212. In response to devastating fires, King John of England declares a law that all the thatched and reed roofs in London must be replaced by fireproof clay tiles. His edict, in large part, launched the mass production of roofing materials that ultimately resulted in the vast selection we have today.

2 Supremely Simple Shingle Repairs

If your roof has passed its second decade and most of the shingles are showing serious signs of age, it's time to bite the bullet and replace the whole thing. But on a sound and solid roof that's years from needing a replacement, these two minor wounds are quick and easy fixes:

- ▶ **Cracks and tears.** Use a caulking gun to run a thick bead of silicone roofing sealant under the crack. Press the shingle down, apply a second helping of sealant over the crack, and spread it out with a putty knife. Then, to prevent a glaring "scar," hold a piece of scrap shingle over the still-moist sealant, and scrape off some granules from the top surface. No scraps on hand? Then check in the gutter for little bits of shingle that have washed down from the roof (they'll resemble colored sprinkles). Gather some up in a small container, and scatter them evenly over the wound. No one will ever guess there'd been a ding!

- ▶ **Curled corners.** As asphalt shingles age, their corners frequently start to curl either up or down. If they're left untended, they'll eventually break off. But if you catch the curve in its early stages, you can head off trouble by simply gluing down the wayward section. Just grab your caulking gun and shoot a dab of silicone sealant under the corner. Then weigh it down in place with a brick or flat rock, and leave it there for at least 24 hours, or until the sealant has dried thoroughly. That's all there is to it!

If your house is more than one story high, your roof is steeply pitched, you're not accustomed to climbing ladders, or you're even a teensy bit nervous about heights, don't even think of getting up on your roof. And if you're reluctant to climb a ladder, don't worry about fussing with your gutters either— pick up the phone and call a roofing pro or an experienced handyman.

CALL A PRO

Tiny Holes Lead to Terrible Trouble

When you evict a former rooftop resident, like an old TV antenna or satellite dish, it's easy to overlook the small holes left behind by the mounting brackets. But those little openings can literally cause the death of your roof. That's because they let in massive amounts of moisture. They do it gradually, though, and by the time you notice obvious signs of a leak, you may have a major case of rot on your hands. On the bright side, those holes are a snap to fix— but not, as you might think, by filling them with caulk. That provides only a temporary bandage. Instead, slide a sheet of flashing under the perforated shingle, with a bead of caulk under and on top of the flashing to hold it in place.

Slide a sheet of flashing under the hole-plagued shingle.

Note: *Whenever you spot any exposed, misplaced roofing nails, pull them out and patch the holes in the same way. Otherwise, as the nails loosen up, water will seep into the openings around them.*

Wait for Goldilocks Weather

Whenever you're doing any kind of work with asphalt shingles, or asphalt roll roofing, choose a dry day when the temperature is not too cold and not too hot. To be specific, when it's below 40°F, the shingles become brittle; they're hard to cut, and they crack easily. As for the upper limit, let your comfort level be your guide, but bear in mind that when it's 85°F at ground level, the temperature on your roof could be in the mid-hundreds. Not only will that make your job miserable, but the asphalt will turn gummy, making it prone to scuffing and generally hard to work with. Also, wait until the morning dew has dried before you climb aloft. And never, ever set foot on a roof that's wet or icy.

Replacing a Damaged Shingle

While it is easy to repair minor dings, a shingle that has missing pieces or is otherwise badly damaged must be replaced ASAP. To do the job, round up a hammer, a flat pry bar, some 1 ¼-inch roofing nails, a tube of roofing cement, and (of course) a new shingle.* Then follow this simple three-step process:

STEP 1. Slide the pry bar under the shingle just above the ailing one, and gently lift it up to expose the nails at the top of its damaged counterpart. Then remove the nails, being careful not to crack any good shingles.

STEP 2. Pull out the dinged shingle, slide in a new one, and secure it with four nails, using the pry bar and hammer. (This way you'll avoid bending the intact versions to the point of cracking.) Put one end of the pry bar on top of the nail and strike the bar with the hammer.

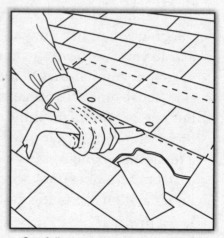

Carefully pry up the shingle above the damaged one and remove the nails.

STEP 3. Spread roofing cement under all the shingles involved and press them down firmly.

* Roofing shingles can't be purchased individually, so if you don't have any left over from an earlier job, you'll have to buy a bundle of them. That'll give you enough to cover about 33.33 square feet of roof surface—so you'll have plenty of spares for your next replacement project! To find the closest possible match, take a piece of the damaged shingle with you to the lumberyard or home-improvement store.

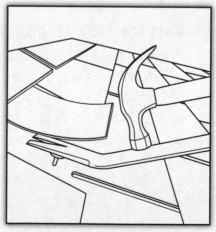

Use a hammer and pry bar to pound four nails into the new shingle.

Temporary Armor

When your roof springs a leak, either of these quick but temporary patches will provide potent protection—even during the heaviest of downpours—until you or a roofing pro can get up there and perform permanent repairs.

- **Aluminum flashing.** Cut a piece that's large enough to cover the damaged area and part of the shingle course above it. Use a pry bar to remove any roofing nails that are in the way, or cut them off with a hacksaw or shingle ripper (see "Replacing a Wood Shingle" on page 201). Apply asphalt roofing cement to the part of the patch that will lie under the undamaged shingles, and slide the "bandage" in place.

- **Heavy plastic sheeting** (the thicker the better). Run a thick, continuous bead of asphalt roofing cement around the damaged area, then press the sheeting into place. If you don't have any roofing cement and there's no time to get some, secure the sheeting by nailing wooden strips around the edges—but use this ploy only if you have to because (of course) you'll be putting more holes in your roof that you'll need to fill later. As a last resort, if you don't have roofing cement *or* nails, use bricks, cement blocks, or sandbags to hold down the sheeting.

AN OUNCE OF

PREVENTION

Make Your Asphalt Roof Veggie-Proof

Copper flashing can work its anti-moss magic on asphalt shingles just as well as it does on the wooden versions (see "Institute a No-Growth Policy" on page 199). But if you're getting ready to install a brand-new asphalt roof, you're in luck. There's an even easier way to fend off moss, lichen, algae, and other vexatious vegetation: When you're shopping for your roofing supplies, go with shingles that contain copper granules. Then you can rest easy, knowing that moss and its water-holding cousins will never get a toehold above your head!

WHEN A TREE LIMB HITS YOUR ROOF

When a raging storm tosses a tree limb onto your roof, don't go charging up there automatically to scope out the damage. Instead, follow this more rational response plan:

• Examine the underside of the roof from your attic or crawl space. If the rafters or plywood sheathing is damaged, call a roofing professional—and your insurance agent. Don't even think of venturing onto the roof yourself.

• If water is leaking in, lay boards across the ceiling joists. Then cover the wood with plastic sheeting, and set buckets, tubs, or pots under the leaks.

• As long as the rafters and sheathing are in good shape, wait until the roof is dry, and climb on up. But before you do, clear away anything on the ground that could be damaged when you send pieces of the limb tumbling down.

• Staying up-roof from the limb (so you're out of harm's way if it shifts or rolls), clip off small branches with long-handled pruning shears. Then use a bow saw to cut the main limb into chunks that you can roll off the roof easily. Don't put more pressure on the saw than you absolutely need to. Remember, it's the back-and-forth movement of the blade's teeth that does the work—if you press too hard on the limb, it could cause more damage than it may have already. And whatever you do, never use a chain saw on a roof, ladder, or anyplace else where footing is the least bit uncertain!

• Once the roof is clear of debris, check the shingles for damage. If you find any, apply a temporary patch to keep water out until you or a roofer can perform a permanent fix (see "Temporary Armor" on page 197).

Note: *If you're not used to climbing ladders or being on a roof, call a professional to get rid of your uninvited "guest" and repair any damage. Likewise, get expert help if the pitch of your roof is any steeper than 4:12.*

WOOD SHINGLES & SHAKES

This Roof Is Not a Restaurant!

There's nothing that wood-eating fungi love better than a roof full of wet shingles or shakes. You can't possibly keep your roof from getting wet, but you can—and must—keep it clean so that the surface can dry out before fungi can move in. That generally means climbing up there and sweeping off leaves, branches, and anything else that can hold moisture. How often you need to perform this life-extending task depends on the weather and the proximity of tall trees. (For more on that score, see "Don't Let Trees Trash Your Wood Siding" on page 142.)

Institute a No-Growth Policy

To lay out a serious unwelcome mat for moss, install copper flashing along the ridge of your roof. When rainwater runs off the metal, it will carry along traces of copper sulfate, a potent natural herbicide that will prevent moss from growing. You can buy rolls of 6- to 7-inch-wide copper sheeting at roofing-supply and home-improvement stores. One band will protect 14 to 18 feet of roof below it. Once you've cleaned off any existing vegetation, follow this simple installation routine:

▶ Use tin snips to cut the copper sheeting into lengths that you can work with comfortably (generally 10 feet max).

▶ Slide a strip under a row of shingles until the metal hits the nails holding the shingles in place. About 2 inches of copper will be exposed.

While straight-line flashing is easy for almost anyone to install (see "Institute a No-Growth Policy," above), putting the stuff in place around chimneys is a complex process that's best left to a pro. As for skylight flashing, don't even think about trying any DIY tricks, especially with a recently installed unit. If you do, you could actually void your warranty.

CALL A PRO

FAST-AGING FORMULA

Help new shingles blend in on an old roof with this timely treatment.

1 lb. of baking soda
½ gal. of water

Mix the soda and water in a bucket. Dip your shingles into the drink, and set them aside. In a few hours, they'll "weather" to an experienced shade of gray. To ensure a long life, coat them with wood preservative before installing them on your roof.

▶ Every 4 feet or so, lift up a shingle and drive a copper nail through the strip. Position the nail so that it will be covered when you lower the shingle.

▶ Continue the process until the stripping spans the length of the roof. If your roofline extends downward 18 feet from that point, add another line of stripping.

Add Years to Its Life

The key to giving your wood roof a long, happy life is to treat it with (surprise!) a wood preservative. Start by cleaning the roof thoroughly (see "Murder That Moss!" on page 202). Then apply a top-quality commercial wood preservative according to the directions on the label. Repeat the routine every five years.

Simple Stopgap Strategies

A couple of common wood-shingle woes can pave the way for trouble on the double. But if you leap into action, you can shore up the fort until there's time to make permanent repairs.

• **Cracks.** Cut a piece of aluminum sheeting and slide it as far as it'll go under the cracked shingle. If necessary, use a wood block and a hammer to drive the "bandage" into place.

• **Curls.** If a shingle curls up, simply nail it down. This trick will resolve the problem for anywhere from a few months to a year or so. The more moisture your roof is exposed to, the sooner you'll have to replace the shingle. But that, too, is light-years removed from rocket science (see "Replacing a Wood Shingle," at right).

Replacing a Wood Shingle

Wood shingles are just as easy to replace as asphalt shingles. Here's the process:

Split the old shingle along the wood grain and remove the pieces.

STEP 1. Wearing gloves and using a hammer and a wood chisel, carefully split the damaged shingle along the wood grain and remove it piece by piece. Then reach underneath the overhanging shingle with a shingle ripper (one of the most useful roofing tools you'll ever find) and cut off the nails that were securing the shingle.*

STEP 2. Measure and cut a replacement shingle that's ½ inch narrower than the opening so that the wood has room to expand.

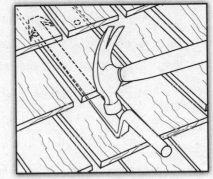

Use a specially designed shingle ripper to cut off the nails.

STEP 3. Set the new shingle into its spot with the slightly curved side up, leaving ¼ inch of space on either side. Then tap it into place, using a wood block to prevent damage. Stop when the bottom edge is about ¾ inch below its neighbors.

STEP 4. Just below the bottom of the old shingle, drive two roofing nails into the new one at about a 45-degree angle. Again using a wood block for protection, tap the replacement upward the final ¾ inch to align with the other shingles in the row. Then cover the exposed nail heads with a little roofing cement.

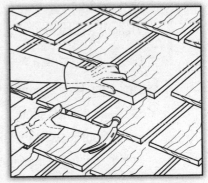

Tap the new shingle into place until it's about ¾ inch below its neighbors.

* *In a pinch, you can use a hacksaw blade to cut the nails off. Wrap electrical tape around one end of the blade to serve as a handle.*

Murder That Moss!

Moss can be deadly for both asphalt and wood shingles. That's because its thick growth, combined with a shallow but invasive root system, keeps its home "ground" damp for extended periods of time. The moisture not only promotes rot in wood shingles, but also erodes asphalt and, in extreme cases, rots the support structure. Fortunately, it's easy to deep-six this sinister stuff, as well as mold, mildew, algae, and lichen. Here's the drill:

- Use a stiff push broom to brush away the moss and tear up its shallow root system. Always brush *down* the roof—never up. Any upward movement could break the bond between shingle layers. And don't step on any wet moss, or you could slide right off the roof faster than a New York minute!

- Mix a solution of 6 ounces of powdered oxygen bleach (such as Stain Solver, available online) per gallon of water. (If you're dealing with algae or other tough stains, up the concentration to 8 ounces of bleach per gallon of H_2O.)

- Using a pump sprayer, apply the potion generously to a cool roof, and keep the surface wet for 30 to 45 minutes, applying more solution as necessary. Be sure that you do this job on an overcast day; in bright sunshine, the cleaner will evaporate before it can work.

- Scrub lightly with a push broom or brush, and rinse well with clear water.

- Once the moss is gone, take a close look at the tops of the vertical slots between asphalt shingles. If the colored ceramic granules are still in place, thank your lucky stars. But if those speckles are gone and you can see the shingle's interior mat, it means that your roof is on death's doorstep.

Note: *Never use chlorine bleach on a roof. It'll remove the natural color from wood shingles (or any other wooden structure). Plus, it will accelerate corrosion of metal gutters and downspouts, and if the stuff runs off the roof, it can kill any plants it reaches on the ground below.*

FLAT ROOFS

Easy Keepers Demand Eternal Vigilance

A flat or gently pitched roof has less surface area to care for than one with a steeper slope. It's also a lot easier and safer to work on. But it holds on to rain and melted snow much longer than its more sharply angled cousins do. And that means you have to be constantly on guard to keep your roof watertight. So every few months, carefully inspect a metal roof for rust or pitting. On asphalt or rubber surfaces, look for holes, tears, blisters, or loose seams. Also check the flashing and, if necessary, secure the edges with roofing cement to make sure that water can't seep in. And, for heaven's sake, whenever it snows, climb up there and shovel off the flakes before they melt!

Brush on Protection

If your roof is covered with asphalt-roll roofing, you can fend off a lot of trouble with a couple of easy-to-apply coatings:

- **Asphalt aluminum paint.** This reflective covering guards against damage from the sun's UV rays. Plus, it lubricates the asphalt to prevent cracking, and provides a waterproof seal.

- **Asphalt roof coating.** If your home's topper sports a crazy-quilt collection of patches, or it needs more than spot repairs, this stuff has your name written all over it. It'll make the roof look like new.

You can buy both products at any store that sells roofing supplies. Whichever one you use, if your roof has any slope at all, start at the highest point and work your way down—carefully!

Listen to the Blister!

Sometimes when flat roofs blister, the bubbles are harmless; other times they're disasters waiting to happen. To find out for sure, press gently on the blister. If you hear no sound, that means all is well. But if the bump goes "Squish!" there's moisture inside, and you need to lance and patch it—now (see "Healing Blisters" on page 204).

Healing Blisters

Delivering blister relief is one of the easiest DIY roof-repair jobs of all. Here's the simple three-step process:

STEP 1. Slit the blister down the middle, and let it dry. Then fill the cavity with roofing cement, and smooth the roofing material flat.

STEP 2. Pound in a row of roofing nails on each side of the slit. Cover it and the nail heads with more roofing cement.

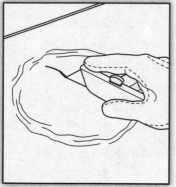

Slit the blister and fill the dried-out opening with roofing cement.

Drive roofing nails on sides of the slit, and apply more roofing cement.

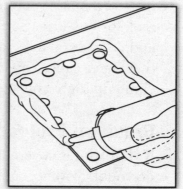

Nail the patch in place, and seal it with roofing cement.

STEP 3. Cut a patch of roll roofing that's 2 inches larger than the slit on all sides. Then nail it on, and seal the edges and the nail heads with roofing cement.

Alleviate Aluminum Leaks

When your aluminum roof springs a leak, buy a roll of fiberglass mesh. Then leap into fix-it action this way:

• Cut two pieces of mesh, each 2 inches larger than the damaged area.

• Thoroughly clean the spot with a wire brush, and wipe away debris. Using a flexible putty knife, coat the surface with roofing cement.

• Press one mesh piece over the cement, then give it another coat.

• Lay the second mesh piece on top of it, and cover it with a final layer of cement.

GUTTERS & DOWNSPOUTS

Toss the Scoop

To keep gutters in good working order, you need to clean them twice a year—in late spring and again in autumn after all the leaves have fallen. That used to mean getting up on a ladder and scooping out the dead leaves and heaven knows what else. But now, thanks to good old Yankee ingenuity, there are scads of tools with telescoping handles that let you get your gutters spanking clean with your feet planted firmly on the ground—even if your roofline is two stories up. And you don't have to get your hands anywhere near the disgusting crud. For example, there are ultra-long attachments that fit onto your wet-dry vacuum cleaner (a.k.a. Shop-Vac®), rotary brushes that fasten onto a cordless drill, washing wands that extend the reach of your garden hose, and giant-size tongs that work like long-distance salad servers. Just do an Internet search for "best gutter-cleaning tools," and you'll find these winners—and a whole lot more.

Down and Out

Downspouts blocked? Don't worry—it happens to the best of us at one time or another. You may be able to clear them out from below with a good blast from your garden hose. Just push the hose up the downspout and turn the water on full force. The pressure should work the blockage loose. Of course, if it does, you may get a little wet, so wear your rain hat! If the garden hose doesn't do the trick, use a plumber's snake.

Look for Leaks

In addition to cleaning your gutters a couple of times a year, it's important to inspect them frequently. The next time you hear the pitter-patter of tiny raindrops, put on your raincoat, go outside, and look up at your gutters. See any water overflowing? Notice any leaks? If you do, make note of where they are. Then wait for a dry day, get out the old ladder, climb up, and take a look.

We all know that gutters can save your home's siding from expensive damage. Well, guess what? This handy home helper can also solve one of your most frustrating clutter conundrums—that is, if you've got a jumbled nest of power cords and cables under your desk. Just screw a length of gutter to the wall or to the inside back legs of your desk. Either way, position it so that the furniture will still fit flush against the wall, while leaving a couple inches of space between the underside of the desktop and the top edges of the gutter. Then gather up those wires and their various connectors and tuck 'em into the trough.

The Pre-Fix Fix

Once you find out where the leak is, but before you start your repair job, you need to prepare the area. Clear any debris from around the leak, and then sand it down and rub the spot with a little paint thinner to clean it thoroughly. Now you're ready to roll.

Stop Leaky Joints

The most common type of gutter leak occurs at a joint, where two pieces meet. And it couldn't be simpler to fix. All you need is a tube of silicone sealant, which you can buy at any hardware store. Just coat the area where the two pieces of gutter meet with the silicone, making sure to apply it to both the inside and the outside of the gutter. Keep in mind that some silicone sealants need to dry for up to two days, so do the job during a stretch of nice dry weather.

Small Potatoes

Patching a small gutter hole (½ inch or less across) couldn't be easier. Simply pick up some roofing cement at your local hardware or home-improvement store. Stuff the cement into the hole, and spread it onto the surrounding area with a putty knife or, in a pinch, a tongue depressor or wooden craft stick. Just make sure your patch extends beyond the hole by at least an inch on all sides.

Bigger Guns

If the hole in your gutter is bigger than ½ inch, the picture gets just a little more complicated. You're still going to cover the whole area with roofing cement, but you'll also need to use a thin piece of rustproof metal to cover the hole. Wait for a dry day to perform your task, and then follow this can't-fail routine:

STEP 1. Gather the following gear: tin snips or heavy-duty scissors, sandpaper, roofing cement, and an empty beer or soda pop can.

STEP 2. Remove the top and bottom of the can and flatten it so that you have a sheet of sturdy aluminum.

STEP 3. Clear the debris from the gutter. Fit the aluminum to the hole from the inside of the gutter (so that it will be invisible from the ground). Trim the can, using the snips or scissors, to get a good fit. Remove the aluminum.

STEP 4. Sand the area around the hole and brush away any dirt. Cover the hole from inside the gutter with roofing cement, and embed the aluminum patch in the cement.

STEP 5. Apply another coat of cement over the patch, and there you have it—a gutter that's as good as new!

Rain, Rain— Don't Go Away!

If you live in an area that's subject to drought and occasional water-usage restrictions (and who doesn't these days?), here's a way to get the most out of your gutters and downspouts: Make sure they drain into good old-fashioned rain barrels. Any watertight container will do, but if you use smaller containers, such as buckets or gallon milk jugs, empty them into a larger barrel frequently. Then, the next time a prolonged dry spell hits, you can draw from your H_2O savings account. It's highly unlikely that you'll have enough liquid assets to irrigate your whole landscape, but you should at least be able to nurse a few treasured plants through the troubled times.

Stem the Sag

When you're cleaning your metal gutters and notice water collecting in one spot, it means that it's sagging—and you need to fix it ASAP. At best, your gutter will become a mosquito maternity ward. At worst, a sagging gutter that's left untended can cause serious damage to your fascia, rafters, roof shingles, siding, and even your foundation. Your plan of action depends on whether your gutters are held up by spikes, in which case you'll see the heads near the top edge, or brackets (a.k.a. hangers or clips), which are invisible from the ground.

▶ **Spikes.** In this system, a long spike is driven through the upper edge of the gutter, through a metal tube called a ferrule, and then through the back of the gutter and the fascia board behind it, and finally into the end of a solid rafter. Over time, spikes generally work themselves out of their pilot holes, thanks to temperature fluctuations that make the gutter expand and contract. The simple solution: Replace the old spike with a new threaded version. For

Replace a loose gutter spike with a new threaded version.

added security, dip wood slivers into epoxy and insert them in the hole before you screw in the new spike. **Note:** *As long as you're replacing one spike, go ahead and upgrade your whole gutter system to screws—because when one of those giant nails comes loose, the rest won't be far behind.*

▶ **Brackets.** Before you try more complex maneuvers, gently bend the bracket upward slightly with a pair of pliers. Then pour a bucket of water into the gutter. If the fluid collects in a puddle, disconnect and remove the affected gutter section, and then unscrew the damaged bracket. Fill the original holes with exterior caulk. Then drill new pilot holes at the same height and as close as possible to the old ones (so you don't risk altering the pitch of the gutter run), and screw on the new bracket. Then, with a helper holding one end of the gutter section, lift it back in place.

Put a Cap On It

Wouldn't it be nice if you never had to clean out your gutters again? Well, that wish can come true if you cover them with metal gutter caps. Leaves and other debris wash over the slick metal surface, while water is drawn into the gutter through a slot just under the downslope edge of the cap. Besides saving you endless hours of cleaning time, these dandy devices increase the strength of your gutters, making them less likely to sag, thereby prolonging their useful lives. There's just one hitch: Top-quality caps cost more than the gutters themselves. So if money is a factor, consider the more budget-friendly alternative in "Why Not to Get Wired" (below). And for good measure, prune back or remove any trees that are close enough and tall enough to drop their leaves on your roof (see "Don't Let Trees Trash Your Wood Siding" on page 142).

If you have problems with birds nesting in your gutters, try this time-tested trick: After you've cleared away an old nest, replace it with a small mirror. The next bird who wants to build a home in that spot will think it's already occupied and find her construction site elsewhere. You couldn't ask for a more effective "No Vacancy" sign!

Why Not to Get Wired

Common assumption: Fitting your gutters with wire-mesh screens is a dandy way to keep leaves out of those channels while letting water drain through the holes in the mesh—at a small fraction of the price you'd pay for gutter caps.

The whole truth: Yes, that does sound like a thrifty, labor-saving idea, but in fact, leaves often cling so thickly to the mesh that water flows right over the surface and onto your siding. Plus, that screening becomes a nuisance when you need to clean the gutters. A better idea: Put a bulb-shaped leaf strainer over each downspout (they're available in home-improvement and large hardware stores). Just be sure to check them every couple of months—and following each major storm—and remove any debris that may have collected in the openings.

Protect Your Attic *and* Save Your Roof!

Get insulated. Besides raising your indoor comfort level, insulating your attic can also help prevent one of the leading causes of roof leaks—ice dams created by melting snow. Adding this protective blanket is a snap! Here's the drill:

- Determine the total square footage you need to cover. Also measure the distance between your attic joists, and buy batts of that width insulation at a lumberyard or home-improvement store.

- Lay a plywood sheet over the joists to serve as a walkway. Using a utility knife, cut the batts into workable lengths by pressing the material into the opening between your walkway and a straight edge.

- Insert the insulation into the space between joists, with the vapor barrier facing down. Make sure it lies flat against the ceiling, but don't compress the insulation or you'll reduce its effectiveness.

Note: *If you have allergies, use nonallergenic cellulose fiber or Miraflex® encapsulated insulation rather than fiberglass. But regardless of the material, always wear a dust mask when you handle the stuff.*

Get vented. Step two in prolonging the life of your roof is to bring fresh air in through vents under the eaves and send it out through other vents near the peak of the roof. Ideally, you should have one square foot of overall vent space for every 150 square feet of insulated attic area. Half of those escape hatches should be in the soffit at the bottom of the roof and half in the ridge or gables near the top. A pro should perform the up-top work, but installing soffit vents is a simple procedure:

- Hold the vent against the soffit and trace around it. Then use a ruler to draw a rectangle that's 1 inch in from all four sides.

- Drill a hole at each of the four corners.

- Cut along the lines of your rectangle using a saber saw.

- Set the vent into the opening and secure it with stainless steel screws.

Outdoor Structures & Systems

Unlike roofs and walls, the other features that adorn the outsides of our homes, like decks, porches, and even driveways, are not life-sustaining necessities. But they sure make things more pleasant—that is, until something goes awry (most often courtesy of Mother Nature). If that happens, then our exterior enhancements can become great big money pits. As always, there will be occasions when you'll need to fork out cash for expert help. But with these tips, tricks, and terrific tonics at your beck and call, those times should be few and far between.

DECKS & PORCHES

A Sweeping Success

Leaves, branches, and other windblown yard debris can spell disaster for a deck because it keeps the wood moist—and moisture is an open invitation to decay. So sweep your deck frequently with a stiff broom, and make sure you get out all the pesky stuff that settles in the openings between the boards. If you have to, get down on your knees and use a putty knife to poke the crud out so it falls to the ground below.

Of course, how often you need to perform this chore depends on the weather and the proximity of generous vegetation around the deck (see "Don't Let Trees Trash Your Wood Siding" on page 142).

Note: *Although a porch is more sheltered than a deck, it's just as important to keep it free of moisture-holding menaces.*

DANDY DECK CLEANER

There are plenty of commercial deck cleaners on the market, but this works as well as any that I've tried. It's perfect for porches and wood fences, too.

1 cup of powdered oxygen bleach*
½ cup of dishwashing liquid
(preferably one with grease-cutting ingredients, like Dawn®)
2 gal. of hot water

Mix the ingredients together in a bucket, and scrub the deck with a stiff broom or brush. Then hose it down thoroughly. Discard any leftover formula—once oxygen bleach is mixed with water, it loses its effectiveness after about six hours.

* Do not combine oxygen bleach with ammonia, vinegar, or any other chemical. Also, never, ever mix it with chlorine bleach or any cleanser that contains chlorine—the combo will create deadly chlorine gas!

Give It a Bath

Once or twice a year, give your deck (or porch) a good scrubbing with a stiff broom and my Dandy Deck Cleaner (at left). Do it on an overcast day, when the wood is cool to the touch, so the formula won't dry out too fast. Move all of your container plants and furniture out of the way, and cover up anything that's planted nearby. Then let 'er rip. If you plan to paint, stain, or seal the surface afterward, let the wood dry for several days.

Note: *Unless you're preparing to apply a restoration coating (see "A Fountain of Youth for an Aging Deck" on page 215), do not power wash a deck or porch. The water's forceful blast can cause the wood to splinter.*

Intensive Care

If you've got an unsealed deck that's sporting algae stains or other stubborn marks, follow this more potent plan. And be sure to do the job on an overcast day when the deck surface is cool:

- Mix 1 cup of powdered oxygen bleach per gallon of warm water in a bucket, stirring until the bleach is completely dissolved.

- Pour the solution into a hand-operated pump sprayer, and saturate the deck surface. Let it soak in for about 20 minutes, reapplying the solution as necessary so the wood stays wet.

- When the time's up, scrub the deck with a stiff push broom, and then rinse thoroughly with a garden hose.

Note: *Do not use this or any other bleach-containing formula on a freshly sealed deck. Instead, clean it as needed with a simple solution of dishwashing liquid and water until the sealer gives out.*

The Finishing Touch

Even if your deck is made of pressure-treated wood, or a rot-resistant type like cedar or redwood, you still need to coat it with a water-repellent sealer or stain every couple of years. (Here's the difference: Sealers are transparent, while stains have colored pigments added to them.) If you're not sure when it's time, here's a clue: If rainwater or a spray from your garden hose beads up on the deck's surface, you're good to go for another season. If the water soaks right in, sealing time is here. There's a mind-boggling array of sealers and stains on the market, so follow these basic shopping guidelines to ensure that you get the biggest, longest-lasting bang for your buck.

▶ **Don't pinch pennies.** It's the same old story: A top-of-the-line product will keep your deck shipshape and looking beautiful for a lot longer than any bargain-basement brand. And that'll translate into massive savings in time, work, and money down the road.

▶ **Choose water-based.** Not only do oil-based stains and sealers make cleanup a mess but—much worse—they're made from natural resins, which algae and mold love to eat. To close the "restaurant," manufacturers lace their formulations with algicides and mildewcides. But over time, these toxic chemicals rise to the surface of the wood and wash away. Not only is that bad for nearby vegetation (and your family's and pets' bare feet), but it leaves your deck defenseless against its archenemies. On the other hand, water-based products are a snap to clean up, and they're made from synthetic resins, which algae and mold won't touch.

▶ **Think semi-transparent.** For the most part, both clear sealers and solid-color stains are especially vulnerable to damage from the sun's UV rays. For that reason, they tend to have shorter life spans and higher maintenance needs than their semi-transparent counterparts. These stains allow some of the wood grain to show through, making them a good choice for wood you want to show off. But if you have your heart set on a clear finish, look for an epoxy-fortified sealer sold under the brand name DEFY®. It contains two cutting-edge chemicals that guard against UV damage.

Note: *New, improved wood stains and sealers are constantly flying out of the laboratories and into the stores. That's why it pays to shop at a local establishment where the expert pros keep on top of the latest developments—and know what will work best in your climate.*

AN OUNCE OF
PREVENTION

Decor to Live For

Believe it or not, the way you handle a couple of purely decorative enhancements can greatly lengthen—or shorten—the life of your deck or wooden porch. Here's the scoop:

Keep it bare. A lot of folks think that rugs or colorful floor cloths make a deck or porch look cozy and homey. Well, that may be, but the material also traps moisture beneath it—and that spells a premature death for any wooden surface. So confine all floor coverings to the great indoors and let your outdoor living spaces breathe freely.

Site plants with care. On a porch, always suspend any hanging plants from the outer—not the inner—edge of the eaves. If you attach planter boxes to your deck rails, hang them so that they're out beyond the deck surface. In either case, you'll ensure that when water drips from the pot, it'll land on the ground, not on your floorboards. It's also important to keep waterproof saucers under any containers that rest on the surface of a deck or porch—and make sure they don't overflow when you water or during periods of heavy rain.

2 Secrets to Better Step Painting

Getting ready to paint the stairs to your deck or porch? If so, the following tips will make the job more pleasant and the finished surfaces safer:

- When you're applying the paint (or stain), coat every second step. When those have dried completely, go back and paint the ones in between. That way, you'll be able to climb those stairs simply by taking two steps at a time, skipping over the wet ones.

- To improve traction, mix ½ cup of clean sand into each gallon of paint or stain. The textured surface—on wood or concrete—will provide better footing when the steps are wet or icy.

A Fountain of Youth for an Aging Deck

What do you do when Father Time and Mother Nature conspire to turn your deck into a cracked, splintery mess? Well, you could have a new one built out of low-maintenance composite lumber. Or—for a tiny fraction of the cost and just a few days of elbow grease—you can roll on a deck-restoration coating that'll make your old warhorse look like a prancing colt again. Best of all, the coating can last up to 13 years without any additional touch-ups. You can find deck-restoration coatings at just about any place that sells paint or building supplies. As for the application procedure, see "How to Restore a Time-Worn Deck" (below).

Be sure to shop for your deck's savior at a local store where you can trust the clerks to give you expert, unbiased advice. That's because the thickness you need depends on the condition of your deck, and the thicker the product is, the less coverage you'll get per gallon. Also, choose your color carefully, bearing in mind that the darker it is, the more heat the surface will absorb and retain.

How to Restore a Time-Worn Deck

Thanks to superpowered restoration coatings, you can revive your deck's youthful good looks—and greatly lessen your maintenance load—in three days. Plan on one day for the prep work and two more days a week later to apply the coating. You'll need a power washer, a jug of deck cleaner, masking materials, several special rollers (one for every 4 gallons or so of coating), and a roller extension handle. The application details vary slightly depending on the brand, but here's the basic procedure:

STEP 1. Break off any large splinters. Then either sink any protruding nail heads or pull them out and replace them with deck screws.

STEP 2. If the surface was previously treated with a stain or sealer, use 80-grit sandpaper to de-gloss and rough up any areas that have been protected from the elements by either furniture or planters.

STEP 3. Scrub the deck according to the directions on the cleaning product label, paying special attention to any greasy areas. Then power wash the whole surface, including the gaps between boards, and let the wood dry for seven days.

STEP 4. Wrap the base of each deck post with masking tape, and cover the rails and the bottom 4 feet of your house siding with plastic sheeting. Also spread plastic sheeting or sturdy drop cloths under the deck to snag any coating that seeps between the boards.

STEP 5. Fill all holes and cracks with either latex caulk or the coating itself, and let it sit for the time specified on the product label (or until the filler is stiff). Then apply the coating to a few boards at a time, starting at one end and proceeding down the length of the deck.

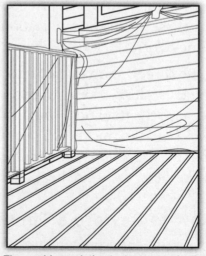

Thoroughly mask the deck posts and rails and the bottom 4 feet of house siding.

STEP 6. Start by dipping the roller into the bucket, then set it on the deck surface and press down to produce a puddle of coating. Roll forward for a few feet. Then lift the roller, reload it, and repeat the process with the next section. Never work the roller back and forth, as you would with paint, or you'll wind up with a covering that's too thin and loaded with air bubbles. As you go along, clean out the spaces between boards using a putty knife or stir stick.

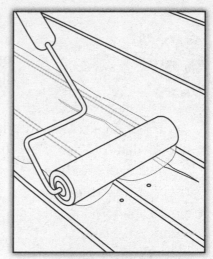

Roll forward only, reloading the roller every few feet.

STEP 7. If you prefer a smooth finish, go over the still-wet coating with a brush, starting at one end of each board and going to the end. Don't lift the brush, or you'll leave unsightly ridges!

STEP 8. Clean up your tools with soap and water, and let the coating dry for three to six hours. When the surface is dry to the touch, repeat the procedure described above. Then let the deck cure for at least 48 hours before you walk on it or put furniture back into place. Don't worry if the first coat looks less than stellar—it'll take the second go-round to deliver the look that you saw in the store sample.

PATIOS & WALKWAYS

Keep It Clean

While accumulated leaves, seedpods, and other debris won't actually destroy a patio as they can a wooden deck, that load of crud can cause a passel of other problems. For one thing, it gives insects a dandy place to hunker down and multiply. It can also leave unsightly stains on concrete, flagstones, or brick pavers. So make it a habit to sweep your patio regularly and periodically give it a good cleaning with a solution of laundry detergent and hot water (see "2 Dandy Down-Home Ways to Clean Your Patio" on page 219).

Before you sweep a patio or any other masonry floor—indoors or out—scatter slightly damp coffee grounds on the surface. They'll clamp onto the dirt so your broom can gather it up without sending dust flying all over the place.

Patio Power-Washing Pointers

A strong shower of pure H_2O from a power (a.k.a. pressure) washer can make an aging flagstone, brick, or concrete patio look like new again. But unless you're careful, that ultra-potent blast can cause more harm than good. To avoid damaging the surface material—or hurting yourself —follow these guidelines:

▶ If you've never used a pressure washer before, have the folks at the rental shop walk you through the process and show you how to handle the unit safely.

▶ Never use a pressure washer that's rated higher than 3,000 psi.

▶ Use a 15- or 25-degree fan-type nozzle—not one that delivers a pinpoint, laser-like spray.

▶ Hold the nozzle 6 to 10 inches away from the surface; if the jet is too close, it can etch lines into the material.

▶ Test the washer on a small area so that you can get used to handling the high-pressure action.

▶ Clean one section thoroughly before moving on to the next one. If you follow a random, overall pattern or try to rush the process, you're likely to see uneven streaks once the surface has dried. Working in a steady, even manner, it should take you about three to five minutes to clean 3 to 4 square feet.

Note: *In most cases, water alone will get your patio (or any other masonry surface) clean. But if you're faced with grease or oil stains, see "Oil's Well That Vanishes Well" on page 231. Don't let anyone talk you into using harsh chemicals in your power washer—and don't even think of using muriatic acid, or you could wind up with a heap of trouble on your hands.*

Seal It and Save It

The sealing of concrete pavers, bricks, or flagstones has what a friend of mine calls a "high glory factor." In other words, the job produces aesthetic and practical results that far outweigh the amount of time and effort involved. To be specific, applying a water-based sealer enhances and protects the natural color of the material; prevents sand erosion; reduces the growth of weeds, mold, and mildew; deters ants and other insects from colonizing the seams; and increases the longevity of the surface. Here's the simple application process:

STEP 1. Power wash the patio thoroughly (see "Patio Power-Washing Pointers," at left), being sure to remove all stains and eradicate any moss or mildew. For that routine, see "Murder That Moss!" on page 202. Then don't do anything for several days so the surface, and the ground underneath, can dry out thoroughly.

STEP 2. Fill the joints with sand. Simply open the bag and spread the sand around on the patio surface. Use a stiff push broom to sweep it into the cracks until the openings are completely filled. Then sweep away any excess.

2 Dandy Down-Home Ways to Clean Your Patio

Or maybe your driveway, pool decking, walkway, or concrete steps. You can buy all kinds of fancy fixes for sprucing up masonry surfaces, but two of the best are right in your kitchen or laundry room. Which one you want to use depends on how dirty the surface is. Here are your choices:

For routine cleaning, mix 1 tablespoon of laundry detergent per gallon of hot water (as hot as you can get it). Hose off the patio and use a stiff push broom to scrub it with the soapy water. Finish up with another good hosing to rinse the suds away.

If the surface is extra-grubby, make a half-and-half solution of whole milk and regular cola (not diet). Pour the mixture on the dirty surface, and scrub with a stiff brush. Rinse with the garden hose.

STEP 3. Use a nylon brush dipped in the sealer to cover all the patio edges. Then spray on the first coat, using a garden-type pump sprayer with a metal fan-style nozzle. When the sealer is dry enough to walk on, spray on the second coat,* using the brush to smooth out any puddles. Throughout the process, keep a light hand on the spray "trigger" because an overdose of sealer can ruin the whole project.

That's all there is to it! Just be sure to wait for the amount of time recommended on the product label before putting any furniture or plants back into place.

* Some brands need only one coat; follow the manufacturer's guidelines.

Hoist That Paver!

Lifting a single paver from its base can be tricky—unless you have a wire coat hanger on hand. To make yourself a set of puller-uppers, simply cut the wire into two pieces, and bend each of them into an L shape, so there's a short, flat piece at one end. To use your hoisting devices, slide one down on each side of the paver, turn them so the flat part is under the target, and lift up. After the first one is free and clear, if you have more to remove, you can easily lift them out by hand.

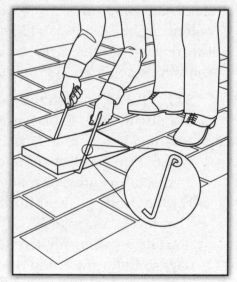

Turn a wire coat hanger into a pair of paver lifters.

Do a Flip-Flop

When patio pavers become pitted from water runoff or from overly enthusiastic pressure washing—or they develop stains that you simply can't get off—don't rush out and buy replacements. Instead, simply flip the defaced blocks over, leveling them with sand if necessary. The fresh side will last just as long as its neighbors.

Drop, Don't Slide!

Whenever you're laying bricks, pavers, or flagstones, drop them directly (but gently!) onto their intended resting places. Sliding them even a short distance across the sand or gravel will wreak havoc with your carefully leveled surface—and you'll have to even out the mini mountains and valleys all over again!

Got Chips Off the Old Blocks?

If so—and the breakage hasn't been caused by dropped objects or other physical trauma—the problem is probably due to poor drainage. Whether pavers are made of concrete, slate, brick, flagstone, or tile, accumulated dampness often causes them to chip and crack. The simple DIY solution is to buy replacements for the damaged pavers and follow this remedial action plan:

- Lift out the still-intact pavers and lean them against a fence or wall in a sunny spot to dry out thoroughly.

- Dig up the patio area to 3 to 4 inches below the depth of the pavers (see the note below).

- Lay down a sheet of water-permeable polypropylene landscape fabric to keep weeds from springing up between the pavers.

- Fill the area with crushed stone, gravel, or coarse sand. Then level it out and tamp it in place, using a carpenter's level to make sure the surface is even.

- Set your pavers in place, fill the joints with sand, and apply a high-quality sealer (see "Seal It and Save It" on page 219).

Note: *Sticking to this depth range is important. If the bedding layer is too thin, the stone or sand can wash or be kicked away and expose the unsightly landscape fabric. On the other hand, if it's too thick, the material will accumulate enough dirt that it will actually encourage weeds to sprout.*

DARN GOOD DEPOSIT REMOVER

When lime and hard water leave unsightly deposits on your flagstone patio—or your concrete driveway, water spigots, planters, or any other hard outdoor surface—get rid of them with this foolproof formula:

½ cup of borax
1 cup of warm water
½ cup of white vinegar

Dissolve the borax in the water, and stir in the vinegar. Sponge the mixture onto the spots, let it sit for 10 minutes or so (longer for really stubborn stains), and wipe the ugly marks away. How's that for a quick and easy fix?

Shop with Care

It's a given that when you're planning a new driveway, walkway, or patio, you want to use materials suited to your visual taste and the architectural style of your house. But if you want that surface to retain its good looks for the long (or even short) haul, you need to keep these two shopping tips in mind:

▶ **Mind your X's.** Regardless of the material you choose, if you live in cold-winter territory, look for pavers that are designated SX, which means they can withstand freezing temperatures. Those labeled MX are intended for milder climates, and the NX versions are for indoor use only.

▶ **Be picky about bricks.** No matter how mild your climate is, don't cover any horizontal surface with building (a.k.a. common) bricks. Even the kind labeled for severe-weather use is not sturdy enough to hold up under constant foot—much less vehicular—traffic.

Foil a Failed Flagstone

A walk or patio made from irregular flagstone looks great, all right. But when you need to replace a stone, finding (or cutting) a new one of just the right size and shape can be mighty tricky. Fortunately, the solution to your dilemma is as close as your kitchen. First, remove the damaged stone (see "Special Handling Required," at right). Then cut off a sheet of heavy-duty aluminum foil that's a little larger than the vacated space, and set it over the opening. Press the foil in carefully, and fold the edges over to make a template that fits the space with just enough wiggle room to hold the sand you'll be packing into the joints. Then look for stone that's as close as possible in size and shape.

Special Handling Required

Flagstone is a whole lot more delicate than it looks. So whenever you need to remove and replace stones, work carefully, following these guidelines:

- To pry up a stone, rest the pry bar against a piece of wood. It'll make the lifting easier and also protect the adjacent stones.

- Never raise a large stone in a horizontal position, even if you have a helper, because the slab could break in two under its own weight. Instead, tilt the stone on one edge before you hoist it up. And to avoid injuring yourself, bend your knees and lift with your legs—not your back—and make sure your partner does the same. If there's no one to share the load, walk the upended flagstone, one corner at a time, to its destination.

- When you set a stone in place, use your hands to press it gently into its sandy bed. Don't jump or stomp on it. If you do, you could crack the stone or hurt your knees—or both.

The Cutting-Edge Cutting Routine

If you have a lot of flagstones to cut, it pays to invest in a good masonry saw. But when your project demands only a few stones, a heavy (preferably mason's) hammer and a brick set or stonemason's chisel will do the trick nicely. Here's what you need to do:

▶ **Draw the line.** Place the stone on top of the one it will abut, and use a carpenter's pencil to mark a cut line where the two pavers will intersect.

▶ **Give it some give.** Set the stone on a resilient surface, like sand, bare ground, or a piece of carpet laid on a more solid base.

Never rest a paver of any kind directly on concrete or any other hard material because your hammer blows will cause the stone to bounce and very likely break in all the wrong places. But a softer bed will absorb and dissipate the energy of the strike and make the stone less prone to jump around.

▶ **Score first.** Wearing protective goggles and gloves, make a shallow cut along the top, bottom, and sides of the stone. Then use a series of progressively stronger blows to split the flag all the way through.

Note: *Sturdy eye and hand protection is an absolute must when you're working with flagstone because it can—and usually does—shatter and send razor-sharp splinters flying through the air.*

WALLS & FENCES

Save That Wall!

Replacing a collapsed retaining wall can cost a bundle—and make a royal mess of your yard during the construction process. The good news is that as long as a wall is built on a solid, level, well-compacted base, you can keep it shipshape for years by faithfully performing these three simple chores:

• **Replace loose stones—fast!** When one works its way loose, it's a sure bet that its neighbors will soon follow. So whenever you find that one or two stones are the least bit wobbly, shore them up immediately, using mortar if necessary to keep them in place. Or if they're chipped, replace them.

• **Evict all plants.** Weeds or the windblown seeds of trees, shrubs, and vines will sprout in the tiniest gaps in a wall. And once they take off, their roots can drastically shorten the structure's life span. Your mission: Yank out any and all seedlings as soon as you spot them. Or if you've got a lot of little troublemakers, let 'em have it with my Tight-Space Weed Killer (at right).

- **Don't settle for settling.** Low spots or excessive settling behind a wall may look harmless, but the water that collects in those areas can seep into the structure and eventually bring it down in a heap. So each spring, remove the mulch or sod on top of the wall and add enough new backfill to bring the cap back to its proper level.

Fend Off Fence Fatalities

Just like a wooden deck, a wooden fence demands constant diligence to retain its good looks and sound structure. At least every couple of months—and especially in the spring or after a period of heavy weather—inspect the whole perimeter closely. In particular, look for and immediately remedy any of these common woes:

▶ **Gaps between fence posts and concrete footings.** Fill them with a top-quality exterior caulk.

▶ **Worn stain, or flaking or peeling paint.** Scrape it off and recoat the bare spots (see note on page 226).

▶ **Rusted or corroded hardware.** Replace any rusted or otherwise weather-worn brackets, screws, or wire ties.

POWERFUL POTIONS

TIGHT-SPACE WEED KILLER

This ultra-potent—and ultra-safe—formula is tailor made for wiping out those annoying weeds that sprout up in impossible-to-dig places, like gaps in retaining walls, the narrow spaces between stepping-stones or pavers, or cracks in a driveway.

1 cup of salt
1 tsp. of dishwashing liquid
1 gal. of white vinegar

Mix the ingredients in a bucket, and pour the solution into a handheld spray bottle. Then hit those pesky weeds hard with a stream of the stuff—not a fan-type spray! For best results, do this job on a hot day when the sun is at its strongest. (Be careful not to get this solution on any plants you want to keep!)

▶ **Loose gate hinges.** Tighten them up, or replace them as necessary. And make sure they're well lubricated.

Note: A wooden fence (unless it's made of unfinished cedar) should be stained or painted every two to three years.

How to Rust-Proof an Iron Fence

An iron or steel fence (or railing) will literally rust to pieces if it's not securely covered in paint. So if you've got one with a coat that's flaking or blistering—or that's unpainted—you need to hop to it. Wait for a clear, dry day,* and follow this three-step routine:

STEP 1. Sand, chip, and wire-brush off all existing paint, rust, and scale to reach clean, bare metal. Then wipe the surface with a soft, clean cloth dipped in mineral spirits.

STEP 2. Immediately spray or brush on two or more coats of a rust-inhibiting primer that's specially made for ferrous metals. Don't delay because once iron or steel is bare, it will start to rust in a flash.

STEP 3. Let the primer dry for at least 24 hours, and apply an acrylic topcoat of the same brand as your primer (so you're sure they're compatible).

* The key to success with this project is to do it when there's no trace of fog or mist in the air. If there is, the dampness will put a fine layer of rust on the metal before you even start priming the surface. And if the sun is beating down, those hot rays will dry the primer way too quickly.

AN OUNCE OF
PREVENTION

Make Water Unwelcome

Letting water sit on top of wooden fence posts is throwing an open house for moss, mold, algae, and rot. Here are two simple ways to say, "No, no, H_2O!":

• Cover the posts with preformed metal or vinyl caps (available in home-improvement stores and from online retailers).

• Trim the top of each post to form a water-shedding point, slope, or curve.

CONCRETE REPAIRS & MAINTENANCE ▬▬

Spray before You Paint

Are you getting ready to paint your home's concrete foundation? Or maybe you'd like to give a new look to a concrete-block retaining wall. If you're using latex paint, the secret to a long-lived coat is to give the blocks a shower before you begin. Here's the easy-as-pie process in a nutshell:

- Choose an exterior paint that's especially made for concrete.

- Clean and roughen up the surface with a wire brush.

- Haul out the garden hose and spray the surface lightly, and then wait until the concrete is merely damp before you start painting.

The reason for this important step is that dry concrete will suck the water out of latex paint as soon as you brush it on, so the paint won't get a chance to harden properly. And before too long, your carefully applied coat will peel right off.

Note: *If you're applying oil-based paint, you can skip the watering step because concrete does not absorb oil.*

The Root(s) of the Problem

Earlier in this chapter, I pointed out the aesthetic damage that fallen tree leaves and seedpods can cause to concrete and other paved surfaces. Well, the roots of woody plants can make an even bigger mess of concrete slabs, creating buckling and cracks to beat the band. So if you've got trees or shrubs growing anywhere near your driveway, patio, walkway, or pool deck, you need to perform a preemptive chopping job at least once each summer. Just plunge a sharp, flat-end spade 6 to 8 inches below the edge of the slab, pull it out, then sink it again, overlapping each cut as you move along. That'll sever the roots before they can do their dirty work—but it won't harm the plants one iota.

Filling Cracks in Concrete

Any opening in a concrete surface is a disaster waiting to happen. Gaps at the base of your house—like the area where a patio, walk, or driveway meets a wall—can direct water onto, and into, the foundation. But even small fissures collect water that can freeze and expand, making the gash larger. So at least once a year, take an inspection tour and fill any cracks and eroding joints with urethane caulk. The exact methodology depends on the size of the opening. Here's the deal:

To fill cracks that are ¼ inch wide or less, load the tube into your caulking gun and draw it down the crack, smoothing the caulk with the tip as you go.

For gaps and joints that are more than ¼ inch across, follow this procedure:

Press the backer rod into the gap with your fingers.

- Buy a length of foam backer rod that's as long as the gap and one size larger in width.

- Press the rod tightly into the gap with your fingers so that it rests ¼ inch lower than the concrete.

- Cut the caulk tube tip at a 30-degree angle to make the opening the same size as the gap. Using a steady motion, fill the crack until the caulk is flush with the surface, beveling the joint if it abuts a wall. Smooth the caulk with the back of an old spoon, periodically cleaning it with a rag dipped in mineral spirits.

Note: *Urethane caulk is extremely sticky, so wear disposable gloves and old clothes whenever you work with the stuff. If you get any of it on your skin, wipe it off ASAP with a rag dipped in paint thinner.*

Use an old spoon to smooth out the new joint.

Finding cracks in a concrete patio or driveway can put a damper on your day. But discovering fissures in your home's foundation can send you into full-blown panic mode. If that's just happened to you, take a deep breath and calm down. There may be nothing to worry about. For example, hairline cracks in poured concrete or in the mortar between blocks are generally no big deal. Likewise, the kind that appear at an L-shaped section, like an area where the foundation steps down to follow a hillside, are generally harmless from a structural standpoint—although you should fill them to keep moisture out of your basement or crawl space.

On the other hand, stair-step cracks in masonry joints are cause for concern, especially If the opening is wider than ¼ inch or the wall is bulging. Horizontal cracks are even more problematic and could indicate severe damage to the foundation. In either of these cases, have a structural engineer assess the situation immediately.

CALL A PRO

Sayonara, Spalling!

A heavy blow can cause a concrete affliction called spalling (a.k.a. chipping or flaking). It can also occur when the concrete mixture contains too much water, or when a newly poured batch is not cured properly. Besides looking like the dickens, a bad case of spalling can turn a walk or patio into prime ankle-turning territory. Fortunately, you don't have to repave the whole shebang. Just spruce up the damaged portion using this three-step process:

▶ **Break up the weakened areas** using light swings with a small sledgehammer. (The impacts will produce hollow sounds.)

▶ **Scrub away the loosened material** with a wire brush. Then rinse the area thoroughly with a garden hose, and let it dry.

▶ **Cover the surface** with latex patching compound, and go over it with a steel trowel (to produce a very smooth surface) or a wood float (for a rougher surface with better traction).

5 Steps to a Fixed-Up Step

Replacing a corner that's broken off a concrete step may seem like a daunting task, but it's actually a quick and easy five-step fix.

STEP 1. Use a wire brush to clean off all the loose debris.

STEP 2. Screw together two short pieces of 1-by-6 lumber to make an L-shaped form, and coat it with cooking oil spray (so the cement won't stick to it). Hold it firmly against the dinged corner, flush with the top of the step, while a helper secures it with long strips of duct tape. (Prop the form up at the bottom if that's needed.)

STEP 3. Brush a generous coat of latex bonding adhesive* onto the broken corner.

STEP 4. In a bucket, mix a small batch of quick-setting cement,* following the directions on the package. Then scoop up a glob with a pointed trowel and press it tightly into the form so that it rises above the corner just a bit.

STEP 5. Let your handiwork sit overnight, and then gently peel off the tape and hang the form on a hook in your workshop.

* Latex bonding adhesive and quick-setting cement are both available at any place that sells building supplies.

> **WELL, WHADDYA KNOW!**
>
> If you think that concrete—the stuff of which sidewalks, house foundations, and superhighways are made—is a modern development, think again. The ever-resourceful Romans invented the stuff in the early years AD. They started with cement, which they made from a volcanic ash called pozzolana, but they quickly found that mixing the stuff with water, lime, and chunks of stone produced a much stronger material. They reckoned they could use it to build sturdy fortress walls and lay down roads that would crisscross their whole empire. And, of course, they proceeded to do just that!

ASPHALT REPAIRS & MAINTENANCE

Asphalt Driveway Sealers: Three of a Kind

Any sealer will increase your asphalt driveway's longevity, but just how long the surface will hold up—and how easy it is to put down—varies depending on the formulation. There are three types, each with its pros and cons. Here's the rundown:

▶ Coal tar sealers resist water, oil, and gasoline penetration and provide protection from the sun's UV rays, which cause driveways to crack and deteriorate. On the downside, they emit odiferous volatile organic compounds (VOCs) during the messy application process, and they will burn your skin on contact.

When There's No Time for Sealing

If you can't spare several days to seal your driveway, then at least dig out any weeds and wayward grass that have sprouted in cracks and fill those holes. That'll hold off further damage until you can do a full-scale cover-up—and it just may save you the cost of a new driveway. For the easy how-to routine, see "2 Crackerjack Crack Fillers" (at right) and "The Hole Story" (on page 234).

▶ **Asphalt-based** products resist water effectively, but they offer reduced protection against oil, gas, and UV rays. They cost a little less than the coal tar versions, and the odor isn't as strong—but they're just as messy, and you'll have to do the job more often.

▶ **Acrylic polymer** sealers are the top of the heap. They cost more than their asphalt and coal tar counterparts, but they can last two to three times longer, and they're virtually odor-free. Plus, unlike the other types, they work just as well on concrete as they do on asphalt. Best of all from the average do-it-yourselfer's standpoint, you can roll 'em on using a regular paint roller and clean up your tools, your clothes, and yourself with plain old soap and water (see "How to Seal Your Asphalt Driveway," below).

How to Seal Your Asphalt Driveway

Using an acrylic-based sealer will make this job a whole lot more pleasant—and give you longer-lasting results. But no matter which type you choose, the basic application process is the same. Do the job on a mild day in spring or fall, when no rain is predicted for at least 48 hours—and preferably 72. Here's all you need to do:

STEP 1. Prep the surface. Use a stiff-bristled broom to sweep away loose dirt and debris. Remove stuck-on dirt with a garden hose. Then fill any cracks or holes, get rid of stubborn stains following the directions in "Oil's Well That Vanishes Well" on page 231, and rinse thoroughly. (Don't skip this step because many stains, including oil and grease, can bleed or bubble up through the sealer and ruin your whole job!)

STEP 2. Use a paintbrush to apply a thin coat of sealer (no thicker than a dime) along the edges of doors, walkways, or other surfaces that you don't want to cover.

STEP 3. Pour a strip of sealer across the highest part of your driveway, and roll it over the surface using a paint roller—again keeping the coat thin. Work in 3- to 4-square-foot sections, moving across the driveway.* Continue the process until you've covered the whole surface.

STEP 4. Let the first coat dry for the time specified on the product label. Then apply a second thin coat at a right angle to the first one.

STEP 5. Erect a barrier to prevent anyone from driving on it for at least 24 hours. (But after about four hours, it'll be dry enough to walk on.)

Roll a thin coat of sealer onto the surface, working in 3- to 4-square-foot sections.

If you use a coal tar or asphalt-based sealer, use a squeegee to pull it across the surface while applying steady downward pressure. Also, bear in mind that if you get this stuff on your shoes, you'll never get it off. So either cover your shoes with sturdy plastic, or wear footgear that you can toss in the trash when the job is done.

2 Crackerjack Crack Fillers

Got a crack in your blacktop driveway? No worries. You can make it vanish in either of these two super-simple ways:

- Buy a tube of (surprise!) asphalt crack filler at a hardware or home-improvement store, and force the stuff into the gap using a caulking gun or a pointed trowel.

- Get a roll of adhesive-backed tape filler made from polypropylene fabric that's impregnated with asphalt. Clean the surface around the crack, and apply the tape as you would a big bandage.

Got some old door, gate, or cabinet handles lying around? If so, you've got a dandy way to make pothole filling a whole lot easier. Just screw two of the handles on opposite sides of a 4-by-4, and hold onto them as you tamp down your patching material.

The Hole Story

Filling a pothole in asphalt requires a different process than patching a crack—but the job is just about as simple. First, buy a sack of cold-patch asphalt patching material and a 4-by-4 to use as a tamper, and proceed as follows:

▶ Use a chisel and small sledge-hammer to remove the damaged asphalt, undercutting the edges so your patch will stay put. Then take out 2 inches of the base, and tamp down the remaining layer.

▶ Fill the hole halfway with the patching compound, level it off, and tamp it down to compact the material. Repeat until the patch is about ½ inch above the adjacent surface.

▶ Cover the patch with sand or a sheet of plywood, and drive over it a few times. Then check the area. If the filler is too low, add more patching material and drive over the spot again. Keep at the task until the patch is at or slightly above the surface.

Note: *If you plan to seal your driveway, wait for a year or so after you've filled any potholes because it takes cold-patch material that long to settle and harden thoroughly.*

INGROUND IRRIGATION SYSTEMS

Three to Get Ready...

For Old Man Winter, that is. If temperatures drop below freezing in your neck of the woods, the most important thing you can do to ensure a long life for your irrigation system is to winterize it in the fall. There is no excuse for shirking this chore because it's a fairly simple three-step process:

- Make sure that all standing water—and I do mean all—is out of the system (see the Call a Pro box on page 236).

- Turn off the water at the main shutoff valve. If it's located in an unheated basement, insulate the valve just to be on the safe side. Wrap it with insulation if it's outdoors above the frost line.

- If you have an automatic system, shut down the timer control, or put it into "rain mode" so you won't have to reprogram it later.

Clear That Clog!

When a sprinkler head refuses to produce H_2O, chances are the problem is a simple clog that you can clean out in a flash. The procedure depends on the type of head.

Impact sprinkler head

▸ First, insert a screwdriver between the cover and the case to dislodge any debris.

▸ Then, to clean the case, pry up the cover and unscrew the head using the wrench that came with your system.

Fixed-head sprinkler

▸ Clear out debris using the corner of an old credit card. Don't use a metal tool, or you could damage the nozzle!

▸ To clean the screen, unscrew the nozzle and lift out the screen. If there are any tears, replace it with a new one that's specifically made for your system. Otherwise, rinse the screen under running water.

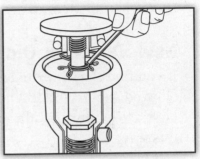
Unscrew the sprinkler head using a specially designed wrench.

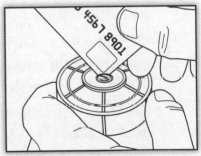
Use a credit card to clean debris from the sprinkler head.

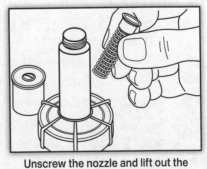
Unscrew the nozzle and lift out the screen.

Call before You Dig

While cleaning sprinkler heads is a clear-cut aboveground job, most other system repairs entail digging. And that can land you in a whole lot of trouble if your shovel happens to hit an underground power or sewer line. So make sure you know their whereabouts before you begin any belowground work. If you installed your system, or had it done on your watch, you should have a map showing those highly sensitive routes. If you can't find it, call your town clerk's office or the local utility company.

New Heads for Old

If you find that a sprinkler head is damaged rather than simply clogged, you're still in luck because replacing it couldn't be easier. First, close the shutoff valve and turn off the timer. Then have at it this way:

- ▶ Cut into the grass around the sprinkler head using a sharp spade, and roll back the sod. Lift out the dirt very carefully to avoid damaging the pipe or connection fitting.

- ▶ Unscrew the old head from the riser. Wrap pipe (a.k.a. plumber's) tape around the threads of the new head, screw the head into place, and tighten it (gently!) with a wrench.

- ▶ Test the spray, and if all's well, refill the hole and set the sod back in place.

When it's time to close down your irrigation system for the winter, it's essential to remove all standing water before freezing weather sets in. In theory, you can do the job yourself using drain valves (either manual or automated). But to guarantee that the pipes and other components are thoroughly empty, have a professional "blow out" the system with a compressor. Otherwise, you could be in for an unpleasant—and potentially expensive—surprise come spring.

CALL A PRO

Replacing a Damaged Pipe

For underground sprinkler pipes, the "livin'" isn't always easy as a summer breeze. And it's not much fun for a lawn tender either when a plastic conduit springs or gets "strangled" by tree roots or crushed by car traffic. Luckily, though, replacing a damaged section of an existing inground irrigation system is an easy and pretty quick fix. Here's the four-step surgical procedure:

STEP 1. After turning off the timer and shutoff valve, slice away the sod in the affected area, remove the soil from around the pipe, and bail out any standing water in the trench.

STEP 2. Cut out the damaged section using a hacksaw or pipe cutter. Then buy a telescoping PVC union and solvent weld coupler unit that's ½ inch shorter than the length of pipe you removed. (You can buy both components at any irrigation-supply store—check online to find a nearby supplier.)

STEP 3. Solvent weld the coupler to one end of the cut pipe and the smaller end of the PVC union.

STEP 4. Pull out the larger end of the union so that it overlaps the other end of the cut pipe by 1 inch, and join the two pieces with solvent. Let it dry for 30 minutes. Then turn the water back on and test the system before filling the hole and replacing the sod.

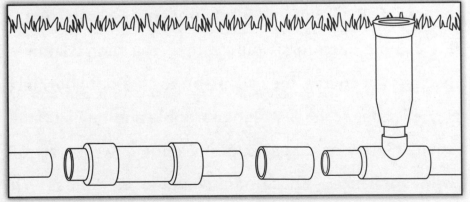

A telescoping union and coupler securely join the two ends of a cut pipe.

PART 3

THE STUFF IN YOUR LIFE

In the first two parts of this book, we focused on features and systems—indoors and out—that are more or less permanent parts of your home. Now I'm going to offer up sound solutions, timely tips, and ingenious ideas for prolonging the useful lives of the more portable things that make your life easier, safer, and more enjoyable. In these pages, you'll find fun and simple ways to care for everything from the curtains on your windows to the clothes in your closet and your new couch to your grandma's china. You'll even discover heaps of life-lengthening maintenance secrets that a lot of manufacturers would rather you didn't know—because, of course, they want you to toss out your (let's say) blender at the first sign of trouble and buy a brand-spankin' new one. Speaking of blenders, we'll start off with appliances—those hard-charging workhorses we rely on every day.

Appliances

You really don't *need* a washing machine—much less a food processor, coffeemaker, or dehumidifier. After all, for thousands of years folks got along just fine without all those fancy contraptions. But we take these modern conveniences for granted, and when they break down, it can send your stress level soaring. In this chapter, I'll show you how to fix many of those glitches so you can go on with life as you know it— without having to shovel out big bucks in the process.

STOVES & MICROWAVES

Code Yellow

If your gas stove's burners are slow to light, you see yellow flames instead of blue ones, or there is no flame at all in some spots, it means just one thing: The holes in the rings' perimeters are plugged with grease or dirt. To cut the clogs, poke each opening with a piece of fine wire, like a straightened-out paper clip or safety pin. Do *not* use a toothpick, matchstick, or anything else that's made of wood because it can easily break off. Then you'll have *real* trouble on your hands.

The Flame Won't Light!

When you push the ignition button on your gas stove and nothing happens, don't panic. The problem is probably a clogged igniter head. When dirt builds up, it blocks the spark between the burner and an electrode that kicks it into action. The simple solution: Turn off the gas and remove the burner head. Dip the head of a retired toothbrush in white vinegar and scrub until the crud washes away.

Got a Burner on the Blink?

Not to worry! In two out of three cases, an electric stove's heating coils are no harder to replace than a burned-out lightbulb. On many models, you can simply pull the burner out of its connection, much as you would pull a plug out of a wall socket. On other types, the element is fastened to the wires with a couple of screws, which you'll need to remove. (Be sure to kill the juice at the fuse box or breaker panel first!) Either take the dead coil and the stove's model number to an appliance store and buy a replacement, or order one from the manufacturer's website. When you've got your new burner, reverse the process and plug it back into the stove top. Then restore the power and turn the burner on. If it still doesn't work, you've got a more serious problem—most likely a broken switch—that demands professional help.

What about the third-case scenario? This is the type of burner that lifts up so you can clean underneath it easily, and the connections are usually soldered in place. Unless you're adept at soldering, you'll need to call an appliance repair guy right from the get-go.

EMERGENCY RESPONSE:

WHEN YOU SMELL GAS

GET OUT! Gas flowing from an open, unlit stove burner—or any other part of a gas range—can turn a closed-up kitchen into an explosive atmosphere in as little as 10 seconds. So if you smell gas, get all people and pets out of the house immediately, and leave the door open behind you. Once you're clear of the building, call the fire department or your gas company. Do not call from your cell phone on your way out, and don't turn on any lights or use a landline telephone, flashlight, or computer. Any of these devices can easily trigger a spark that could blow the place sky high.

Smooth Sailing Isn't Guaranteed

Smooth-top electric ranges win popularity contests for their sleek good looks and easy-to-clean glass or ceramic surface. But they have one major flaw: If you don't treat that top with kid gloves, it'll pick up more scratches than a leopard has spots. Deep scratches are nearly impossible to hide, but in many cases, you can minimize surface scrapes so they become virtually unnoticeable. Wait until the stove top is completely cool and use one of these remedies:

▶ **Automotive scratch remover.** Apply it with a soft cloth and buff gently. Let the compound dry and wipe it off with a dry cloth.

▶ **Baking soda.** Mix it with enough water to make a paste, and buff with a soft cloth. Then rinse with water and dry the glass with another soft cloth.

▶ **Maas® metal polish.** Put a dab of the cream on a cotton ball or soft cloth, and rub it over the affected area using small, circular motions. Then wipe with a clean, damp cloth. If the scratch remains, repeat the process using a gentle scrubbing pad. **Note:** *Maas® metal polish is available online and in hardware and home-improvement stores.*

Whichever product you use, if the scratch hasn't vanished after the second try, don't keep scrubbing away at it. You could wind up with a more permanent dull area that will be even less attractive than the original wound.

Smooth Stove Tops Are Sissies

There's no getting around it: Smooth cooktops demand special care. To avoid making a mess of the surface, follow these guidelines:

• Use only the kind of cookware recommended by the manufacturer. In virtually all cases, glass, ceramic, stone, and cast-iron pots and pans are all no-nos because they can scratch the surface faster than you can say "Oops!" Copper-bottomed pans can leave a residue that looks like scratching, but it comes right off if you wipe the burner immediately after it's cooled down.

SMOOTH-TOP STOVE CLEANER

This lemony mixture will safely get your old (or new) smoothy bright and clean.

¼ cup of white vinegar
2–4 drops of lemon essential oil
Baking soda

Mix the vinegar and oil in a small spray bottle. Sprinkle the baking soda over the dirty areas of the stove top, and spray the vinegar and oil over the soda. It will fizz. Wait for 10 minutes, or until the mixture becomes pasty, and wipe it away with a soft, damp cloth. The dirt will go with it!

- Never slide any pot or pan—or anything else—over the surface.

- Always wipe off the bottom of a pot or pan before you set it on a burner. Even the tiniest particles of grit or burned-on food could scratch the stove top.

- Never use an abrasive cleanser or scouring sponge when you clean the stove top. Instead, for routine cleanups, wait until the surface has cooled completely, and wipe away spills with a soft, damp cloth. The one exception: Go after any sugary spill as soon as the burner is cool enough to touch safely. Otherwise, the sugar will pit the glass.

- To remove burned- or dried-on food, use my Smooth-Top Stove Cleaner (above).

Only You Can Prevent Kitchen Fires

Caked-on grease can start a fire at the drop of a spark. This simple routine will get rid of those crusty old trouble spots in a hurry:

▶ Sprinkle a thick layer of salt over the grease.

▶ Cut a lime (or several, as needed) in half and squeeze the juice over the salt, and let it sit for about five minutes.

▶ Scrub with a sponge to loosen the grease, and then wipe it away with a damp rag or paper towels.

And from now on, don't let greasy spills sit around long enough to dry! Keep a bottle of my Dandy Double-Punch Degreaser close at hand, and use it to clean up splatters as soon as they appear. You'll find the super-simple recipe on page 244.

Replacing an Oven Heating Element

The metal loops at the bottom and top of your electric oven may look intimidating, but on most models replacing a baking or broiling element that's gone kaput is just about as simple as installing a new stove-top heating coil (see "Got a Burner on the Blink?" on page 240). Here's what you need to do:

STEP 1. Turn off power to the stove's circuit and make sure the entire range is cool. Then pull the oven racks out to free up working space. Loosen the screws on the element's mounting bracket on the back wall of the oven, and pull the element toward you as far as it will go. But don't pull too hard! If the manufacturer used push-on wire connectors instead of screws, those plastic pieces could pop off, sending the wires through the hole in the back of the oven and beyond your reach. Then your easy-as-pie fix will turn into a major project—or a pricey repair call.

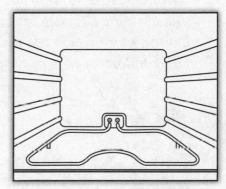

Remove the mounting screws at the back of the oven.

STEP 2. Prevent a vanishing act by clipping a clothespin to each wire. Or tape the wires to a piece of cardboard that's too big to fall through the hole. Then remove the screws or pull off the connectors that secure the element to the wires.

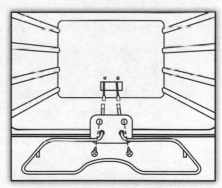

Remove the screws that hold the baking element to the terminal wires.

STEP 3. Take the element to an appliance-supply or hardware store and buy a replacement of the same size. Make sure the spacing of the terminals is the same so they'll fit through the back of the oven.

STEP 4. When you get home, slide the new element's terminals through the holes in the mounting bracket, and screw the terminals to the wires (or refasten the push-on connectors). Then remove the clothespins or cardboard you've attached to the wires, and screw the mounting bracket back in place.

STEP 5. Turn the power back on and give the oven a test run. If it still won't heat up, most likely the problem is in the control mechanism—and you will need professional help with that.

Note: *As with all appliances, stoves vary in their construction details. For example, on some ovens, you need to remove the back to reach the terminals. And some newer models have the baking element concealed under a panel. So before you undertake this or any other repair, take a look at your owner's manual. If the process looks too complex for your DIY comfort level, turn the job over to a pro.*

POWERFUL POTIONS

DANDY DOUBLE-PUNCH DEGREASER

This acidic combo teams up to quickly cut through any kind of grease and oil splatters your kitchen can deliver.

2 cups of white vinegar
½ cup of lemon juice

Mix the ingredients together in a spray bottle. Keep it in the kitchen, and the minute any grease spills onto your stove, in your oven, or on any other surface, spritz it with the solution and wipe the spot away with a paper towel. (Wait until the stove top or oven has cooled down first!)

It's Elementary...

Or is it? If your electric oven isn't performing as it should, the problem could be a defective baking or broiling element. On the other hand, the culprit could be the thermostat or the temperature-selection switch. To find out for sure, place an oven thermometer in the middle of the oven and set the control to "Bake" at 450°F. The bottom element should light up to an even shade of red, and the thermometer should top out at 450°F. Then turn the dial (or push the button) to "Broil" at the highest temperature setting. The upper element should glow like a stoplight, with the thermometer reaching the digit you selected.

If only one of the elements fails to heat up, replace it with a new one (see "Replacing an Oven Heating Element" on page 243). But if they both stay cool, or if the temperature is off by more than 35 degrees, the fault lies with the thermostat or the selection switch. And either one of those glitches demands professional attention.

"Self-Clean" Means What It Says!

This is one time when the lazy way really is the best way. Using a chemical oven cleaner on a self-cleaning oven can damage its interior. So for goodness sake, let the oven do the work for you. And while it's getting itself spruced up, remove the racks and give them a no-mess bath this way:

▶ Put each rack in a large, heavy-duty plastic trash bag.

▶ Add 1 cup of white vinegar, ⅓ cup of dishwashing liquid, and hot water to almost fill the bag.

▶ Then seal the sack tightly and put it in a bathtub full of warm water for 60 minutes or so.

▶ Remove the rack from the bag and scrub it with a brush or scouring pad. Then rinse the rack with water and let it air-dry.

Note: *Whatever you do, never leave racks in the oven while the self-cleaning process is under way; the ultra-high heat could warp the metal.*

Curses—Foiled Again!

True or false? Lining the floor and the racks of your oven with aluminum foil is a dandy way to ease your cleanup chores.

Very true. That will make for fast, easy oven cleaning—but you'll pay for that convenience in several ways:

• Covering the racks will hinder the flow of air that food needs in order to cook efficiently and effectively.

• The heat reflected by the foil can throw off your thermostat.

• Lining the floor of your oven can damage both the heating element and the oven lining.

The bottom line: Spending a little time and elbow grease suddenly sounds a lot more appealing!

FIRE!

Any electric or gas-powered appliance can turn your home into an inferno. Follow these guidelines to stop flames in their tracks:

Sparking appliance. Cut the power at your electric panel, and either replace the device or have it repaired before you turn it on again. If flames are coming out, douse them with a fire extinguisher of either the C or ABC type. And (of course!) if they don't go out right away, call 911.

Oven fire. Turn off the oven and kill the juice to the circuit. After that, simply keep the oven door tightly closed, and the fire will eventually die from lack of oxygen.

Burning pan. Never carry a burning pan to the sink! Instead, turn off the range and exhaust fan, slide a large metal pan lid over the flames, and leave it on until the heating element, the pan, and its contents are cool. As long as the burner or the oil in the pan is still hot, lifting the lid even a hair could supply enough oxygen to restart the fire.

Stove top. When oil or grease ignites on the cooking surface, smother the flames with a thick layer of baking soda or salt. Do not douse any cooking fire with water or flour!

Give It a Head Start

Whenever possible, start your oven's self-cleaning cycle immediately after baking or roasting, when the oven is still good and hot. This way, powering up to the necessary heat level will put less wear and tear on the appliance—and also a little less padding on your utility bill.

Jump-Start Your Microwave

It's annoying, all right: You pushed the start button on your microwave oven, and it sprang right into action. But when the appropriate nuking time was up, you realized that the food inside was still icy cold. Time to ante up for a new machine? Maybe. Then again, maybe not. It could simply be that the thermostat has tripped itself up. When that happens, the oven will make its usual whirring, humming sounds, but the cooking feature goes AWOL. So before you haul the thing to the dump, try this: Pull the plug out of the outlet, wait for 30 to 60 seconds, and plug it back in. If your lucky stars are with you, during that time-out the thermostat will reset itself. If it doesn't, well, nothing ventured, nothing gained.

The Merry-Go-Round Won't Move

If your microwave's carousel stops turning, a good cleaning just might put it back in business. Here's how to go about it:

- Remove the glass platter and wheeled turntable. You'll see a round track with a notched wheel in the middle. Close the door, turn the oven on, and peek through the glass.

- If the wheel is moving right along, turn the machine off, pull the plug, and clean the carousel track and turntable well with my Dandy Double-Punch Degreaser on page 244. Then put a drop of mineral oil on each of the wheels, and put everything back together again.

- On the other hand, if the wheel is not turning, you'll need to get professional help—or a new microwave (see "Sometimes It Pays to Say 'Uncle'" on page 248).

Micromanage Spills and Splatters

Unfortunately, microwave ovens don't come with a self-cleaning option. But you don't really need one. Either of these no-muss, no-fuss formulas will remove dried-on food from the walls and floor of the oven. (Needless to say—I hope!—in both cases you need to use a microwave-safe container.)

▶ Mix 2 tablespoons of baking soda in 1 cup of water and cook it on "High" for two to three minutes.

▶ Stir 3 tablespoons of lemon juice into 1½ cups of water and nuke it on "High" for five to ten minutes.

Whichever mixture you've used, at the end of the cooking time, remove the container and wipe the oven's now-moist interior clean with damp paper towels.

A Thin Rim Could Do You In

We all know that you should never use metal pans in a microwave oven. What you may not realize, however, is that even a thin gold or silver rim on a porcelain plate could cause an electric arc that, besides damaging the oven, could easily start a fire. The same goes for the remnants of a metal freshness seal on a glass bottle, like maple syrup that you want to warm up for your waffles, or the wire in a twist tie that you might grab to seal a cooking bag. (For a no-risk alternative to a twist tie, use butcher's twine or dental floss—just remember to cut a small slit in the bag for ventilation.)

Deodorize Your Microwave

Unlike baked-on food, strong odors don't pose a fire hazard in your microwave, but they can put a serious damper on your appetite. The quick fix: Pour a teaspoon or two of vanilla extract into a bowl and nuke it on "High" for 60 seconds. Now your morning oatmeal won't smell—or worse—taste like last night's fish.

Sometimes It Pays to Say "Uncle"

Most microwave oven fixes are not DIY projects. And unless you have an ultra-high-end model, there's a good chance that professional repairs will cost more than the price of a new machine. In fact, with prices starting at under 40 dollars these days, it could cost a whole lot more. If your ailing nuker is anywhere near the normal microwave life span (4 to 10 years with average family use), you're better off replacing it.

REFRIGERATORS & FREEZERS

Keep Your Chiller Chilling

Your refrigerator is like any other appliance: The harder it has to work, the sooner it'll wear out. But by following these simple guidelines, you can help keep it chilling longer—and save money on your electric bill to boot:

- Clean the condenser coils at the back of the refrigerator at least once a year, using either a brush or a vacuum cleaner. Dust and dirt that accumulate on the coils will make the unit work a lot harder than it needs to.

- Open the door as seldom and as briefly as possible. This way, the cool air inside will stay cooler.

- Make sure the refrigerator temperature stays between 36°F and 40°F, and the freezer temperature remains between 0°F and 5°F. Keeping the unit any colder than necessary will make it work harder than it needs to—and consume up to 25 percent more energy in the process.

- Position the fridge out of direct sunlight and away from heat-producing appliances, such as ovens and dishwashers. And make sure the casing is at least a few inches away from the surrounding walls or cabinets so that air can circulate freely around the condenser coils.

- If you have a freezer that must be defrosted manually, do the job on a regular basis. Ice that builds up on the coils will make the compressor run longer and work harder.

If your refrigerator suddenly starts to smell, and you've ruled out the obvious culprits like forgotten, weeks-old produce or a too-high temperature, it could be that your breaker strips are damaged. These guardians prevent moisture from entering the insulation between the inner and outer walls of the appliance, and when they're compromised, it diminishes the cooling efficiency of your refrigerator and also causes an unpleasant aroma. Unfortunately, there is no DIY fix for this dilemma, so get on the horn to your local appliance store pronto and ask someone there to recommend a pro who can solve the problem for you.

CALL A PRO

Make It Even, Steven

A refrigerator operates most efficiently when it's on a perfectly level footing. If your floor can't provide that kind of surface, don't fret: Appliance manufacturers take these domestic imperfections into account at the factory. To set things right, look at the bottom of the unit (you may need to remove the toeplate first). If your model

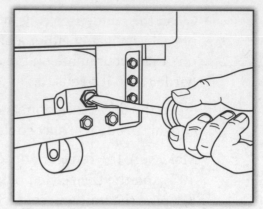

Raise or lower your refrigerator to make it level.

has stationary feet, raise or lower them using an adjustable wrench. Adjust castors by turning their leveling screws with a screwdriver. Then check the results with a carpenter's level, and make further tweaks as needed.

Tighten Up and Chill Right

Each door of your refrigerator and freezer has a molded rubber gasket that keeps cold air in and warm air out. At least, that's what it's supposed to do. If your fridge is running more frequently than it used to, it's probably because the gasket is leaking. To find out for sure, perform this three-part test:

- ▶ **Eyeball the gasket.** If you see condensation or spots of blackish mold anywhere near the strip, it means that it's time to replace the gasket. No visual problems present? The trouble could be in its early stages, so proceed to part 2.

- ▶ **See where the buck stops.** In several different spots, close the door on a dollar bill, and slowly pull it out. If it shows any resistance, it means that the gasket is in good shape. But if that currency slides right out, you've definitely got a leak on your hands. You may or may not need to replace the gasket—it depends on what you learn in part 3.

- ▶ **Inspect the doors.** If one of them is sagging, it may be causing the gasket to seal poorly. As long as the gasket is pliable and fairly new, realigning the doors could solve your problem (see "Line 'Em Up," below). On the other hand, the out-of-kilter door may have put so much strain on the gasket that you will need to replace it. For that routine, see "Replacing a Refrigerator Door Gasket" (below).

Replacing a Refrigerator Door Gasket

The longer you let a defective gasket stay on the job, the sooner you'll have to shell out for a new fridge, or at least major repairs. To find the right replacement, call a local appliance-parts store or visit the manufacturer's website. You'll find all the relevant details in your owner's manual or on the manufacturer's identification plate inside your fridge, either on or near the door. You'll also need a jar of petroleum jelly and, depending on your refrigerator, a hex head screwdriver that matches the size of the screw heads on the door (you can find a hex head driver in any hardware store).

STEP 1. Put the new gasket in hot water, in either a bathtub or the kitchen sink, to soften up the rubber and make it easier to work with.

STEP 2. Once the gasket is pliable, unplug the refrigerator and begin working on one section

---

PREVENTION

Line 'Em Up

A sagging refrigerator or freezer door can prevent even a new gasket from sealing tightly—and that'll make the appliance work harder and wear out sooner. Fortunately, realigning one or both doors is a simple DIY fix. The exact details vary depending on the make and model, so consult your owner's manual or the manufacturer's website for specific instructions. Basically, though, all you need to do is pry off the hinge cap, loosen (don't remove!) the hinge screws, shove the door into alignment, and verify your success with a carpenter's level. Bear in mind that moving a lower door will affect the door above it, so you may have to adjust that one, too.

Note: *Remember to take everything off the door shelves before you start!*

at a time. Lift the inside edge of the old gasket and loosen (don't remove!) the hex head screws in the metal retainer strip. Then pull out the old gasket and slip the new one into place over the strip and tighten the screws. If there is no retainer strip, simply remove the existing gasket and snap the new one into place (it works much like the press-on seal on a plastic storage bag).

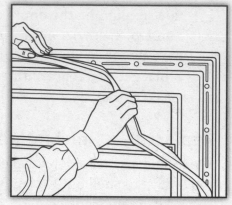

Remove the old gasket and install its replacement one section at a time.

STEP 3. To reduce gasket drag, rub a very thin layer of petroleum jelly onto the hinge side of the gasket—but not onto the other sides.

Fill That Freezer

A freezer, whether it's a stand-alone model or the one that's attached to your refrigerator, performs most efficiently with less wear and tear on its working parts (and on your electric bill) when it's filled to capacity. So at shopping time, buy a unit that's big enough to suit your needs—but no bigger. And when you do find yourself with empty freezer space, fill it pronto. Some of the fastest filler-uppers are milk cartons or plastic jugs filled with water. As a bonus, besides enhancing your freezer's performance, they'll keep your food cold longer during a power outage.

Don't Fill That Fridge!

At least not all the way. Unlike a freezer, a refrigerator does its best work when air can circulate freely around the contents. As a general rule, that means you don't want to use up any more than three-quarters of the inside space. Also be sure to keep beverages and moist foods covered tightly so that the moisture can't escape into the unit. The more humid the air is, the harder the refrigerator has to work to keep it cool.

Going Down!

If you're expecting a hurricane or other heavy weather that's likely to trigger a power outage, set your refrigerator and freezer at their lowest-possible temperatures. The colder your food is when the lights go out, the better chance it will have of staying chilled and edible until the power is restored.

A Freaky Fix for Funky-Tasting Drinks

Have your ice-cold drinks started tasting funny? If you answered, "Well, yeah, kinda," then I have another question for you: When is the last time you changed your refrigerator's water filter?

If you can't remember—or if you didn't even know your fridge had a water filter, you've found the root of your problem. Every refrigerator that has an automatic ice cube maker or water dispenser also has a water filter inside the cabinet. If it's not changed every three to six months, it gets clogged with impurities, the water flow slows down, and bacteria can breed in the cartridge. When the population gets high enough, the water not only begins to taste foul, but it can also make you sick. So get with the program: Stop by your local appliance store, pick up a package of replacement filters, and mark the change dates on your calendar. The location of the filter varies, but on most machines it's either near the top of the interior refrigerator compartment or behind the bottom grille. As always, you can find all the details in your owner's manual or on the manufacturer's website.

Store Help Close at Hand

When any appliance—large or small—goes on the blink, very often your owner's manual can help you solve the problem in a flash—but not if you can't find the danged booklet. So to save yourself a lot of time, frustration, and possibly money, corral all of your owner's manuals and product warranties in an accordion file folder, and stash it where you can easily get your hands on it.

WASHERS & DRYERS

Keep Your Washer Washing

Believe it or not, the way you handle your laundry can spell the difference between a washing machine that gives you years of trouble-free service and one that turns into a worthless pile of junk before its time. Whether you're laundering bed sheets, heavy-duty work clothes, or delicate lingerie, always follow these three important guidelines:

- **Wash full loads whenever possible.** A washing machine is designed to run most efficiently when it's set for its highest water level and filled to the maximum. Check your owner's manual to determine your washer's load capacity in pounds; depending on the model, it could be anywhere from 10 to 20 pounds. Then weigh a few loads to see how heavy the pile is. (It will vary considerably, of course, depending on whether you're washing, let's say, bath towels and blankets, or summer dresses and T-shirts.) In a very short time, you'll know just by looking when you've got the right amount to maximize your load.

- **Don't overload the machine.** Overloading strains the motor and therefore shortens your washer's life span. Regardless of the weight of your load, it should never be above the top of the agitator axle. Don't pack it down to cram in more stuff. In order to get clean, the fabric needs room to spin around freely inside the drum.

- **Handle partial or tiny loads properly.** For example, if you need to wash a single blouse or pair of jeans to wear tonight, set the water level on high—or at least at a higher level than you think you need. Without enough water in the tub, the fabric will get wrapped around the agitator. That'll cause wear and tear on the agitator seal—not to mention the damage all that twisting and turning will do to your duds. The extra pennies you might save on your water bill will be nothing compared to the cost of new clothes or a new washing machine!

Give Old Hoses the Heave-Ho

Old washer hoses can burst, spewing water all over the laundry room, and making a royal (and possibly expensive) mess of everything. So if your hoses are starting to show signs of experience, replace them with flexible, steel-wrapped versions that are guaranteed never to burst. (They're available in plumbing-supply stores or from your local plumber.) These babies aren't cheap, but take it from me: The peace of mind you gain will be worth every penny you spend!

Chump the Chips

When the enamel coating inside a washing machine or dryer drum gets chipped, nasty rust spots can form on the bare metal—and, before long, your laundry will be decked out in orangey streaks and splotches. So as soon as you notice the stains, trot down to your local hardware store and buy some porcelain enamel touch-up paint. Dab some onto each ding and let it dry, following the manufacturer's instructions. While you're at it, touch up any chips around the machines' doors, too, because rust can set in there when you move damp laundry.

AN OUNCE OF
PREVENTION

Don't Let Detergent Be Your Downfall

Using too much detergent won't get your clothes any cleaner—but it could make your wallet thinner. The damage could come in one of two ways: An overload of detergent will send the water spilling over the rim of the tub and into the drive motor, causing it to burn out. What's more, the suds can push small items over the top of the drum, where agitation will pull them into the outer tub and from there quite possibly into the water pump. Either scenario could land you with a bill for major repairs or a new washer.

So how much detergent should you use? Well, according to a veteran washer repairman I know, in most cases, you don't need to use any at all. Unless your clothes are visibly dirty, the agitation process is all it takes to get them spankin' clean. In cases when you do have actual dirt to deal with—or you just can't bear to go totally soapless—use half the amount recommended on the container.

2 Simple Keys to Longer Washer Life

As odd as it may seem, these two ultra-easy maneuvers can greatly extend the life of your washing machine:

▶ **Keep it on the level.** One of the simplest ways to prolong the life of your washing machine is to make sure that it stays on a level footing, from side to side and front to back. Otherwise, it may literally start to "walk" around the room with your clothes. Not only will that stroll damage your floor, but it can also wreak havoc on the machine's inner workings. To raise the legs of your washer, turn them clockwise. To lower them, turn them counterclockwise. It's that easy!

Level your wobbly washer by turning its legs.

▶ **Keep minerals on the move.** Minerals in your water can accumulate in your washer's hoses, inlet valves, and pump. Over time, the buildup restricts water flow, increases friction—and shortens the life of the machine. To fend off trouble, periodically fill the drum with cold water, add 1 cup of vinegar (no soap and no clothes), and run the washer through a complete cycle. Performing this ploy about every three months should keep your machine's mechanism free and clear, but do the job more frequently if your water is hard and/or you average more than eight to ten loads of laundry a week.

How to Winterize Your Washing Machine

When you're closing up a summer cottage, you can't just close the door and leave your washer in unheated quarters. If you do, any water that's left in the pipes, inlet valves, and pump could freeze and expand—and you could come home to a badly damaged appliance and some mighty unpleasant collateral damage. So before you take off, follow this simple hibernation-preparation routine:

STEP 1. Turn off the hot- and cold-water faucets.

STEP 2. Disconnect and remove both water inlet hoses (the ones that run from the water supply to the washer). Then shake them gently over a bucket to release any water.

STEP 3. Remove the drain hose from the wall and let any water drain into the bucket. Holding the hose in an upright position, pour 1 cup of propylene glycol (a.k.a. nontoxic RV-type) antifreeze into the opening. Keep the hose upright for at least 60 seconds while the antifreeze flows into the drum of the machine's pump.

STEP 4. Pour 1 quart of the same antifreeze into the washer and run it for two minutes or so (not for a full cycle). The water remaining in the system will mix with the antifreeze to coat the machine's interior.

STEP 5. Turn off the washer, unplug it, and put the two inlet hoses into the machine's tub.

STEP 6. When you open your summer place, reconnect the hoses and power supply. Then run the empty washer through a full cycle with detergent to clean out any residual antifreeze. Presto—you're good to go for another season!

> ## WELL, WHADDYA KNOW!
>
> No one knows exactly who invented the washing machine, or when. The basic concept goes back centuries, to the days when sailors on long sea voyages would stuff their soiled clothes into canvas sacks, tie them to ropes, toss them overboard, and let the ocean waves tumble them clean. One thing we do know is that as early as the 1700s, women in western Europe were doing the family laundry by putting it into a wooden box, which they filled with soap and water and tumbled by hand with a crank. The first electric clothes washers appeared in England and the United States in 1915 and featured a motor that rotated a metal drum pierced with holes. These pioneer machines still demanded a fair amount of hard labor, including hauling wet laundry out of the tub and running it through a wringer. Then in 1939, the first truly automatic washers came on the market, complete with pre-set water levels, variable sturdiness cycles, and timing controls. And housewives from coast to coast stood up and cheered!

HOMEMADE DRYER SHEETS

You can make your own dryer sheets and get the same anti-cling power of store-bought kinds, but at a fraction of the cost.

Liquid fabric softener
Water
Washcloth

In a medium-size mixing bowl, combine 1 part fabric softener and 1 part water. Mix thoroughly. Soak the washcloth in the mixture for a minute. Wring it out, and use it in your dryer to prevent static cling. You can reuse the washcloth several times before laundering it and recharging it with a new batch of softener.

Sure Doesn't Look Like a Window!

Expanding polyurethane foam, which comes in an aerosol can, is designed to seal up air leaks around window jambs. But it can also solve a common—and highly annoying—wash-day problem: water-supply pipes that bang against laundry room walls during the spin cycle, making a dickens of a noise in the process. To nix those knocks, pick up a can of the foam at your local hardware store and spray it onto the pipes where they meet the walls. It may not make your laundry chores any more fun, but it will make the process a lot quieter!

4 Signs That Your Dryer Is a Ticking Time Bomb

Clean your dryer vent or have a specialist inspect the system immediately if you experience one or more of these danger signals:

▶ **Your duds are still damp!** If drying time is increasing with each cycle, it means there's an overload of lint in the vent—and the machine has to work harder and longer to push the hot air out.

▶ **Ouch—that's hot!** If your clothes are much hotter than usual at the end of a cycle and/or the outside of the dryer is hot to the touch, it means the vent is not exhausting properly—and you could soon find yourself in very hot water.

▶ **The flap won't flip!** An outside vent that doesn't flip open when the dryer is running means that lint (or possibly some other obstruction) is restricting the airflow.

▶ **Something's burning!** If you detect a burning odor when you run your dryer, disconnect the thing instantly and don't even think of turning it back on until you've had the problem checked out and resolved.

Lose the Lint

Lint is a dryer's worst enemy, and it could be yours, too: When it builds up in the screens, filters, and vents, it can foul up the appliance's mechanism and shorten its life span. What's even worse, backed-up dryer lint is a leading cause of home fires. To keep your dryer on the job—and a roof over your head—attend to these routine chores:

• Clean out the lint screen after each load of laundry.

• Every month or so, wash the lint screen in warm, soapy water. If you use dryer sheets, scrub the screen with a retired toothbrush to remove the microscopic fibers and chemicals that these "miracle" softeners deposit in the filter (see note below).

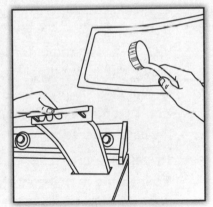

Wash your dryer's lint screen with a brush every month.

• Every four months or so, use a stiff-bristled brush to scrape built-up lint from the outdoor vent.

• Twice a year, remove the exhaust duct from the back of the dryer and have at it with a vacuum cleaner. (Don't forget to unplug the dryer before you start. If it's a gas-powered model, turn off the fuel valve.)

Note: *Dryer sheets can also work their way into your dryer's exhaust vent. So whenever you toss one in with a laundry load, be sure to remove it when the cycle's finished.*

When dryer lint is clogging up the dryer's screen and vent, it's a genuine household hazard. But elsewhere around the old homestead, it can be mighty useful stuff. Here's a trio of excellent examples:

Soil-building material. As long as the lint came from 100 percent cotton or linen fabric, toss it into your compost pile, or bury it in your garden or flower beds. In no time at all, it'll break down into valuable humus.

Fire-starter nuggets. First, cut a cardboard egg carton into 12 sections, and fill each one with dryer lint (but only from 100 percent cotton or linen fabric). Then melt down old candle stubs or paraffin sealers from homemade jelly, and pour a layer of melted wax on top of the lint. When it's time to light your fireplace, charcoal grill, or campfire, set one of your nuggets in the kindling or briquettes, and hold a match to the cardboard edge.

Tick eliminators. Soak any kind of lint in a pet shampoo that contains a flea and tick killer called permethrin. Then pull off a small wad, and push it into a toilet paper tube. When you've filled a half dozen or so tubes, set them out in brushy areas or other sheltered spots where tick-carrying mice are likely to find them. The mice will take the fuzzy stuff home to line their nests, and the disease-spreading ticks will be history!

Deal with the Seal

Just like every other front-opening appliance, your dryer has a seal (a.k.a. gasket) around the door to keep the inside air at the right temperature. If you notice dampness on the outside of the door, you'll know that replacement time is at hand. So jot down the model number of your dryer and pick up the appropriate seal and some heat-resistant adhesive at a local appliance-parts store. After that, the process is as easy as 1, 2, 3:

- Pull or (depending on the model) pry off the old seal.

- Remove any residual adhesive with mineral spirits.

- Attach the new seal using the new adhesive.

That's all there is to it!

HUMIDIFIERS & DEHUMIDIFIERS

Vinegar: The Drink of Air-Moisturizing Champions

Each kind of humidifier performs its work in a slightly different way, but to function at peak efficiency—without spewing germs into the air—they all need regular cleaning with vinegar. The exact procedure depends on the type of mechanism. Here's the deal:

▶ **Rotating.** Most portable humidifiers work by rotating either a permanent sponge or a disposable filter through a water reservoir and then past a fan that blows air through the wet object, thereby sending moisture into the room. In either case, you need to clean the water reservoir every day to keep mold from growing. To do that, first turn off the unit, empty the reservoir, and wash it with hot, soapy water, then rinse. Every third day, wipe the container with white vinegar to break up any mineral deposits. Rinse and dry the container before you fill 'er up with fresh water. **Note:** *If your humidifier has a disposable filter, check it every three days, and replace it as soon as it turns gray.*

▶ **Ultrasonic.** These babies use a metal diaphragm (a.k.a. nebulizer), which vibrates at an ultrasonic frequency to create a mist that's released into the air—along with bacteria and other crud if the water's not clean. So each time you fill the reservoir, wash it out with white vinegar. And at least once a week, remove any clogs in the diaphragm by soaking it in vinegar for 20 minutes, and then rinsing it with clear water.

▶ **Steam-powered.** This type boils water and mixes the resulting steam with air that cools it, in the process releasing a warm, gentle mist. It's the safest system from a health standpoint because the heat kills germs lickety-split. On the downside, mineral deposits tend to build up in the boiling chamber, decreasing the unit's efficiency (and, therefore, its life span). The simple solution: Clean that cavern every week or so with a soft brush dipped in a half-and-half mixture of vinegar and water.

3 Keys to a Healthy Dehumidifier

A dehumidifier works just like an air conditioner: It uses a fan to draw air over cold evaporator coils, and a condenser pulls water out of the air. Like an AC unit, a dehumidifier works better and lasts longer if you keep its inside parts in tip-top shape. Here's how:

- Once a day (more often in humid weather), empty the water container so that it doesn't overflow or become stagnant. Better yet, install a hose so the machine empties into a floor drain.

- At least once a month, wash the water container and the filter in warm water with a few drops of dishwashing liquid mixed in. Let both bathers dry completely before putting them back on the job. (If the filter is showing signs of wear, replace it.)

- At the beginning of each season, lubricate the fan motor per the owner's manual instructions. No manual? Then check for lubrication ports in the motor and add a drop or two of SAE 20 oil to each opening.

It's an Inside Job

Always keep your windows closed when your dehumidifier is running. Otherwise, it'll try to dry up all the air coming in from the great outdoors—and die an early death from the struggle. Also close the doors to any rooms that are not on the machine's target list, and make sure your clothes dryer is not vented into the basement or wherever the dehumidifier is stationed.

Higher Humidity Helps Your Furnace Live Longer...

And lowers your heating bills, too! Adding even a small portable humidifier to your household can cut your furnace's on-duty hours, thereby reducing wear and tear. How so? Because increasing the air's humidity in the winter makes people feel comfortable at lower temperatures. For example, when the air is dry, most folks prefer a temperature that's between 75° and 80°F. But when the relative humidity is 50 percent, that same crowd will be comfortable at 70°F— so your heating system won't have to work so hard.

VACUUM CLEANERS

When the Suction Goes South...

There's usually a quick and simple fix. Of course, the remedy depends on what the problem is. Here are the possibilities:

▶ **A clogged brush.** Very often, a reduction in cleaning power is caused by string, thread, or hair that's gotten wound up in the rollers. So just cut through the tangled mess with a seam ripper or sharp scissors and pull out the strands.

▶ **A blocked hose.** If suction power plummets when you're using a cylinder (a.k.a. canister) model, you may have sucked up something that's stuck in the hose. Turn off the cleaner and start removing the hose, section by section, beginning with the one farthest from the canister. After you remove each one, switch the machine back on and check the suction. If it springs back to life, you'll know you've got a blockage in the segment that you've just removed. See "Clear a Hose with a Hose" on page 264 for further marching orders.

▶ **Full or torn dust bag.** This is a no-brainer: Toss the thing out and put in a new one. If you don't have any, go out and buy some—don't try to patch a ripped bag with tape! These sacks are not meant to be reused.

▶ **Clogged filters.** If you're using a bagless vacuum cleaner, either an upright or canister type (and you've emptied the dust container), the filters are the most likely culprits. The solution: Clean the nasty things or—easier and more pleasant by far—replace them.

▶ **Splits in the hose.** If you've already investigated all of the above possibilities and the suction is still sluggish, carefully inspect the hose for cracks or slits. Even a barely visible opening can greatly reduce the machine's pulling power. Cover any damaged areas with duct tape, pressing it firmly between the ridges if the hose is corrugated.

Replacing a Broken Drive Belt

When your vacuum cleaner's beater bar (the roller with brushes) suddenly stops rotating, the cause is almost always a broken or jammed drive belt. Having it replaced will cost you a pretty penny at a repair shop, but a new belt should cost you only a few bucks and installing it is a simple DIY fix. Here's the ultra-easy four-step routine:

STEP 1. Pick up a new belt at a hardware or appliance-parts store. If yours isn't in the inventory, check the manufacturer's website.

STEP 2. Unplug the vacuum, remove the cover over the sweeper section, and slide the roller out of the housing.

STEP 3. Slip the new belt in place, using a screwdriver to pull the belt over the drive pin and, at the same time, push the roller back into the housing.

STEP 4. Screw the cover plate back on, plug in the machine, and you're back in business.

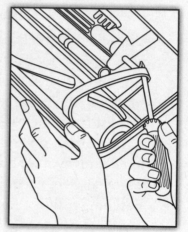

Use a screwdriver to pull the new belt over the drive pin.

Clear a Hose with a Hose

The most effective way to clear a blockage from your vacuum cleaner hose is to shove a dowel, broom handle, or nice, long stick in there, right? *Wrong!* That could easily ding the hose, and then you'll have more trouble on your hands than you have already. Instead, use a strong but gentle alternative: a garden hose. First, detach the blocked hose from the vacuum cleaner and feed the garden hose into it until you reach the clog. Then give it a few gentle shoves. If it refuses to budge, pull your pusher out and try again from the other end. Keep at it, alternating ends until the channel is free and clear.

If nothing you can do will budge the obstacle, simply slice into the hose at the site of the blockage, pull the troublemaker out, and repair the incision with duct tape.

Listen Up!

A loss of suction power isn't the only thing that could indicate an obstruction in your vacuum cleaner. If the sound abruptly leaps to a higher pitch, unplug the machine and immediately inspect the filters, bag, and hose for uninvited guests.

Don't Fill 'Er to the Top!

A fully loaded vacuum cleaner bag (or dust container on bagless models) puts excess strain on the motor and makes it more likely to go belly-up before its time. So make it a point to empty those dirt collectors when they reach about the three-quarters mark.

SMALL APPLIANCES

The Problem Could Be the Plug

If an appliance starts working intermittently, there could be all sorts of reasons. But there's a good chance that it simply needs a new plug—and you can supply one in a matter of minutes. First, cut off the old plug, taking a few inches of cord with it so you can buy the right version at the hardware store. When you get home, your DIY mission depends on which of these two kinds of cord you're working with:

- **Flat.** You're really in luck here because you can buy quick-connect plugs that make a perfect connection with no tools required. Just slip the new plug cover over the cord. Spread the prongs on the inner piece to open it up, and shove the cord into it. Then squeeze the prongs closed. Tiny spikes inside will pierce the insulation and dig into the wire to complete the connection. Slip the cover in place, and you're good to go.

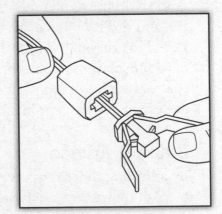

Slip the cord into the inner plug and slide the cover over it.

- **Round.** Pull the cord through the opening in the plug. Slice the cord down the middle for about 4 inches and remove the insulation. Tie the two wires into an Underwriter's knot, as shown in the illustration. Then pull the cord flush with the top of the plug and pop the cover in place over the prongs.

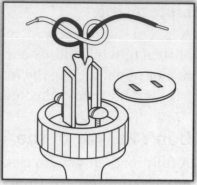

Slit the cord, and tie the two wires into an Underwriter's knot.

Detachable Damage Control

When an appliance with a detachable power cord starts working sporadically, the problem may be the plug that goes into the device rather than into the wall. If the plug is held together with screws, as many are, open it up and tighten the connections inside. Then test it. If it still fails to perform—or if you couldn't get it open to begin with—order a replacement cord from the manufacturer. And from now on, keep it attached to the appliance. Plugging it in and pulling it out time and again puts undue wear on both the plug and the socket.

Loose Cords Live Longer

And so do the appliances they're attached to. That's because when a power cord is coiled or wrapped up while a device is turned on, the heat can't dissipate properly. If it builds up enough, it could melt the cord's insulation—or even start a fire. As you might expect, appliances that draw a lot of amps, like toasters, hair dryers, and space heaters, are especially susceptible to coiled-cord catastrophes.

Blanket Advice

By adopting these two simple habits, you can keep your electric blanket delivering toasty warmth for years: Never tuck the wired portions under the mattress, and don't put anything heavy on top of the blanket—whether it's on your bed or in storage. If you do, you could easily damage the delicate wires that run through the fabric, and that in turn will reduce the blanket's heating power and send it into early retirement—or to an early grave.

A Terminal Case

Is your electric blanket refusing to heat up—even though you've treated it with kid gloves for its whole life? If so, it could be that the terminals on the plug are dirty. Just sand them lightly with extra-fine-grit sandpaper, and they should perk right up. The same trick works to put a heating pad back on track when it's running too hot or too cold. In this case, you want to sand the switch contacts on the temperature-control unit.

Get Rid of a Bitter Brew

If your electric coffeemaker is producing java that tastes bitter or sour, here's your quick fix:

- ▶ Fill the well to capacity with a half-and-half solution of water and white vinegar.

- ▶ Install an empty filter to catch any crud that comes out, and run the machine through a normal brewing cycle.

- ▶ "Brew" three or four batches of clear, fresh water to remove all traces of vinegar.

As you might expect, how often you need to perform this coffee-maker cleaning routine depends on the quality of the water you use and how many pots of coffee you make—so just trust your taste buds to tell you when it's time.

Appliance cords can make a tangled mess of drawers or—worse—open shelves or countertops. But resist the temptation to bunch each cord up and fasten it snugly with a twist tie. That tight bond could weaken and break the inside wires. Instead, loosely fold up the cords and stuff them into empty toilet paper tubes. Presto—end of mess with no risk of internal damage! (If plain old cardboard is too raw-looking for your taste, cover each tube with wrapping paper or contact paper that blends with your decor.)

Bitter Brew, Take 2

If your coffee tastes bitter—and you grind your own beans—the foul taste may not be the fault of your coffeemaker. It could be that residue from all those grinding sessions has accumulated under the blades. To make sure that aging dust doesn't wind up in your mug, run a cup of raw white rice through the grinder once a month.

Caring for Your Keurig

Keurig® brewers have attracted a large and loyal following because of their ability to produce a single cup of coffee, tea, or hot chocolate at the press of a button. The basics to keeping your Keurig crankin' out cuppas couldn't be simpler. Here's the routine:

- **Clean it regularly.** Every week or so, wipe down the outside with baking soda (see "Think Inside the Box" on page 270), and wash the water reservoir and its lid in warm, soapy water. The drip tray, the funnel, and the piece that holds the K-Cup® can go right in the dishwasher. Also use a paper clip or toothpick to remove any clogs that may be building in the unit's exit needle.

- **De-scale it.** Periodically fill the water reservoir halfway with white vinegar and run the brewer (minus K-Cups) through several brewing cycles until the container is empty. Then rinse it, fill it with clear water, and run it again until all the water is gone. As with regular coffeemakers, how often you need to perform this chore depends on how much you use the machine and how hard your water is. Some models have an indicator light that goes on when it's time for de-scaling.

CALL A PRO

If your coffeemaker (or other small appliance) is still under warranty, do not attempt any DIY repairs before you check with the manufacturer or read the fine print in your owner's manual. In some cases, the appliance will even feature a warning against owner servicing on the baseplate or back of the device. Any fiddling could instantly make your warranty null and void.

Restart the Drip

When the water in the top of your drip coffeemaker stops trickling down or it comes out in spurts, the problem is probably clogged holes at the base of the water tank (a.k.a. spread plate) and/or the drip control bar. In most cases, it's a fast and easy fix: Just turn the coffeemaker upside down and use a toothpick or a straightened paper clip to unplug the holes in both components. If that doesn't do the trick, you may be able to order replacements from the manufacturer or from an online appliance-parts dealer. To find one, search online for "coffeemaker replacement parts."

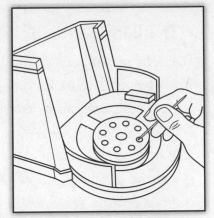

With the coffeemaker turned upside down, clear out clogged holes with a toothpick or straightened paper clip.

Guidelines for Great Grinding . . .

And a longer life for your coffee grinder. There's nothing like the taste of fresh-ground coffee. But to keep that supply coming, remember these three simple operating rules:

▶ **Press and release.** Grinding for more than 30 seconds at a time, or for more than 60 seconds in any five-minute period, can overheat the motor. So always use a pulse action, pressing and releasing the switch, so the mechanism starts and stops every few seconds.

▶ **Grind warm beans.** If you store your coffee beans in the freezer, let them come to room temperature before grinding them. They'll break up more easily and evenly, putting less strain on the motor. Never run an empty grinder. When no beans are in the bowl, the blades can spin too fast and damage the motor.

▶ **Don't give it a bath!** Immersing the body of a coffee grinder—or any other small appliance—in water is the surest route to its early death. Instead, use a soft cloth to wipe out the bowl and a toothbrush to clean the blades. (Of course, it's perfectly okay to wash the plastic lid in warm, soapy water.)

Blender Blades Can Lose Their Bite

If your blender takes forever (or so it seems) to whirl your fruit into a smoothie, the most likely reason is that built-up sediment is obstructing the blades. This stuff is all but impossible to remove with routine cleaning, so try this extra-strength approach: Mix ½ cup of baking soda with ½ cup of warm water, pour the mixture into the blender, and let it sit overnight. In the morning, run the blender at full speed for 30 seconds or so.

If that doesn't restore the machine's former oomph, it probably means that food residue has seeped past the seal and into the motor's bearings, causing the lubricant to congeal. So take the blade assembly apart and clean it in hot, soapy water. Dry it thoroughly, and lubricate it with mineral oil.

Note: *Your owner's manual should show you the procedure for disassembling your particular model's blade system. If it doesn't—or if you don't have the manual—check the manufacturer's website for guidance.*

You Can't Keep Good Bread Down

It's frustrating, all right: You're trying to make toast, but the "elevator" refuses to stay at the bottom floor of the machine. It could be simply that the GFCI outlet has switched into "no-go" mode, but if you've already ruled out that cause, the problem could be that crumbs have built up between the toast holder and the electromagnet that keeps it in the down (a.k.a. toasting) position. One of these two maneuvers should put that holding force back in action:

- With the toaster unplugged, reach into its innards with a new, dry toothbrush or paintbrush and loosen the crumbs. Hold the toaster upside down over the garbage disposal or trash can and shake it hard to release the residue. Then plug the machine back in and push the "Down" button. Still a no go? Try this:

- If your toaster's cover is removable, take it off. You'll see the electromagnet—the large block at the bottom of the toaster. Clean the top of the magnet and the bottom of the toast holder with a soft cloth moistened with rubbing alcohol. Replace the cover, plug the toaster in, and retest the button. If the mechanism still doesn't hold, bid your no-longer-trusty toaster a fond farewell.

Ammonia Axes Toaster-Oven Troubles

Whether your annoying challenge is on the inside or the outside of your toaster oven, old-fashioned ammonia can save the day.

▶ **Inside.** Got stuck-on food that you can't scrape off? Unplug the oven and let it cool down. Then put a bowl of full-strength ammonia inside, close the door, and leave it overnight. Come morning, remove the bowl, and wipe the inside of the appliance with a soft, damp cloth. Let the oven air out completely before using it again.

▶ **Outside.** We've all been there: A plastic bread bag melts on the outside of the toaster oven. Again, pull the plug and wait until the appliance is completely cool. Then cover the melted bag with a cloth soaked in ammonia. Wait a few minutes, and scrape the stuff off with a plastic scraper or plastic scouring pad.

AN OUNCE OF
PREVENTION

Be Careful What You Process

Never use a food processor to chop up anything that's really hard, like coffee beans, vanilla beans, raw grains, or ice. That can—and over time will—damage the blades. Likewise, avoid gummy or sticky foods, such as dried fruits, which can clog up the works and strain the motor. No matter what you're processing, cut it into small chunks, add the pieces a few at a time, and don't fill the bowl beyond the level recommended in your owner's manual. Otherwise, the motor will have to work harder than it needs to, and there's a chance that it'll opt for an early retirement.

Pertinent Problem-Solving Ploys for Small Appliances

It's a sad but true fact of 21st-century life that small appliances have become disposable items. Even if you can find someone to fix whatever problem your machine is having, if the gizmo costs less than 100 dollars, it's all but guaranteed that the service charge will outweigh the price of a new one. But that doesn't mean you have to toss an ailing appliance out the window! Quite often, a simple tweak will put it right back on track—or prevent a derailment to begin with. Here's a roundup of quick fixes for some of the most common pint-size helpers:

Heat-Control Headaches

When it comes to the heat controls, Murphy's Law is in full effect: The danged thing always burns out just when you most need to use the appliance. Luckily, help may be close at hand. Before you toss (let's say) your electric frying pan, try plugging in the heat control from a waffle iron, griddle, electric wok, or slow cooker. If the sensing element and terminals match, that pan'll be fit to fry again.

Rampaging Rust Spots

Sooner or later a non-stainless-steel electric wok or frying pan is bound to pick up rust spots. To make them vanish, dip the end of a cork in scouring powder, and rub the marks away. Wash the pan with warm, soapy water (but don't immerse it!), then dry it thoroughly, and season the surface with a thin coat of mineral oil.

An Unwaxed Waffle Iron

Your brunch guests are due in half an hour and your waffle iron's nonstick surface has given up the ghost. No problem! Just put a layer of wax paper between the plates of the appliance for a few minutes while it heats up. The wax will be transferred to the surface, and your waffles will pop out as usual. (This isn't a permanent fix, but it will get you through a culinary crisis.)

A Broken Cord

One of the quickest ways to send any small appliance to its grave is to yank on its power cord to disengage the plug from its socket. Even a gentle tug puts undue strain on the wires, and eventually they'll fray. So always grip the plug and pull it straight out of the socket.

1 2 3 4 5 6 7 8 9 10 12 13 14

Furniture

We can all take comfort knowing that our furniture will never suffer the kinds of mechanical problems that can make electric appliances give up the ghost. But chairs, couches, and tables can—and routinely do—collect their own fair share of woes in the form of scrapes, scratches, stains, and broken legs (or seats). The good news is that, armed with the fabulous formulas, timely tricks, and sound strategies coming up, you can fix or head off most of those mishaps.

WOODEN FURNITURE

Your Table Has a Drinking Problem

When you spill beer, white wine, or any other alcoholic beverage on wooden furniture, a stain can form almost instantly. So act fast! Wipe up the spill immediately, and rub the spot vigorously with the palm of your hand. Then dip a soft cloth in a little furniture polish, rub the area gently, and wipe it clean with a dry cloth.

Ring around the Table

No matter how often we remind our nearest and dearest to use coasters and napkins, those white circles always seem to appear, as if by magic. If the ring is new, simply put a little mayonnaise, white (not gel!) toothpaste, or salad oil on a soft cloth. Then rub your homemade weapon of choice over the spot, and wipe it dry with a soft, clean cloth. For a really stubborn stain, dip a soft cloth in hot water with 2 or 3 drops of ammonia added to it. Wring out the cloth well, and rub the ring lightly to make it disappear.

HOMEMADE FURNITURE POLISH

This classic mixture is as old as the hills, but it cleans and shines wooden furniture as well as any newfangled polish!

½ cup of linseed oil
½ cup of malt vinegar
1 ½ tsp. of lemon or lavender oil

Mix all of the ingredients together in a clean glass jar with a screw-on lid. Then wipe the polish onto the wood with a soft, clean cotton cloth. Buff to a shine with a second cloth.

Paper on the Table

Got paper stuck to a wooden tabletop—courtesy, perhaps, of a spill that hasn't been mopped up promptly? No problem! Dampen the paper with baby oil, give it a few minutes to soak in, and you'll be able to pull it right off.

What's My Line?

With the exception of water rings (see "Ring around the Table" on page 273), white marks on wood furniture are generally caused by one of three things: liquids containing alcohol, heat, or water. You should be able to get rid of them for good, but your method will vary with the amount of damage done. Here's a trio of potential fixes:

▶ **Ashes.** Dip a dry, clean cloth in a half-and-half mixture of cigarette or wood ashes and either lemon juice or salad oil (not both). Wring the cloth out, and rub the white mark vigorously.

▶ **Ammonia.** This trick is especially effective for alcohol marks. Dip a soft, clean cloth in warm, sudsy water and then add a few drops of ammonia. Wring out the cloth, and rub the white mark gently. Dry with another soft, clean cloth.

▶ **Get serious.** If the methods above don't budge the spots, call out the big guns: Moisten a soft cloth with lighter fluid, followed by a mix of salad oil and rottenstone. Wring out the cloth, and rub the white mark gently. Then wipe it dry with a soft, clean cloth. **Note:** *Rottenstone is a silica-based abrasive that's like pumice, but softer in texture. It is not hazardous, but it can be rough on the hands, so wear gloves when you're working with it.*

Don't Burn, Baby!

There are few sorrier sights than a burn mark on a beautiful wooden table. To get rid of the nasty thing, you have two choices:

- Rub the burn with a paste made of baking soda and boiled linseed oil, working with the grain until the spot disappears.

- If that doesn't work, dip a cotton swab in paint thinner, dab the burn gently, and then scrape it away. Drip a bit of clear nail polish into the dent. Let it set for a few minutes, then add more nail polish until the indentation is level with the rest of the table.

Felt Pads Can Fool You

Sticking self-adhesive felt pads on the bottoms of lamps, vases, and other potential scratch makers seems like the ideal way to protect the finish on your tabletops. There's just one problem: Sometimes the adhesive can seep through the felt and stain the wood surface. And, unfortunately, it's all but impossible to tell what furniture may be susceptible to the glue. So play it safe: Get some felt at a craft or fabric store and cut it to whatever sizes and shapes you prefer. There's no real need to attach the pads to the objects' bottoms, but if doing that makes you feel more secure, use plain white glue (such as Elmer's®) or double-sided tape.

Removing Dripped Wax from a Tabletop

Glowing candles are a homey, comforting sight—until they drip all over one of your favorite tables. The good news is that waving wax on its way is easy.

STEP 1. Scrape as much of it as possible off the furniture with a plastic scraper or an old credit card. (This is a great use for those cards that keep showing up, uninvited, in the mail!)

STEP 2. Put a few ice cubes into a plastic bag, and hold it on the remaining wax. The stuff will crumble, and you can wipe it away. Just make sure to also wipe away any moisture from the ice bag, or you'll have *real* spots on your table!

This trick works just as well with chewing gum as it does with wax.

When it comes to cleaning and polishing wooden furniture, not all rags are created equal. The best ones are made of the same stuff you like to have next to your skin: Soft, absorbent, 100 percent cotton. And that gives you a great chance to give new life to some of your favorite old belongings—such as:

- Diapers
- Dishcloths and tablecloths
- Flannel shirts, pajamas, and sheets
- Napkins
- Percale sheets and pillowcases
- Sweaters and all-cotton sweatshirts
- Terry cloth towels and bathrobes
- T-shirts

Grease Is the Word

Getting rid of grease stains can be tricky because the longer they sit, the tougher it is to remove them. But these methods will arm you with the artillery you need to battle just about any kind of greasy goo. Here's the plan of attack:

▶ **If you're Johnny-on-the-spot** when grease and your furniture get together, grab some salt pronto and pour it over the spill. Let it sit for a few minutes to absorb the mess, then gently wipe it away with a soft cloth.

▶ **If the stains attacked behind your back,** place a blotter (or folded towel) over the spot, and press with a warm iron until the mark disappears.

▶ **If heat doesn't do the trick,** turn to mineral spirits. Saturate the area with the spirits, and set an old absorbent cloth over it to soak up the grease. You may have to repeat this exercise a few times, but I guarantee it'll send that grease packin' for good!

Hit the Nail on the Head

When you spill a little nail polish on a tabletop, you should simply reach for the nail polish remover, right? *Wrong*! That'll ruin your furniture's finish in a flash! Instead, blot the stain immediately with a soft cloth or blotting paper. Then rub the spot with extra-fine steel wool dipped in furniture wax, and wipe dry.

Inky Dinky Do

When ink leaks or spills onto your wood table or desk, soak up the excess fluid immediately. Then clean the surface with a damp cloth. Water-soluble ink should disappear. If the ink's not water-soluble, it will probably leave a stain. To remove it, mix rottenstone with enough vegetable oil to make a paste. Rub the mixture into the mark with a soft, clean cloth, then dry with another soft, clean cloth. (For more on rottenstone, see "What's My Line?" on page 274.)

Removing Spilled Paint from a Tabletop

You may not cry over spilled milk, but spilled paint could be another story. If the paint's still wet, it's a snap to save the day: Just wipe away water-based paint with a damp cloth. For oil-based paints, use mineral spirits. If the paint has had time to dry, here's your three-step mission:

STEP 1. Cover it with boiled linseed oil and let it stand until the paint has softened.

STEP 2. Remove it with a cloth covered in still more boiled linseed oil.

STEP 3. Finally, scrape off any residue with a plastic scraper.

Whatever you do, don't use paint remover—it'll ruin your finish faster than you can say "Whoa, Nellie!"

If your dinged, broken, blemished, or wobbly piece of furniture is a valuable antique or artisan-made item, don't try any DIY tricks. Instead, ask a reputable antique dealer to recommend a professional furniture restorer who can get your treasure back in shape. In the case of a contemporary gem, if at all possible, have the item's creator perform any repairs. An original, one-of-a-kind piece of furniture can plummet in value (for both insurance and resale purposes) if anyone other than the originating artisan works on it. The same goes for original works of art and high-end crafts such as wood carvings and textiles.

CALL A PRO

3 Slick Tricks for Treating Marble Stains

Marble-topped tables are magnets for all kinds of stains. Just follow these de-magnetizing guidelines:

Beverages. Mix 1 part 3% hydrogen peroxide to 4 parts water. Dip a sponge in the solution and rub the spot, then wipe it off. Repeat as necessary until the mark has vanished. Make sure you act fast to prevent the fluid from soaking in!

Non-beverage stains. Cover the spot with salt and wait a minute or two for the salt to absorb the liquid. Then brush it away and add more. If the salt hasn't soaked up the stain after three or four tries, move on to the stubborn-stain treatment below.

Stubborn stains. Cover the area with salt and pour sour milk on top of that. Let it sit for two to three days, and wipe it off with a soft, damp cotton cloth.

Note: *If you don't have any sour milk on hand, mix 1 tablespoon of vinegar with enough fresh milk to make a cup. Let it stand about five minutes to thicken.*

6 Winning Ways to Nix Nicks

When a tabletop, dresser, or any other piece of wooden furniture picks up a shallow scratch, dust the piece off, and then reach for one of these down-home remedies:

- **Serve it salad dressing.** Mix ¼ cup of vinegar and ¾ cup of olive oil together, and wipe it onto the surface with a soft, clean cloth.

- **Color it gone.** Hide a scratch by rubbing it with shoe polish, an eyebrow pencil, or a crayon that matches the color of the wood.

- **Condition it.** Pour a few drops of hair conditioner on a cotton cloth, rub the wood, and buff with a second cloth. It'll hide the scratches and give the wood a soft glow.

- **Say "Nuts!"** Rub fresh walnut or pecan meat over the ding, or apply a little walnut oil.

- **Grab the iodine.** To heal a scratch in dark-colored wood, dip a cotton swab into the bottle, and dab that ding away.

- **Pass the peanut butter.** Smear a little onto the mark, leave it for 60 minutes or so, then wipe it off and buff the area.

Note: *Test any of these tricks in a hidden spot first.*

Demolish Deeper Dings

If your wood's wound is a little too deep for a simple rubdown (see "6 Winning Ways to Nix Nicks," at left), go at it with one of these more intensive cures:

▶ Grate a crayon into a bowl, and put it in the microwave or into a pan of boiling water to melt the wax. Then dribble the wax into the gouge and smooth it out with a flat knife or plastic scraper. If necessary, mix shavings from several crayons to get the right shade for your wood.

▶ Lay a damp dish towel over the dent and gently run a warm iron over it. Work slowly, and peek under the towel periodically to make sure you don't scorch the wood. The moist heat should plump up the wood fibers enough to even out the surface.

Tighten Up Wobbly Chair Legs

Continuing to use a wooden chair (or stool) that has loose legs can send the piece downhill fast. So at the first sign of a wobble, take that seat out of service until you have time to perform this four-step surgical procedure:

STEP 1. Pull out each stretcher where it joins a shaky leg. (If you need help getting it out, tap the leg gently with a rubber mallet—never with a regular metal hammer.) Then sand or scrape off the old glue from the stretcher end and its socket. Wipe off any remaining glue using a half-and-half solution of vinegar and warm water and let the wood dry thoroughly.

STEP 2. Test-fit the joints. If any stretcher moves in its opening, glue a small strip of cotton to the end to build it up a tad.

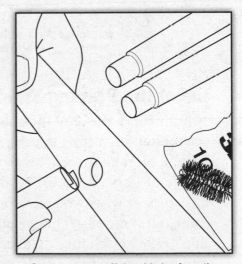

Sand or scrape off the old glue from the stretcher and its socket.

STEP 3. Apply carpenter's glue to both surfaces of the joint, and shove the stretcher end (a.k.a. the tenon) into place. Use a clean, damp cloth to wipe away the glue that oozes out of the socket.

STEP 4. To hold the joints in place while the glue dries, use bungee cords or a web (a.k.a. band) clamp, available in hardware stores. Easier yet, buckle a couple of belts together, wrap them around the chair's legs, and fasten them as tightly as you can. Let the glue dry for at least 24 hours before removing the clamp.

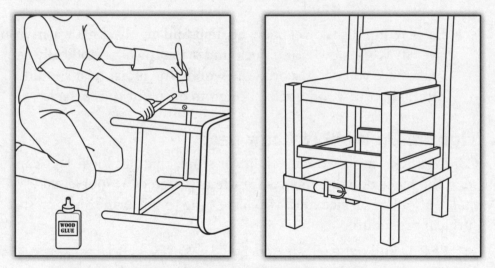

Apply carpenter's glue to both surfaces of the joint, then strap two belts together to hold the joints in place while it dries.

Level the Playing Field

A floor that's the least bit unlevel can add undue strain to the joints of wooden furniture, putting it out of commission before its time. As you might expect, a heavyweight champ like a china cabinet, hutch, or bookcase is especially vulnerable. If the piece rocks on its base or feet when you push on it, you know you've got a problem. But even if it doesn't budge an inch and it looks perfectly straight, don't take any chances: Check the position with a carpenter's level, and if it's out of kilter, slide a shim under one side or under one or two legs to put the load on an even keel.

Slide, Darn Ya, Slide!

When you furnish your rooms with old wooden furniture, it's a frustrating fact of life that the drawers don't always glide in and out as smoothly as you'd like. And sometimes they won't budge at all. So what do you do to put them back into full action? It depends on how stubborn they are. Here are two options:

- Many times, you can coax a reluctant drawer into gliding smoothly by rubbing the runners with a bar of bath soap. If that doesn't do the trick, sand the runners with fine-grit sandpaper, and reapply the soap.

- If the drawer constantly sticks all the way around, clean and sand all of the outside surfaces. Coat them with shellac (available in many hardware stores), let it dry, and rub the entire exterior of the drawer with paraffin. From then on, you'll have smooth sailin'!

POWERFUL POTIONS

SHELLAC SHAPE-UP FORMULA

You never see shellac finishes on newer furniture, but it's hot stuff at flea markets and in vintage-furniture stores. If you've got some shellacked treasures at your place, give them a coat of this fabulous formula once a year or so. In between coats, dust the pieces with a dry cloth or your vacuum cleaner's brush attachment. Don't ever use water or commercial furniture polish to clean a shellac finish because moisture—even high humidity—tends to make the stuff sticky.

1 part boiled linseed oil
1 part mineral spirits

Mix the ingredients together in a small bucket, then dip a sponge or soft cotton cloth into the solution and rub it evenly over the wood surface. (Make sure you wear gloves.) Wipe away the excess with a soft, dry cloth. If it's been more than a year since you've cleaned the furniture—or if you've just acquired a piece that hasn't seen loving care in a while—you may need to repeat the process to remove all of the dirt. When you're through, wash your gloves and cleaning cloths in hot, soapy water.

WOOD VENEER

Beat Bubble Trouble on the Double

It's a common problem with veneered furniture: A patch of the glue that holds the topper to its base wood gives out and a bubble pops up on the spot. One of these two ploys should heal that blister in a hurry:

▶ **Iron it out.** The glue on older veneer can usually be reactivated with an iron set on medium heat. Lay a damp towel over the bubble, press the iron onto the cloth, hold it for a few seconds, then remove it. Repeat the process two more times. If the surface is flat, take away the towel, and hold the iron directly on the veneer for two seconds—no longer, or you could damage the finish!

▶ **Lance the blister.** Using a utility knife, slice into the bubble along the grain. Slide yellow carpenter's glue under the veneer with a toothpick. Press down lightly, and wipe off any excess glue. Lay a sheet of wax paper over the incision, topped with a few heavy books, and let the glue dry overnight.

AN OUNCE OF
PREVENTION

Fragile—Handle with Care!

Veneered furniture is far more delicate than its solid wood counterparts. Dings, water rings, and other blemishes are harder to remove or camouflage. So to keep your pieces looking their best, follow these guidelines:

• Dust frequently, using a barely damp cotton or microfiber cloth. Immediately dry the surface with an all-cotton cloth. To remove dirt, add a drop of mild soap (such as Murphy® Oil Soap) to the water.

• Don't use any furniture polish that contains wax, silicone, or ammonia. It could destroy the finish or cause the veneer to crack, split, and fade.

• Never set hot, heavy, wet, or rough-bottomed objects directly on the veneer surface—always use protective pads. And wipe up spills *immediately*.

• Avoid placing veneered pieces in very sunny spots. If that's not an option, use shades or curtains to provide protection from the sun's rays.

• Whenever you need to move veneered furniture, wrap it snugly in thick, sturdy mover's pads.

We Have Liftoff!

But in this case, it's nothing to cheer about: A corner of the veneer on your favorite tabletop has parted company from its base wood. Never fear—you can arrange a reunion in a jiffy. Here's all you need to do:

STEP 1. To soften the veneer slightly (so it won't break off as you work on it), lay a damp towel over the loosened area. Set an iron on "Low," and hold it lightly on the terry cloth, checking every 5 to 10 seconds to make sure you're not scorching the veneer. Continue until it's pliable.

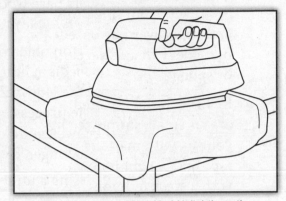

Set an iron on "Low" and hold it lightly on the towel-covered veneer to make it pliable.

STEP 2. Gently reach under the raised corner and scrape away the old glue with a utility knife or single-edge razor blade. (Don't lift the veneer up any farther than it is already, or—even though it's been softened—it could snap right off!) Clean both bonding surfaces with benzene or naphtha to remove any remaining glue. Finally, sand the surfaces lightly with fine-grit sandpaper, and wipe them with a soft cloth moistened with mineral spirits. (Yes, I know this routine sounds like overkill, but trust me—any old glue that's left on either the wood or the veneer will reject the new adhesive, and you'll be right back where you started!)

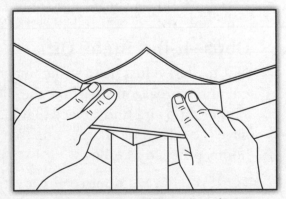

Sand both surfaces with fine-grit sandpaper.

STEP 3. Use a toothpick or wooden craft stick to spread carpenter's glue onto the wooden substrate. Press the veneer down, smooth it out with your fingertips, and wipe away any oozed-out glue with a damp cloth or sponge.

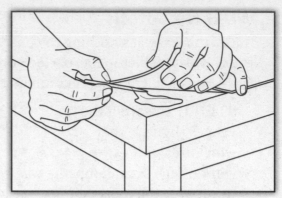

Spread carpenter's glue onto the wooden base with a toothpick or craft stick.

STEP 4. If the repaired area is small, simply secure your fix with masking tape and weight it down with a stack of books. To attach a larger space, cover it with wax paper, top it with a piece of wood that hangs over the edges just a tad, and fasten it on with C-clamps. (If your clamps don't have rubber pads, put wood scraps or cardboard between the clamp and the bottom surface of the tabletop.) Let it sit overnight. Come morning, remove the hardware and admire your job well done!

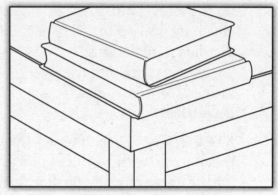

Secure the repaired area overnight with C-clamps or a stack of books.

Oops—It Did Break Off!

Not to worry! Just use a straightedge and utility knife to make a clean cut at the break-off site. Take the sliced-off triangle to a woodworking-supply shop and find a piece that matches it as closely as possible, or have the salesperson order one (see the note at right). When you get home, proceed as follows:

- If you haven't done so already, remove the old glue from the wooden substrate (see Step 2 of "We Have Liftoff!" on page 283).

- Using a sharp utility knife or a veneer saw, cut a piece of veneer in the same shape as the blank space, but a bit larger, so it hangs over the edges a little.

- Apply a thin coat of carpenter's glue to the wood surface, and quickly press the patch in place. Wipe off any excess glue with a damp cloth. Then cover the area with wax paper and weight it down overnight. Come morning, sand off the overhanging edges.

Note: *At a woodworking shop, you should be able to compare your piece to various samples before you place your order. But matching colors online is a bit of a gamble. So if your repair site is small, order a sample kit that contains a variety of shades. Most likely, there will be a piece in the kit that's a close-enough match for your project.*

WICKER

Ah, Wicker!

Every time I see an old-fashioned porch, all decked out with wicker tables, chairs, and rockers, it takes me right back to my childhood. Apparently a lot of folks feel the same way because wicker is more popular than ever—indoors and out. But if you want it to look its best and last for years, you need to give it some routine TLC. Here's how:

▶ **Keep it under cover.** Wicker furniture can't stand up to the elements the way that teak, redwood, and metal versions do. Even in its ideal summer home—a covered veranda—wicker needs more attention than tougher materials. If you know that a storm is brewing, whisk your furniture indoors to avoid damage from wind and water.

▶ **Keep it clean.** Once a year (more often if it's exposed to dust and grit) vacuum your wicker furniture with the machine's soft brush attachment, or do the job by hand with a soft brush.

▶ **Keep it moist.** To do this, follow your annual brushing with the technique described in "There's the Rub!" (see page 286).

It's Not Tough Stuff

Well-made wicker furniture can last for generations—but not if you expect it to put up with the same rough-and-tumble treatment that its wooden counterparts can handle. In particular, follow these sensible safety guidelines:

- **Don't step on it!** When you need to fetch something from a high shelf or cabinet, do not reach for a wicker chair, stool, or ottoman. Your feet could go right through it. At best, it's all but guaranteed that you'll weaken or splinter the reeds that you stand on.

- **Don't lean back!** Some folks just can't resist treating every chair like a recliner. But tilting back in a chair—even a sturdy wooden model—that's intended to remain upright puts enormous strain on its back legs. When your pretend La-Z-Boy® is made of much more delicate wicker, you're beggin' for big trouble!

- **Hands off the arms!** When you get up out of a wicker chair, simply lean forward and stand up—don't put your weight on the armrests. That'll weaken the reeds and, with repeated pressings, crush them.

- **Play musical chairs.** If you use wicker chairs around a dining table, and the same people routinely sit in the same seats, rotate the chairs every few weeks. How come? Because the repeated strain of those folks' weight will warp and wear out the furniture—and probably sooner rather than later. (Picture, for example, your 200-pound hubby plopping into his chair at each meal.)

There's the Rub!

To keep your wicker looking and performing its best, use this routine once a year:

- Remove all dust with a soft brush.
- Then mix equal parts of boiled linseed oil and turpentine in a wide-mouthed glass jar.
- Rub the solution into the reeds with a soft cloth, paying special attention to all the little nooks and crannies.
- Then use a fresh, dry cloth to remove any excess formula.

2 Ways to Shore Up Sagging Seats

Over time, the seats of cane and wicker chairs tend to sag. Well, don't fret—and don't rush 'em off to a repair shop. Either of these DIY fixes will get those fanny holders back in shape fast:

▶ Wash down the seats with a half-and-half solution of white vinegar and hot water. Then set the chairs outside to dry in the sun. As the cane dries, it'll tighten right up.

▶ Soak a seat-size cloth in hot water. Then flip the chair over and lay the cloth on the underside of the seat. Leave it for 20 minutes or so, then remove the cloth and let the cane dry. Repeat two or three times if necessary to firm up the material.

If neither of these maneuvers works to your satisfaction, take the chairs to a repair shop that specializes in cane and wicker (do an Internet search for one near you or ask an antique dealer to recommend one).

Seaworthy Wicker

If you live in a coastal area and you use wicker furniture outdoors, protect it from salt damage with a coat of flexible rubber paint. Many brands are available, in both spray and liquid formulations, at paint, hardware, and home-improvement stores. This heavy-weather "gear" is also a life-lengthening boon for aluminum, metal, and wooden furniture that spends much time where salty breezes blow.

UPHOLSTERED FURNITURE

Unzip at Your Peril

The zippers on the backs of chair and sofa cushions are there so you can take the fabric off the foam padding and toss it in the washing machine or send it to the dry cleaner, right? Wrong! Even if the material is washable, you could be asking for trouble in one of three forms:

• The zipper area and the rest of the cover dry differently, even on a clothesline, and depending on the fabric content, that may cause wrinkles that no amount of ironing can remove.

- Repeated washings—or dry cleanings—will fade the fabric, so that it no longer quite matches the rest of the chair or sofa.

- The fabric may shrink, and then you'll really be in trouble!

So instead of undressing those cushions, vacuum them regularly (along with the rest of the piece) using your machine's upholstery attachment. And to treat spots and spills, use one of the stain-removal tricks at right. If that doesn't work, or if the fabric is especially valuable or delicate, call in a pro.

Sack the Scent

You got a steal of a deal on a beautiful, high-end couch at a flea market. Then you got it home and discovered why it was priced so low: The fabric has a lingering odor of cigarette smoke. Well, don't rush out and have the piece reupholstered—at least not before you try this simple trick: Sprinkle a thick layer of baking soda or clay cat litter on the fabric. Let it sit for three or four hours, and then vacuum the stuff up. The unpleasant aroma should go right with it.

Note: *This odor-removal plan also eliminates musty smells—like those from upholstered furniture that's been in storage for a while.*

Keep Your Couch from Having a Bad-Hair Day

If you find that the tops of your sofa and chairs get soiled from mousse, gels, sprays, and heaven knows what else people put in their hair these days, borrow this idea from the 1850s: Drape a piece of coordinating, washable fabric over the area where heads tend to rest. When the covering gets dirty, just toss it in the wash with the rest of the laundry. The old-timers knew this as an antimacassar, so named because it was originally intended to protect furniture from Macassar, a popular hair pomade in the 19th century.

Note: *Of course, you could make your gunk guards from the same fabric that covers your furniture, provided it's washable. Just be aware that with repeated washings, those protectors will fade and no longer quite match your upholstery.*

Erase that Smudge!

Got smudged upholstery? Take a trip to the art-supply store. A rubber eraser will erase some stains, such as pencil marks and fingerprints, from light-colored fabrics. But don't even think of using an eraser that's pink or any other color—it's all but guaranteed to leave a smudge of its own.

4 Slick Stain Fighters

Before a greasy stain has a chance to soak into your upholstery, apply a poultice to soak it out. Here's a quartet of top performers:

▶ **Cornmeal.** It's perfect for light-colored upholstery. Put enough on to cover the stain, and let it sit for a half hour. Then vacuum or brush the cornmeal away. If a stain remains, dab it with a little mild detergent solution and rinse.

▶ **Fuller's earth.** If the upholstery is dark colored, go to your local pharmacy and buy some fuller's earth, a natural clay product that's used in the manufacturing of fabrics. Apply it in the same way as the cornmeal.

▶ **Cornstarch and talcum powder.** These finer-textured absorbents work as well as cornmeal at removing stains, but they can be harder to remove from some upholstery. Sprinkle a generous layer onto the spot, let it sit for at least 30 minutes, then use your vacuum cleaner's upholstery attachment to get it all up.

POWERFUL POTIONS

PERFECT UPHOLSTERY SHAMPOO

This formula will get your upholstered furniture clean for a fraction of the price you'd pay for store-bought upholstery shampoo.

¼ cup of dishwashing liquid
1 cup of warm water

Combine the soap and water in a bowl. Then whip the solution with a whisk until dry suds start to form. With a soft cloth, massage the suds into a hidden spot on the upholstery, and let it dry. If you see no change in color, keep on cleanin'. When you've finished the whole piece, let it dry, then wipe it with a soft cloth dipped in warm water and wrung out thoroughly. Make sure the fabric is dry before you let anyone take a seat—otherwise, it'll get dirty all over again! (To speed up the drying time, use a fan to "blow-dry" the fabric.)

Note: *If the manufacturer's label says "no water-based cleaners," you won't think of even testing this formula!*

Camouflage a Burn

While a burn on a wooden tabletop can be a fairly quick fix (see "Don't Burn, Baby!" on page 275), it's a whole different ball game when you're dealing with upholstered furniture. When a wound goes all the way through the fabric, your only options for true concealment are to have the piece reupholstered or to put a slipcover on it. If a scorch mark isn't too severe, you may be able to disguise it. Here's the drill:

- Dab the mark with a wet paper towel. (Don't rub, or you'll damage the fibers further!) Then blot with a dry paper towel or clean cloth.

- If that doesn't get all the charring out, put a drop of mild liquid laundry detergent on a wet paper towel and press it onto the spot. Blot with another wet paper towel to remove the detergent, and follow up with a dry paper towel to absorb the burned fibers.

How to Cover a Chair Seat

Dining-chair seats looking worn and haggard? Well, you could pay a pro a tidy sum to reupholster them. Or you could do the job yourself at a fraction of the price. For each chair, you'll need new fabric and a seat-size piece of medium-density polyurethane foam. The thickness is your call, but 2 inches is standard. Also round up a screwdriver, a sharp knife, contact cement or spray adhesive, scissors, and a staple gun. Then follow the seven-step procedure at right:

AN OUNCE OF
PREVENTION

Read but Verify

Any piece of upholstered furniture that was made after 1969 should have a label telling you what types of cleaning formulas you can safely use on the fabric (for example, water-based liquids or foams, or water-free dry-cleaning solvents). That precautionary note is usually on the frame under a cushion, or on the underside of a covered chair seat—that is, if the tag hasn't been removed. But even if you find it and read it, don't take any chances: Always test any cleaner—commercial or DIY—on an inconspicuous spot, like the inside of a skirt or the rim of fabric that's covered by seat cushions. Otherwise, you could wind up with more visual discord than you had to begin with!

STEP 1. Flip the chair upside down and unscrew the seat from its base. Then remove the old fabric. If the padding is in good shape, leave it in place and proceed to Step 3. Otherwise, pull it off, too.

STEP 2. Cut the foam to size, using the seat as a template, and glue the padding in place. (An electric carving knife makes a dandy cutting tool.)

STEP 3. Center the seat, with padding attached, on the wrong side of the fabric. Trim the material, leaving enough cloth to fold over the sides of the seat.

STEP 4. Fold the fabric over the seat, and mark the center of the material at front, back, and sides. Then pull it taut and shoot a staple into each of the four marks.

STEP 5. Starting at the center of each side and moving toward the end, hold the fabric taut and staple it to the wood.

STEP 6. As you come to each corner, pull the fabric tightly toward the opposite side of the seat and fold the remaining material diagonally over the top. Staple it into place and continue along the perimeter until the seat is firmly covered.

STEP 7. Trim off the excess fabric, leaving about ½ inch on each side. Then reattach the seat to the chair's frame.

Note: *For an extra-soft seat, add a layer of fiberfill batting on top of the foam. You can find both materials in craft-supply and fabric stores.*

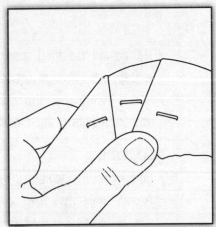

At each corner, staple the folded material.

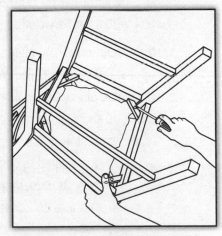

Reattach the seat to the chair's frame.

Don't Let Stains Be the Death of the Party

Whether you're throwing a New Year's Eve bash or just having a few friends in for cocktails, your upholstery can do its share of involuntary imbibing. Fast action on your part can head off a hangover. Here are some easy remedies:

BEER AND WHITE WINE

- Soak up a fresh spill with paper towels, then sponge the area with cool water until all traces of stain are gone.

- If the stain has dried, sponge it with equal parts of white vinegar and water, then blot up the residue, rinse with clear, warm water, and blot dry.

RED WINE

- Pour or sponge white wine onto the freshly spilled red, then cover the area with salt. Let it sit for 10 minutes and vacuum it up. Or douse the spill generously with club soda and blot with clean, dry cloths.

- If the stain refuses to budge, pick up a stain remover called Wine Away (available online and in many wine and food shops, supermarkets, and housewares stores). It's specially  formulated to remove not only its namesake spills but also dark fruit juices, coffee, and tea.

THE HARD STUFF

- If you're Johnny-on-the-spot, simply pour club soda on the area and wipe it until the whiskey, rum, gin, or what have you is gone.

- Sponge dried or persistent stains with a mixture of 2 tablespoons of ammonia per cup of water. Rinse thoroughly, then dab on a solution of 1 part white vinegar to 2 parts of water. Blot up the fluid, and rinse with clear, warm water.

SOFT DRINKS & SWEET MIXERS

- Soak up fresh spills, then sponge club soda onto the stain, and blot it with paper towels or clean cloths until the mark is gone.

- Treat dried stains in the same way, but follow up by applying a solution made from ¼ teaspoon of dishwashing liquid per ¼ cup of warm water, with a few drops of ammonia mixed in. Blot it up, rinse with cool water, and blot again. **Note:** *Never use hot water on a sugary stain—it'll set the mark permanently.*

LEATHER & VINYL UPHOLSTERY

Routine TLC

By and large, leather furniture is a pretty easy keeper—as long as you're diligent about performing these two chores:

▸ **Dust** both upholstered seating pieces and leather-topped tables at least once a week, using a clean, soft cotton cloth. Otherwise, the pores will become clogged with dust particles.

▸ **Clean** the upholstery every few months with a commercial leather cleaner, followed by a conditioner. Or use my Double-Duty Leather Cleaner & Conditioner (see page 294).

Note: *Uncoated leathers absorb liquids like a sponge, so stick to dusting and, when absolutely necessary, a gentle wipe with a damp cloth. Also, read the instructions that came with it before you use any cleaning formula because some newer finishes need special treatment.*

Saddle Up!

While most leather upholstery should be cleaned with commercial leather cleaner or a comparable DIY version, there is one exception: furniture that's covered with the same heavier leather that's used for saddles and baseball gloves. If you're lucky enough to have some of these couches or chairs at your house, keep them shipshape by using (you guessed it) saddle soap or baseball mitt softener. Give the pieces a good rubdown once or twice a year, depending on how much use they get and how dry the air is in your home.

Mark Off Scratches

Got an unsightly scratch on your leather couch or tabletop? Cover it up with a permanent felt-tip marker in a matching color. As always, test it on an inconspicuous area first, and work slowly and carefully during your coloring session. Also, be sure to use a medium or fine-point marker. An extra-fine tip could deepen the scratch, while the thick version is all but guaranteed to color outside the lines, leaving visible evidence of your cosmetic fix-up.

Note: *For the largest color selection, buy your scratch concealer at an art-supply store. Shop in person—not online—so you can match the shade to a swatch of the leather or a matching throw pillow.*

POWERFUL POTIONS

DOUBLE-DUTY LEATHER CLEANER & CONDITIONER

There are many leather cleaners and conditioners on the market—most of them with pretty high price tags. But few can match this two-in-one formula.

> **¾ cup of white vinegar**
> **½ cup of olive oil**
> **Essential oil (optional)***

Pour the vinegar and oil into a handheld spray bottle, and shake well to blend the ingredients. If you like, add a few drops of essential oil for fragrance, and shake again. Set the nozzle on the spray—not stream—setting. Gently spritz about a square-foot section of the leather, then wipe it with a soft, clean cotton cloth using circular motions. Periodically shake the bottle to keep the ingredients well blended. Just remember these precautions: If the floor under the furniture is carpeted, cover it with old towels or drop cloths before you start. And (yes, I'm saying it again) test an out-of-the-way spot first.

* Lemon, orange, and eucalyptus are all good choices, but go with whatever scent your nose fancies most.

Don't Sweat Stains

As long as you blot up spills quickly, using an absorbent cloth or sponge, liquids rarely leave their mark on leather. More good news: Even if the fluid has had time to soak in, the leather will absorb and diffuse the stain—just as human skin does.

2 Timely Touch-Ups

While leather is virtually unstainable, it is susceptible to these two boo-boos—both of which are a snap to send packin'.

- **Water marks.** Simply wipe them away with white vinegar (after testing a dab in a hidden spot, of course).

- **Scuff marks.** Rub 'em out with a white or gum eraser. (Not pink!)

Life in the furniture lane doesn't get much easier than that!

Do the Vivacious Vinyl Two-Step

Most folks who buy vinyl-covered furniture choose it because of its image as a family-friendly, ultra-durable material. Unfortunately, your friendly family could send the stuff to an early grave. How so? Because over time, the body and hair oil that your nearest and dearest deposit whenever they sit on—or even touch—the furniture will make the upholstery harden and crack. So to keep your vinyl-clad pieces on the job for the long haul, perform this two-step procedure regularly:

STEP 1. Dip a soft cotton cloth in white vinegar and gently wipe the whole surface. This will cut through and weaken the ornery oils.

STEP 2. Mix a few drops of dishwashing liquid in a bucket of water. Then dampen a cloth with the soapy water and wash the vinyl, paying special attention to major contact points, such as the arms and back. Rinse with clear water, and dry with another soft cotton cloth.

Moo Juice Vanquishes Vinyl Stains

Got stubborn marks on your pseudo-leather upholstery? Move 'em on out by rubbing the blemishes with a cloth or sponge dipped in milk. Whole, fat-free, or anything in between will work just fine. Then wash the surface with soapy water as described above (see "Do the Vivacious Vinyl Two-Step," above).

OUTDOOR FURNITURE

An Iron-Clad Guarantee

Well-made iron furniture will give you years of faithful service if you guard against its biggest enemy—rust. Inspect your pieces carefully at the beginning and end of the summer (or every few months if you live where the outdoor-living season goes year-round). When you find spots where the paint has chipped off, tend to them immediately using this three-part formula:

▶ Wipe on a coat of white vinegar and let it dry (no need to rinse).

- Repaint the worn areas with a high-quality, rust-resistant paint. I find spray paint the easiest to work with, but some folks prefer the brush-on kind.

- Dip a soft cloth in car wax, and rub the whole piece of furniture with it. Repeat this rubdown yearly, and your rust worries will be a thing of the past.

Give Rust Spots the Rub-Off

You say you got a steal of a deal on a piece of metal furniture or a barbecue grill at a tag sale, but it's got rust spots all over it? Not a problem! Just ball up some aluminum foil, dip it in Coca-Cola®, and scrub those spots away!

But I Don't Want to Wear It!

Aluminum furniture wins popularity contests for its light weight and reasonable price tag. Unfortunately, though, aluminum has one glaring flaw: Left untreated, the surface oxidizes, and develops a powdery, white residue. This ugly stuff, in turn, leaves equally ugly gray marks on clothes, tablecloths, and seat cushions. To ensure that your aluminum furniture keeps itself to itself, wipe it down with a solution of equal parts of vinegar and water. Let it dry, then spray on a coat or two of either clear lacquer or exterior paint.

Drill Rust Away

Metal lawn chairs with contoured seats were big favorites in the 1940s and '50s, and they still are because they're comfortable, durable, and economical (not to mention retro-chic). There's just one downside: The slightly concave seat collects every raindrop that falls from the sky—and where there's rain, there's rust. The simple solution: Drill drainage holes in the seat. Then deburr

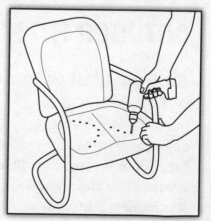

To prevent rusting, drill holes in the contoured seat of a metal lawn chair.

the openings and paint the chair with rustproof paint, paying special attention to the holes' raw edges.

Tweak Your Teak

As far as I'm concerned, you can't find a better furniture bargain than teak. That's because, expensive as it is, it will stand up to decades of wear and tear with almost no maintenance. It does need one little bit of attention, though: Once a year, you should coat the legs with a water repellent. (The ones made for decks work fine.) Here's the simplest way I've found to do this chore:

> **WELL, WHADDYA KNOW!**
>
> Teak garden furniture wears mighty fancy price tags these days, but the first crop came from a scavenger's brainstorm. At the end of World War I, the British Royal Navy started breaking down its battleships, and some enlightened soul shouted, "Save those decks!" Well, the Navy honchos listened. The wood was so drop-dead gorgeous that people started making garden benches from it—and it was so sturdy that, in gardens all over England, those very same benches are still being sat on today.

- Pour about 6 inches of water repellent into a clean coffee can.

- Place one leg of a table or chair into the can and leave it there for two or three minutes.

- Repeat the process until each furniture leg on your deck or patio has had its turn in the can.

Note: *This same procedure keeps redwood furniture from wicking up destructive moisture.*

Don't Spread the Stain

Before you install new redwood furniture on your deck or patio, set each piece on your lawn and give it a thorough rinsing with a garden hose. This will get rid of any excess stain that could run off in the first rain shower—leaving ugly marks on your outdoor seating surface.

Home Furnishings

Let's face it: "Home furnishings" is just about as broad as a term can get. In the space we've got, we can't even begin to cover the whole territory. But in these pages, I will deliver heaps of handy hints and goof-proof guidance on caring for and fixing up many of the hardworking helpers and cherished treasures that truly make your house a home.

WINDOW & FLOOR COVERINGS

Geared for Inaction

Venetian and mini blinds operate by way of a gear that regulates the control cord. When that gear seizes up—as it is prone to doing periodically—one of two things happens: Either the blinds sag on one side when you open or close them, or they refuse to move at all. Fortunately, it's pretty easy to make the gear release its grip. Here's your how-to plan:

▶ Raise or lower the blind all the way, and then lower or raise it into position again. Repeat the process a few times until it stays on an even keel.

▶ If that doesn't work, climb up on a stepladder so you're at eye level with the bar at the top of the blinds. Inside the hole where the control cord enters the bar, you'll see a small metal gear or lever. Just reach in there with a small flat-head screwdriver, lift the tiny thing up, and pull the cord out. Bingo—your blinds are back in business!

The Magic Went Out of the Wand!

Problem: The wand (a.k.a. tilter) that opens and closes the slats on your mini blinds turns normally, but the slats won't move. This means that the wand has become disconnected from the tilting mechanism. Your simple fix-it strategy depends on the position the strips are stuck in.

- **Down.** Turn the wand counterclockwise while, at the same time, pulling down gently on the back strand of the ladders (the string assembly that supports the slats).

- **Up.** Turn the wand clockwise and gently pull down on the front ladder string.

That should restart the action. If it doesn't, order a replacement wand that works with your kind of blinds and install it following the manufacturer's directions. It's a simple process, but the details—and the type of wand you need—vary from one brand and style to another. Several online companies sell replacement parts for all types of blinds and shades. You can find them by searching for (you guessed it!) "window blind replacement parts."

A Tense Situation

Traditional cordless window shades are attached to an aluminum tube, inside of which is a coiled spring that calls the shots. When you pull down on the shade, the tension on the spring increases until you stop pulling. Then a ratchet engages with a pin to keep the window covering where you left it. To open the shade, you simply give it a slight downward tug. This releases the pin, and your cover rolls back up to reveal the great outdoors. So what do you do when the system doesn't work the way it's supposed to? You perform one of

Read before You Fix

If your window blinds are still under warranty, don't attempt any DIY fixes before you read the fine print on the warranty document or check with the manufacturer. Why? Because even minor fiddling could void the warranty and possibly leave you forking out cash for repairs—or new window coverings.

these two simple procedures:

- ▶ **It won't roll back up.** Unroll it another 24 inches, then lift the tube off its mounting brackets. Roll the shade back up by hand, being careful to keep it even from side to side. Put it back in the brackets, and pull it down. If it still won't go back up, repeat the process until it's rolling smoothly again.

- ▶ **It won't stay down.** This means the spring is coiled too tightly. Take the shade down and unroll it about 24 inches. Then put it back in place and give it a "test drive." Repeat the procedure as necessary until the tension is back in proper operating mode.

How to Give Your Blinds a Bath

Slatted blinds can collect a good amount of grime, especially if they hang in front of open windows. To keep them at their peak of good looks, give them a thorough cleaning once a year. If they're made of aluminum or vinyl, you can do the job in your bathtub. Here's how:

STEP 1. Line your bathtub with towels. Then add 2 tablespoons of dishwashing liquid as you fill the tub with warm water.

STEP 2. Turn the blind's slats to the open position, remove it from its brackets, and lay it gently into the sudsy water. Let it soak for five minutes or so, and then wipe the top and bottom of each slat with a clean blind-cleaning brush or a soft cotton cloth or glove.

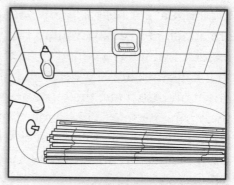

Let the blind soak for five minutes in sudsy water.

STEP 3. Drain out the sudsy water, and turn the showerhead on warm to rinse the blind.

STEP 4. Replace the wet towels with dry ones, and let the blind air-dry for 30 minutes or so.

STEP 5. Reinstall the blind following the manufacturer's step-by-step directions. Then wipe each slat with a clean cotton cloth to remove any residual moisture. Easier yet, use a hair dryer.

Note: *If the slats are too long to fit in your bathtub, do the job outdoors. Apply the soap solution with a bucket, and rinse with a gentle spray from the garden hose. In the case of long vertical blinds, you may find it easier to wash them in place at the window or door.*

Bath Time Follow-Up

When your freshly washed blinds are fully dry and back on the job (see "How to Give Your Blinds a Bath," at left), wipe each slat with a fabric softener sheet. This will help repel dust—for a while, that is. Eventually, you will have to do that job again . . . and again. But don't let that thought bog you down. Remember: The more often you dust your blinds—followed by a dryer-sheet chaser—the less time-consuming the annual bath will be.

Don't Give Wooden Blinds a Bath!

A soak in the tub will warp them—and put real, and faux-wood blinds out of commission in a hurry. So when they're ready for more than routine dusting, clean them while they're hanging at the windows. Use a solution of a few drops of oil-based soap (such as Murphy® Oil Soap) per gallon of water. Dampen a blind-cleaning brush, cotton gloves, or a soft cloth in the mixture, and carefully wash both sides of

AN OUNCE OF
PREVENTION

Clean Down—Not Up!

The slats of vertical blinds are attached to the top frame by open-ended hooks, so at dusting time and for deeper cleaning, always wipe or vacuum with downward strokes only. Any upward movements could detach the hooks and send the slats crashing to the floor. At best, it'll be a time-consuming nuisance to reattach them. At worst, they could be damaged in the fall—or break any fragile objects they hit on the way down.

each slat. Rinse with clear water using a fresh version of the same tool. During both washing and rinsing steps, rinse your wiping implement frequently in clear water to keep it—and therefore the wood—clean and fresh. Then dry the slats thoroughly with a clean, lint-free cloth.

Note: *Check the manufacturer's directions before you use water or any liquid cleaner on wooden blinds. If you can't find the directions, play it safe and use dusting spray and a soft cotton cloth to shine up the wood.*

How to Train Your Curtains

Formal, pleated draperies are designed and constructed to hang in neat folds. Loose curtains, on the other hand, are a different kettle of fish. Even when the rings are spaced at regular intervals, the panels don't always fall evenly. But with a little tough love, you can whip that fabric into shape. Here's all you need to do:

STEP 1. Close the curtains completely. Then move the fabric in each panel around until you're pleased with the depth and interval of the waves.*

STEP 2. Bunch each section up and loop strips of plastic wrap around it every 24 inches or so down the length of the curtain.

STEP 3. Leave the bunches in place for three days. (If you can't cope with bare windows for that long, hang sheets over the curtain rods.)

STEP 4. Release the fabric from its bonds and admire your well-behaved curtains!

* If you have a steam cleaner, intensify the action by giving the fabric a thorough treatment from top to bottom and wrapping it before it's cooled down.

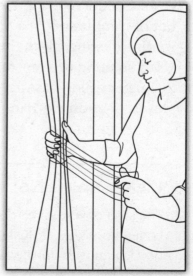

Loop a length of plastic wrap every 24 inches or so down the length of each bunched-up curtain panel.

Make Your Drapes Gel

Your new cotton draperies or sheer curtains may be marked "washable," but there's a good chance the fabric will emerge from the washer so wrinkled that you'll have to spend hours at the ironing board. Well, don't do it— and don't toss 'em either. Instead, run them through the machine again, only this time dissolve 1 tablespoon of plain gelatin in 1 cup of boiling water and add the mixture to the final rinse cycle. You may still need to press out a few creases, but they'll be a lot fewer and farther between.

Note: *This formula also restores the shine to polished cotton curtains, pillow covers, and tablecloths.*

Beat It!

Area rugs collect dust, dander, pet hair, and who knows what else every day. And over time, that crud can wear out the fibers. So get it out the old-fashioned way: Hang the rug over a deck railing or a taut clothesline and whack it hard. An old tennis racket makes a fine tool for this job, but a genuine rug beater is even better—and you can pick up a vintage one for peanuts on eBay or at an antique store.

Ruffled and Ready

After you've washed your ruffled curtains, do the frills seem to start drooping right before your eyes? You don't have to put up with that nonsense. Just spritz the ruffles with aerosol hair spray as soon as you take the curtains out of the dryer. They'll stay at their peak of perkiness until it's time for their next "bath." (This trick works just as well to keep ruffled bedspreads and pillow covers looking new and fresh.)

Salt That Soot

Oops! When Santa came down the chimney, he left some ashes and soot all over your hearth rug. No worries! Do what Mrs. Claus does with the old gent's clothes: Just rub salt and a little all-purpose household soap, such as Fels-Naptha®, into the stain, and then rinse it clean with lukewarm water.

Pups Will Be Pups

Did Fido mistake your heirloom rug for his personal potty? Don't despair—but do act fast! If the waste product is solid, scoop it up gently. Then lay the rug, upside down, so the soiled spot is over a bucket. Pour clear water through the underside of the stain and into the bucket until the mark is gone—emptying the container as necessary. This treatment will eliminate either urine or fecal stains without damaging the delicate fibers, as scrubbing could do.

2 Amazing Anti-Moth Maneuvers

Clothes moths don't confine their egg-laying activity to clothing. Any natural-fiber object in your house—including carpets and rugs—can be a moth maternity ward. If larvae are lingering in your floor covering, spring into action in one of these two ways:

- Sprinkle the invaded surface with a healthy layer of salt, then vacuum it up.

- Saturate a bath towel with water, wring it out, and spread it out on the rug. Then grab your iron, set it on "High," and press the towel until it's dry. You don't need to push down hard; it's the steamy heat, not the pressure, that kills the pesky little pests.

BED, BATH & TABLE LINENS

Freshen Up Your Bed Covers

Every time you wash or dry-clean your blankets and bedspreads, a little bit of the life goes out of them. So the next time they're looking less than fresh, but they're not actually soiled, just give them a good dose of fresh air. Wait for a dry day with a gentle breeze. Then either hang the coverings over a clothesline, or drape them over a porch or deck railing (clipping them in place with clothespins so they don't sail away!). An hour or so in the great outdoors will leave those bedclothes smelling as clean and fresh as a mountain stream—without the life-shortening stress of tumbling around in the washer and dryer.

Safe and Simple Storage

To safely store special-occasion table linens or out-of-season curtains, first pad the bar of a cedar suit hanger with a cotton hand towel (the cedar will help repel moths). Cover it with a piece of acid-free tissue paper (available in craft-supply stores), and drape your folded fabric over that. Hint: If the pieces will be in long-term storage, take them off their hangers and refold them every month or so. This will prevent discoloration and wearing along the creases. For extra protection, hang a couple of moth-repellent sachets over the hanger (see "Make Some Moth Chasers," below).

Make Some Moth Chasers

You can buy herbal sachets that will keep moth larvae from turning your treasured linens into hole-ridden clutter. But it's a snap to make your own. Just sew up some little cotton bags or buy them at a craft-supply store. Or cut the feet off some old panty hose. Then fill the pouches with any or all of these dried herbs. Use whatever combination pleases your nose—moths hate 'em all!

- Lavender *(Lavandula)*
- Santolina *(Santolina)*
- Southernwood *(Artemisia abrotanum)*
- Tansy *(Tanacetum)*
- Thyme *(Thymus)*
- Wormwood *(Artemisia absinthium)*

Rehab · Revamp · Revive

So what do you do when an old blanket, bedspread, or comforter gets too worn to use on your bed—or picks up a stain that you can't remove for love nor money? Donate it to your car. That cover will come in handy when you need to load or unload the trunk and your vehicle is, shall we say, less than pristine. Just drape the blanket over the back of the trunk and the bumper, and proceed with your task—confident that you won't mess up your clothes in the process.

Keep Your Towels Terrific

How long even premium bath towels stay on the job depends on how you treat them on laundry day. Specifically:

- Every time you wash your towels, add 2 cups of white vinegar to the rinse water. They'll stay as soft and fluffy as almost anything this side of a five-star hotel!

- Don't ever put towels (or sheets or blankets) away unless they're completely dry. Even a tiny bit of moisture could cause them to mildew or start to smell less than fresh.

A Toothy Cleaning Tip

Need to get a stain out of a comforter or pillow? To avoid washing the whole big thing, isolate the mark with dental floss. Just push the filling out of the way, gather up the soiled area, and tie it off tightly with the floss. Then proceed with the appropriate stain-removal treatment (see "Stain Removal 101" on page 335).

Note: *A rubber band will also work.*

Gather the stained fabric section together, and tie it off tightly with dental floss.

POTS, PANS & KITCHEN GEAR

How to Season Cast-Iron Pans

A cast-iron pan will last forever if you treat it right, and you can get the pan good and hot without worrying about damaging it. And did you know that when you cook in cast iron, you're getting some of your daily dose of iron? That's right: Some of the iron actually gets into the food and makes your meal better for you. There's just one hitch to using cast iron: Before you cook with a new pan, you have to give it a little pretreatment or food will stick to the surface, and the iron will rust. This little ritual is called seasoning, and here's all there is to it:

STEP 1. Set oven to 300°F.

STEP 2. While the oven's heating, wash the pan in warm, soapy water, and dry it thoroughly. (After you wipe it with a dish towel, put the pan on the stove top on very low heat for a couple of minutes to make sure it's absolutely dry.)

STEP 3. Using a paper towel, coat the inside of the pan lightly with peanut oil or vegetable shortening. Then pop it into the preheated oven for 60 minutes.

STEP 4. When time's up, remove the pan from the oven and wipe off any excess oil. (Don't forget to wear a sturdy oven mitt!)

AN OUNCE OF
PREVENTION

Filter Out Rust

Let's face it: Any kitchen delivers its fair share of moisture—which, in turn, can produce rust on cast-iron pots and pans. Your ultra-simple prevention policy: Keep a coffee filter in each piece of non-enameled cast-iron cookware in your kitchen arsenal. The paper will absorb dampness and fend off those dreaded orangey stains.

Cast-Iron TLC

After you cook in a seasoned cast-iron pan, never wash it with soap or scrub it with scouring powders or pads. If you do, you'll destroy that protective coating you spent so much time applying. Instead, clean your pan by pouring boiling water into it. When it's cooled down enough so that you won't get burned, wipe off any food residue with a wad of paper towels or a clean (soapless!) dishcloth or sponge. Then dry the pan thoroughly.

If some stubborn cooked-on food refuses to budge, put the pan on the stove top and add a little water. Bring it to a boil, and use a plastic or rubber (not metal!) spatula to remove the splotches.

What do you do if some well-meaning kitchen helper gets carried away and cleans your favorite cast-iron skillet with soap and steel wool? Or you find a great, but clearly mistreated, iron pot at a tag sale? Just reseason that baby (see "How to Season Cast-Iron Pans," at left) and she'll be rarin' to go!

Revive an Old-Timer

To restore an old, rusted, greasy iron skillet to its prime, set it in a plastic tub and pour in enough Coca-Cola® to cover the pan—about three 2-liter bottles should do the trick. Let it soak overnight to loosen the gunk, and then give it a good going-over with a stiff plastic brush. Wash the pan with warm, soapy water, pat it dry, and it's all set for reseasoning (see "How to Season Cast-Iron Pans" on page 306).

Pop! Goes the Haze

Enameled cast-iron cookware isn't nearly as picky about its care and handling as the "undressed" kind is. Over time, though, that shiny, protective coating can get dull and hazy looking. To brighten it up, pour soda pop into the pan (any fizzy flavor will do). Let it sit for about 10 minutes, then rub the surface with a nonabrasive plastic scouring pad or a soft toothbrush. Bingo—the grime'll be gone.

4 Quirky Copper Cleaners

If you're a real cooking enthusiast, you know that nothing beats copper pans when it comes to conducting heat. And, it looks as good as it cooks, as well it should,

WELL, WHADDYA KNOW!

On February 23, 1886, a young Oberlin College graduate named Charles Martin Hall perfected a process for inexpensively producing an aluminum compound that could be cast into cookware. (We know the exact date because Mr. Hall jotted it down in his laboratory notebook.) He founded his own company and began turning out lightweight, easy-to-clean pots and pans with remarkably even heat distribution and a durability that prompted the firm's name: WearEver.

American housewives were reluctant to trade their tried-and-true iron and tin pots for this newfangled stuff, and major retailers refused to stock it. That all changed in the spring of 1903, when the renowned Wanamaker's department store staged the first public demonstration of aluminum's cooking prowess. Hundreds of women gazed in amazement as a professional chef made apple butter *without stirring*. When the ladies confirmed up close that the ingredients had neither burned nor stuck to the pan, they were hooked. By the time Mr. Hall died in 1914, his WearEver line had earned him a tidy 30 million dollars.

considering what it costs. To keep your cookware looking like all it's worth—or to spruce up copper that's gotten tarnished—reach for one of these out-of-the-ordinary cleansers:

▶ **Cream of tartar and lemon juice.** Mix 'em into a thick paste, rub it onto the copper with your fingers, and let it sit for about 10 minutes. Wipe off the paste, wash and dry the pan, and buff it with a soft cloth.

▶ **Salt and vinegar.** Fill a spray bottle with vinegar and 3 tablespoons of salt, shake until the salt dissolves, and give the copper a good spritzing. Let the pot sit for 10 minutes and then scrub it clean.

▶ **Worcestershire sauce.** Soak a sponge in the sauce and rub it over the metal surface. Wait one to two minutes and then wipe the pot clean. Rinse thoroughly with water, and dry.

▶ **Half a lemon and salt.** This trick is just the ticket for removing stubborn stains. Simply dip lemon halves in salt and rub-a-dub-dub the marks away.

The End of the Rainbow(s)

We all know how aluminum pots get those annoying rainbow marks inside. But maybe you don't know how easy it is to get rid of them. Just fill the pot with a solution of 1 tablespoon of vinegar per quart of water, and heat the concoction on low for three or four minutes. You'll get a shine you can see yourself in!

POWERFUL POTIONS

AMAZING ALUMINUM CLEANER

This DIY cleanser will keep aluminum pots and pans looking brand-spankin' new. (It'll also work on your aluminum outdoor furniture!)

½ cup of baking soda
½ cup of cream of tartar
½ cup of white vinegar
¼ cup of soap flakes (such as Ivory Snow®)

Combine the baking soda and cream of tartar. Add the vinegar, and mix to form a paste. Stir in the soap, and transfer the mixture to a glass jar with a tight-fitting lid, and label it. Apply the paste with a plain steel wool pad, and rinse.

3 Freaky Fixes for Food Frustrations

Here are some oh-so-easy solutions to a trio of common cookware conundrums:

- **Burned grease on the bottom of pots and pans.** Fill 'em with water, and drop in six antacid tablets. Soak for an hour, and wash.

- **Crusted-on food on a baking pan.** Pour a teaspoon or two of fabric softener into the pan, fill the pan with water, and let it sit overnight. The next morning, wipe the gunk away.

- **Stubborn stains on nonstick cookware.** Cover the bottom of the pan with water, and add 2 tablespoons of baking soda and a slice of lemon. Simmer the mixture until the stains disappear.

3 Remarkable Rust-Removal Routines

There's nothing more frustrating than reaching for a favorite tool, kitchen knife, or cast-iron pan, and finding that it's splotched with rust. Well, don't fret—and don't rush out and buy a commercial rust remover. Instead, use one of these kitchen-counter cures:

- ▶ **The quick method.** Make a paste from 2 parts salt and 1 part lemon juice. Rub the paste onto the metal until the spots vanish, and rinse with clear water.

- ▶ **The slower but easier way.** Soak your "stricken" pieces overnight in full-strength white vinegar. The rust will dissolve like magic.

▶ **An inside job.** When the trouble spots are on the inside of a pan or skillet, put 3 cups of sliced rhubarb into it, and pour in just enough water to cover the rusted areas. Cook the rhubarb over low heat, stirring occasionally until the rust drifts off the metal surface. (How long this takes depends upon the thickness of the rust layer.) Toss the contents into your compost bin, or bury it in a flower bed, then wash the pan and dry it thoroughly.

CHINA & CUTLERY

Hands-Off Plate Repairs

Thanks to today's high-tech superglues, mending a broken plate and putting it back in full dinner-table (or wall-decoration) action can be a piece o' cake. There's just one problem: It's mighty tricky to get the pieces in exactly the right position and hold them there while the glue dries—that is, unless you use this slick trick:

STEP 1. Fill a large pan or flat-bottomed bowl with sand and set the largest section of the plate in it with the broken edge facing up.

STEP 2. Mound the sand tightly around the piece until it can stand straight up on its own.

STEP 3. Attach one section at a time, following the glue manufacturer's directions.

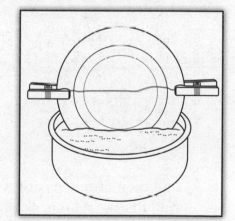

Stand the plate upright in tightly packed sand, and hold the joined pieces together with clothespins.

STEP 4. Use clip-type clothespins to hold the joined pieces together while the glue dries.

Nail Those Stains!

Your bone china has served you well for years—picking up a motley array of stains in the process. Well, don't go out and buy a replacement set. Instead, moisten a cotton ball with nail polish remover and rub the

If your treasured china teapot spends most of its time at the back of a kitchen cabinet, it's bound to get its fair share of bumps from the dishes up front. To protect the spout, cover it with the thumb from an old, thick woolen mitten or glove. No over-the-hill hand-wear on hand? Then slip a toilet paper tube over the spout and secure it with masking tape. (Also be sure to use one of these protective devices whenever you're boxing up a teapot for a move or long-term storage.)

spots away. (Do the job very carefully, though, because this is powerful stuff, and it can damage synthetic fabrics, wood finishes, and plastics.) When you're finished, wash the dishes. They'll be ready for the fanciest dinner party in town.

2 Simple Steps to Sparkling Silverware

It's your turn to host the whole family for Christmas dinner, and you want to use the good silverware your grandma left you. But you don't want to use one of those smelly chemical polishes—and besides, in the midst of the holiday rush, there's no time to sit down and do the job. No problem: Here's your easy-does-it two-step plan:

STEP 1. Line the bottom and sides of your kitchen sink* with aluminum foil, and toss in ½ cup each of baking soda and table salt.

STEP 2. Fill the sink with enough freshly boiled water to cover your silverware, and then drop the cutlery into the drink. Let the mixture sit for 30 minutes to an hour. As if by magic, the grime will be pulled from the silver onto the foil. If any grayish spots remain, you should be able to wipe them off with a damp dishcloth. Just be aware that a heavy coat of tarnish may require a few more treatments, or an overnight "bath."

* Or use a baking pan that's big enough to hold the flatware in a single layer. To de-tarnish taller objects, such as candlesticks or vases, use a container that's high enough and broad enough to contain the piece(s) with about an inch to spare all around.

No Foiling!

What's that? You're fresh out of foil, company's coming to dinner in an hour, and you need to polish your favorite silver cake plate? Piece o' cake! Any of these quick tricks will work:

- Rub white (non-gel) toothpaste onto the surface and scrub it with a soft, damp cloth.

- Rub the silver with the inside of a banana peel. To remove extra-stubborn tarnish, puree the peel in a blender, and massage the paste onto the metal. Then wipe it with a soft, clean cloth.

- Pour about a cup of baking soda into a bowl and add enough water to make a thin paste. Then rub the paste onto the silver, rinse it off, and buff with a soft cotton cloth. (If you don't use all of the paste in one go-round, put it into a glass jar with a lid and save it for next time—or just pour it down the drain to keep it free and clear.)

The Simplest Way to Shine Your Silverware . . .

Is to use it on a daily basis. Just by giving those knives, forks, and spoons the jobs they were designed to do—and then washing and drying them afterward—you'll keep tarnish at bay. Don't put your silver in the dishwasher, though. The extreme heat and harsh detergents will eventually turn the metal dull and white, and you'll need to have the stuff professionally refinished. Always hand-wash your silver using phosphate-free detergent with no lemon scent added to it. Then dry the pieces immediately to avoid spotting.

AN OUNCE OF

PREVENTION

Your Terrific Tarnish-Prevention Plan

Even if you take your silver flatware out of storage and put it to work (see "The Simplest Way to Shine Your Silverware . . . ," above), it's not likely that you'll use every piece every day. So give it added protection by setting a small bowl of uncooked rice or a few untreated charcoal briquettes in the drawer. Either guardian will absorb tarnish-causing moisture. The same trick works just as well to keep dampness from building up inside a silver coffeepot or teapot. In this case, tuck a briquette or a spoonful of rice inside the pot.

LAMPS & DECORATIVE ACCESSORIES

Keep Parchment Lamp Shades at Their Peak

Parchment shades don't ask for much in terms of TLC. Just dust the surface frequently with a soft cotton cloth, and use a white eraser to remove any spots or splotches. When the grime is too intense for that approach, give your lamps a change of "headgear" (see "How to Re-Cover a Lamp Shade," below).

How to Re-Cover a Lamp Shade

Lamp shades that have seen better days can make even the most beautiful room look frumpy. Fortunately, you can put life back in those lights quickly and easily—and for a whole lot less cash than you'd shell out for new shades. Just choose your new fabric, remove any decorative trim from the old shade, and follow this simple five-step process:

STEP 1. Make a template. Lay the shade, seam side down, on a piece of craft or wrapping paper. Using the seam as your starting and ending points, roll the shade slowly along the paper, tracing the top and bottom edges with a pencil as you go. At each end, use a straightedge to draw a line connecting the upper and lower borders.

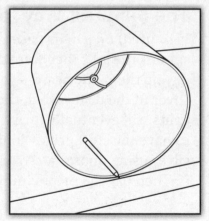

Trace the top and bottom edges of the shade to make a paper template.

STEP 2. Cut out the template. Spread your fabric, right side down, on a flat surface. Put the template on top, and move it around until the material's pattern (if there is one) is aligned the way you want it.

STEP 3. Cut the fabric, leaving an extra 1 to 1½ inches around the perimeter, and iron it to remove any wrinkles. Also fold over and press one of the short ends to serve as the finished seam.

STEP 4. Lay the shade on its side, seam side up, on the fabric. Starting at one end, spray aerosol fabric adhesive* onto a small section of the shade. Smooth the fabric over the surface, pressing out any wrinkles, and move on to the next section. When you've worked your way all around the shade, attach the raw end of the fabric with spray adhesive, then overlap the material with the finished, pressed-over end and secure it with fabric glue.*

STEP 5. Fold the cut edges of the fabric under and tuck them between the fabric and shade. Use quick-release tape to hold the fabric as you go. Then run a thin bead of fabric glue on the shade near the fold line and firmly press the fabric into place.

You can buy spray fabric adhesive and fabric glue in craft-supply stores and from numerous online retailers.

Spray adhesive onto a small section of the shade and press the fabric onto the surface.

Fold the top and bottom edges under and secure them with fabric glue.

Learn to Live with Lost Lacquer

Oops! You hauled your brass candlesticks out of storage and discovered that the lacquer finish is damaged. No problem—just strip off the old coating by rubbing it with nail polish remover on a soft cloth. Then leave the brass in its natural state and keep it shiny and bright by rubbing the surface periodically with either of these two DIY polishes:

▶ A slice of lemon sprinkled with baking soda

▶ A cloth moistened with white vinegar and sprinkled with salt

Whichever combo you choose, follow up by rinsing the brass with a cloth dipped in warm water, and then buff it dry with a soft cotton cloth.

BRAVO BRASS CLEANER

This marvelous mixture will keep your brass accessories and hardware shining like the morning sun. And, unlike commercial formulas, it contains no harsh chemicals. (It works the same magic on copper cookware.)

> ½ cup of all-purpose flour
>
> ½ cup of dry laundry detergent (without bleach)
>
> ½ cup of salt
>
> ¾ cup of white vinegar
>
> ¼ cup of lemon juice (fresh-squeezed or bottled)
>
> ½ cup of hot tap water

Mix the flour, detergent, and salt in a bowl. Add the remaining ingredients, and blend thoroughly. Dip a soft, clean cotton cloth into the mixture, and rub it onto the brass, taking care to get into all the nooks and crannies. Buff with a second cloth. Store any leftover cleaner in a jar with a tight-fitting lid.

Darn That Tarnish!

Unlacquered brass that's sporting a heavy coat of tarnish demands a more intensive cleanser—like either of these winners:

- **Non-gel toothpaste.** Just squeeze a big squiggle of it onto an old, soft toothbrush, and scrub the crud away.

- **Ketchup.** Put the victims in a saucepan, cover them with ketchup,* and heat it on high until it comes to a boil. Lower the heat and simmer until the brass is bright and shiny again.

Whichever method you use, rinse the brass with warm water and dry.

Note: *Hot-pepper sauce will work, too, but it costs more.*

A Sure Cure for Bronze Disease

Despite its name, this ugly green corrosion can attack both bronze and copper when moisture reacts with the metal. Fortunately, in its early stages, it's a snap to halt the chemical reaction that's causing the color change. At the first sign of greenish patches or speckles, stop trouble in its tracks this way:

▶ Soak a soft, clean cloth in either straight buttermilk or 1 cup of hot vinegar with ¼ cup of salt mixed into it.

▶ Wrap the item with the cloth, or lay the cloth on the affected area and let it sit for 15 minutes.

▶ Wash the "patient" in warm, soapy water; rinse with clear water; and dry the metal thoroughly before you put it back on display or into storage.

Your Bathroom-Container Protection Policy

We've all seen pictures in glossy magazines of bathrooms that are chock-full of storage containers made of unprotected metal, or cardboard covered with decorative paper or fabric. And there are all shapes and sizes of canisters with fancy, preprinted paper labels that say things like "Cotton Balls" or "Bath Salts." Well, take my advice: Except for a guest bathroom that's only used once in a blue moon, or a half bath with no tub or shower, forget those fragile things. If you put them in a bathroom that sees action every day—even by only one person—you're asking for a lot of rust, rot, or mildew. Instead, look for containers made of materials that can stand up and say "Boo!" to high humidity and splashing water. Any of these will work just fine:

- Breathable basketry
- Ceramic
- Glass
- Plastic
- Stainless steel
- Wood

Before you spruce up any dingy, tarnished *objet d'art*, consider how much you know about its history. If a (let's say) copper weathervane, silver vase, or bronze statue that you snagged at an estate sale turns out to be a genuine antique, removing what the experts call the "natural patina" could reduce the item's value by thousands of dollars. So unless you know for certain that you're dealing with a modern reproduction, don't reach for any polish—commercial or DIY—until you've gotten the green light from a specialist at a museum, auction house, or antique shop.

CALL A PRO

CHRISTMAS DECORATIONS

Hair's to a Festive Christmas!

As odd as this may sound, hair spray can keep some of your favorite decorations looking merry and bright for the whole 12 days of Christmas—and then some. Here's a trio of ways to put it to work:

▶ Before you hang a wreath outside, spray the ribbons and bows with super-hold hair spray and let it dry. The trimmings will stay clean and perky. (Just don't hang the wreath where it will get rained on, or the hair spray will wash off.)

▶ Help your tree keep its needles longer by spritzing it from top to bottom with hair spray (either the pump or aerosol kind will work).

▶ If you have satiny tree ornaments and the threads are beginning to unravel, spritz them with hair spray and press the stray ends back into place.

A Sweet Way to Hold the Needles

Got no hair spray on hand? Then follow this routine to help your tree hold on to its needles: When you bring the tree home, cut an inch or two off the bottom of the trunk, and immediately set it into a bucket of cold water with 1 cup of molasses mixed in. Let the tree soak for two or three days before you move it to a stand and trim it.

Yuletide Water Ways

These timely tips will help prolong the life of your Christmas tree—and possibly your house to boot:

• For maximum safety and longevity, use a tree stand that holds at least 1 gallon of water (that is, unless your tree is a mini model).

• Just before you put the tree in its stand, cut at least ¼ inch off the base to remove any sap and allow the maximum amount of water absorption. This is important even if you gave the evergreen a preliminary soak (see "A Sweet Way to Hold the Needles," above).

CHRISTMAS TREE SURVIVAL TONIC

Every year my Grandma Putt poured this elixir into our Christmas tree stand to keep that ol' tree fresh and green throughout the holidays. I've never found a better formula!

2 cups of clear corn syrup
4 tbsp. of chlorine bleach
4 multivitamin tablets with iron
1 gal. of very hot water

Just before you set up your Christmas tree, cut an inch or two off the bottom of the trunk (so it will absorb moisture more efficiently). Then mix all of the ingredients together in a bucket, and pour the mixture into the stand. Deliver a fresh dose whenever the water level starts going down, and your evergreen will stay as fresh as a daisy right into the new year!

- Site the tree away from fireplaces, radiators, and other heat sources that could dry it out.

- Top off the water supply daily.

Save the Ornaments

A few scratches on your glass ornaments can add character—and maybe bring back fond memories of Christmases past. But if the paint is peeling off in big patches, that's another story. You can still save those decorations, though. Just strip off the old paint with a half-and-half solution of ammonia and water. Then rinse with clear water. When the baubles are completely dry, paint them with glossy enamel (brush or spray it on; it's your call), and hang 'em on the tree.

Note: *Be sure to wear gloves for the stripping phase of this project—and any other time you're working with ammonia.*

More Glass Acts

Make that non-acts. Always keep glass tree ornaments away from water, cleaning sprays, and waxes. Any liquid or oily substance can damage or discolor the finish. A light swipe with a microfiber cloth will bring back the shine of most modern ornaments—but don't try it on hand-painted or antique versions. Their finish is so unstable that even a wet cotton swab can wipe it away.

Time to take down your real Christmas tree? These cast-offs can make the job easier:

• Before you start untrimming the tree, spread an old sheet around the base. That way, any loose needles will fall onto the fabric. When you've removed all of the ornaments, wrap the sheet around the tree, and haul it outside for your neighborhood recycling pickup. Or deck it out with edible treats for the birds.

• When you're ready to clean up the needles that escaped the sheet, pull a panty hose leg over the nozzle of your vacuum cleaner. The needles will stick to the nylon surface instead of clogging the inside of the vacuum. When you're through with the job, just peel off the stocking, and throw it away.

Put Your Tree to Bed

If you have an artificial Christmas tree, you know how hard it can be to get the thing apart after the holidays are over. End that yearly struggle by dipping the end of each branch into petroleum jelly before you insert it in the tree trunk. The decorated limbs will stay snugly in place until you're ready to "un-decorate." They'll glide right out! Wipe away the petroleum jelly before storing the branches. And keep in mind that flocked or white trees are sensitive to heat and humidity. So keep them out of the attic!

ART & COLLECTIONS

Photographs and Glass: A Sticky Wicket

Whenever you frame photos, don't ever let them touch the glass! Over time, moisture can creep into the frame, and even the smallest bit can make the pictures stick. Always use an archival, acid-free mat or, if you've chosen a decorative, stand-up frame, insert spacers that keep the surface of the photo from coming into contact with the glass. (You can buy spacers at art-supply and framing stores.)

Note: *This same caution applies to watercolors, prints, posters, and all other works on paper.*

DON'T MOAN OVER MILDEW

It's happened to most of us: You come upon some forgotten treasures in your basement, but they've picked up some mildew in that damp cellar. Don't fret—just go after the foul stuff using one of these techniques:

Mildew Victim	Recommended Treatment
Book covers	Sponge alcohol on the spots, and set the books in sunlight until the splotches disappear.
Books	Sprinkle cornstarch throughout the pages. Wait several hours until the moisture has been absorbed, and then brush out the starch. **Note:** *Do this job outdoors, so the mildew spores don't invade your house!*
Fabric (washable)	Brush off the mildew spores outdoors. Soak the item overnight in buttermilk, then wash and dry it.
Leather	Wipe the mildew away with a solution of equal parts of rubbing alcohol and water. Follow up with a good leather conditioner
Small wooden objects	Soak them for 10 minutes in a bucket of warm water with ½ cup of bleach and 1 tablespoon of laundry detergent added. Then set them out in the sun to dry.

Must Get That Mustiness Out!

Drat! That collection of old trunks and suitcases you found in your attic would be perfect for storage in the rest of the house—if only they didn't smell musty inside. The simple solution: Put half a dozen untreated charcoal briquettes inside each case, and close it up. (Put them on sheets of paper or plastic to keep the black powder from rubbing off onto the lining.) Then every few days, take out the charcoal and replace it with a new supply. Depending on how aromatic each piece is, the deodorizing process could take anywhere from a couple of days to several weeks.

If you have original historic documents or other important, but fragile, pieces of history, consult with a professional conservator about how you should store or display them. An antique dealer or someone on the staff at your local museum should be able to point you in the right direction.

Nix the Negatives?

True or false? There's no reason to hang on to negatives anymore because you can always have a new print made from the original photograph.

It all depends. While it is true that any photograph, new or old, can be duplicated, there is one catch: You have to have the original. If it's been destroyed in a fire or flood, or lost in a move, you're out of luck. My advice: Don't take any chances with photos that are especially near and dear to your heart—say, your children's baby pictures, or snapshots of your favorite family vacations. Keep those negatives in a sturdy, fireproof box or, better yet, in your safe deposit box at the bank.

Do Not Laminate!

You may think you're doing your loved ones a favor by having a special piece of paper laminated—maybe the front page of the newspaper on the day they were born. But according to the folks in charge of preserving documents at the Library of Congress, laminating is a big-time no-no because it damages the paper. Instead, they say that if you want to display the image, you should make a photocopy, and store the original in a flat, custom-size box (available in stores and on websites that carry archival supplies). Keep the box in a place where it's safe from heat, moisture, pollutants, dust, and pests.

The Art of Survival

Correction: Make that the survival of your art. Whenever you need to store pictures of any kind, keep them safe and sound by following these guidelines:

▶ **Vacation quarters.** If you rotate your collection, be *very* careful how and where you store the off-duty pictures. Never, ever put paintings, prints, drawings, or photographs in an attic or basement. High humidity levels and fluctuating temperatures can damage them in a hurry. Instead, keep them in a closet that has a relatively constant temperature and humidity level. Wrap framed pieces in bubble wrap or thick blankets.

▶ **Longer-term storage.** When you need to tuck unframed artwork away for longer periods of time, put each piece between sheets of acid-free paper, and tape a piece of foam board to each side. Write a description of the picture on the foam board so you'll remember what's in there. Then either stand your "sandwich" upright in a safe location, or slide it under a bed or sofa.

The next time you use the last of a liquid cleaner that comes in a trigger-type spray bottle, hang on to the empty bottle. Wash it and let it dry thoroughly. Then use it to blow the dust off ceramic figurines, fancy picture frames, carved furniture, or anything else with hard-to-get-at nooks and crannies.

Picture-a-Weigh

Problem: You need to determine the weight of a picture so you know what kind of hanging hardware you'll need—but you don't have a scale on hand. Not to worry! Just remember my practically foolproof picture-weighing system: Simply lift the picture, then use these guidelines:

• If you can hold it in one hand, it probably weighs less than 10 pounds.

• If you can lift it easily with two hands, it weighs around 20 pounds.

• If you need to bend your knees, but you can still lift it without a strain, it's less than 50 pounds.

• If you need help, chances are it weighs between 50 and 100 pounds—and you're going to need some high-powered hardware!

How to Build a Better Book Safe

The Internet is swarming with instructions on turning a thick book into a hiding place for valuables by carving out a compartment from the inner pages. You can also buy highly realistic commercial versions. But in either case, there's just one problem: Even *War and Peace* won't give you a whole lot of stashing space. Enter this variation on the theme, which can conceal a fairly sizable container. The one caveat is that its top is clearly visible. For that reason, you have to keep it on a shelf that's well above eye level—and that has enough other books on it to provide good camouflage. But if you've got that kind of choice real estate, you're in luck. Here's all you need to do:

STEP 1. Find or build a wooden box of the size you need. (It can be lidded or not—it's your call.) Then gather up enough books to cover one side of the container.

STEP 2. Using a fine-toothed power saw, cut off the covers and pages of each book to within about 1 inch of the spine. If the sides of your assemblage will be visible—even partially—retain the book covers on the left and right sides, as shown in the illustration.

STEP 3. Glue the spines to the box, stash your loot inside, and tuck the whole shebang on a high shelf.

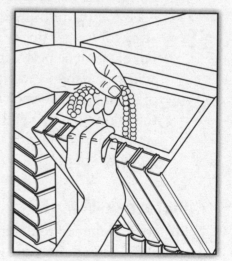

Glue a line of book spines to your box, and you've got yourself a safe.

Librarians Know Books Best

Your treasured books can last for generations if you heed these tips from the folks who are trained to make them do just that:

▶ **Shun the sun.** Keep books out of direct sunlight to prevent the covers and bindings from fading.

▶ **Give 'em air.** Long-term book survival demands good air circulation. Don't pack volumes tightly together on the shelves. Leave room between the tops of the books and the shelf above, and always align the spines at the front edges of the shelves. Pushing books to the back of the case is begging for mildew invasions.

▶ **Don't turn corners.** It destroys a book's value. Instead, use bookmarks made of paper, ribbon, or leather. Avoid paper clips or clip-on bookmarks because they can leave permanent marks on the pages.

▶ **Support the spines!** If a row of books doesn't reach from one end of a shelf to the other, use substantial bookends to hold the volumes upright and stable. If they're allowed to lean, the added pressure on the spines will break them down. Also, whenever you take a book off its shelf, grasp and pull it from the sides, not the top of the spine.

▶ **Wash your hands!** Whenever you handle books, make sure your hands are clean. Any dirt or oils from your skin can mar the cover and pages.

▶ **Don't write in your books.** Any mark—even your name written on the inside—automatically decreases a book's value in the eyes of a dealer or private collector. (The exception: If you happen to be a famous person or the author of the book, your autograph could increase its worth.)

▶ **Store 'em right.** Store books (and all important paper items) away from dirt, excessive dust, extreme temperatures, and extreme humidity or dryness—and never in a basement or garage. Also, always pack books flat, whether for storage or a long-distance move. When the spine faces up and the pages hang down, their weight puts stress on the binding and, over time, will destroy it.

▶ **Deal with dampness.** To keep damp books from getting mildewed, sprinkle cornstarch throughout the pages. Wait several hours until all the moisture has been absorbed, then brush out the starch. If any trace of moisture remains, repeat the process.

The Geography of Storage

What on earth does that mean? Just this: For many types of home furnishings and collectibles, one guaranteed way to ensure an early death is to store them in either the attic or the basement. Consider these particulars:

BASEMENT

This is no place for anything that could suffer harm from dampness, dirt, or pests (not to mention plumbing leaks or full-scale floods). The roster of items includes:

- Antiques, art, or photographs
- Audio- and videotapes
- Books
- Carpets and rugs
- Clothes, quilts, and other fragile textiles
- Fire hazards like gasoline, kerosene, and oil-based paint
- Functioning electronics
- Fur and leather
- Important papers
- Luggage
- Musical instruments
- Vinyl records

- Anything that would cause you heartbreak or financial woe if you lost it

ATTIC

Although this is an ideal place to store gear that you don't need to keep close at hand, remember that temperatures in that lofty spot can reach as high as 150°F in the summer. And in the winter, temps plunge. If your attic is not temperature-controlled, and you've stashed anything delicate or fragile under the rafters, get it outta there—and do it *now*! The attic no-no list includes:

- Audio- and videotapes
- Candles and anything else that's made of wax
- Computer discs
- Fireworks, firecrackers, and sparklers
- Flammable substances of any kind
- Food, including any in cans or jars
- Musical instruments
- Original artwork
- Photographs and photo albums
- Vinyl records and CDs
- Wool blankets and clothing

Clothing & Accessories

Even if you don't come close to wearing the "fashionista" label, it's probably safe to say that you've got a pretty penny or two invested in your clothes and accessories. Who doesn't these days? Unfortunately, it's not likely that you can make any of your duds last as long as, let's say, a dining room table. But with some sound and simple TLC and occasional timely tweaks, you can keep your wardrobe at the peak of "health" for years.

CLOTHES ENCOUNTERS

The Dastardly "Dry-Clean-Only" Lie

When you see the words *dry clean only* on a garment label, it's only natural to think that if you ignore that warning, you'll wind up with clothes that would fit a two-year-old. Well (to quote Ira Gershwin), it ain't necessarily so. If you follow these guidelines, you can do the job yourself, and your clothes will come out just fine—without the use of harsh chemicals that could potentially hasten the demise of your duds (and put a major crimp in your pocketbook, to boot)!

Critter-derived fabrics, including alpaca, angora, cashmere, mohair, and wool.

▶ Gently hand-wash in lukewarm (100°F) water with mild soap.

▶ Rinse in cool water with a teaspoon of white vinegar added to it.

▶ To dry the garment, lay it flat, and stretch it to its original shape and size.

Silk fabric.

▶ Fill a basin with 100° to 120°F water, and mix in a little gentle castile soap, which has a neutral pH.

▶ Swirl the article around in the soapy water, then rinse with clear, cool H_2O.

▶ Dry the item on a hanger indoors. Never hang silk outdoors—or near a sunny window—because the sun's UV rays can damage it.

▶ Hang the garment in a steamy bathroom to smooth out any wrinkles, or iron it on low, using a piece of white or pale-colored 100 percent cotton to cover the silk.

POWERFUL POTIONS

ALL-NATURAL LAUNDRY SOAP

Laundry detergents are intended for use on synthetic materials such as polyester and acrylic. But natural fibers, like cotton, linen, silk, and wool, keep their good looks longer when you wash them with a soap-based formula. This is one of the best.

1 cup of soap,* grated
½ cup of borax
½ cup of washing soda**

Mix all of the ingredients together, and store the mixture in a lidded container. Use 1 tablespoon for a small load or lightly soiled laundry and 2 tablespoons for a large or heavily soiled load. For a sinkful of hand-washables, use about 2 teaspoons.

* Fels-Naptha®, Octagon®, and Ivory® are all good choices.

** Available in the laundry products aisle of your supermarket.

Keep the Color

Modern-day fabrics tend to be a lot more colorfast than they were in days gone by. Still, unless you're absolutely sure the dye will stay put, it doesn't pay to take chances. So before you wash a new, bright-colored garment for the first time, soak it for about 15 minutes in a solution made from ⅔ cup of white vinegar per gallon of cold water. Then wash and dry the article according to the guidelines on its care tag.

Winning Ways to Whiter Whites

We all know that over time, white clothes tend to take on a dull, grayish tone. Chlorine bleach can restore the brightness—but it will also weaken the fabric, thereby (of course) shortening the life of the garment. But these easygoing treatments will accomplish the same objective with no nasty side effects:

- Add 1 cup of white vinegar to your washer's rinse cycle.

- Soak the dingy garment for 30 minutes or so in 1 gallon of hot water with either 1 cup of baking soda or five aspirin tablets mixed into it.

- To keep your whites white, dissolve four aspirin tablets in 1 cup of hot water, and add it to the regular warm-water wash cycle.

Join the Darker Side

Just as white fabric turns gray over time, darker colors tend to fade into dull, dingy tones—and often quite quickly. But don't rush out and replace your formerly vibrant duds. You can keep your dark washables looking crisp and sharp for years. Here's how:

▶ **Black.** Add 2 cups of brewed coffee or strong black (not green!) tea to the rinse cycle.

▶ **Other deep shades.** For navy blue, dark brown, or burgundy, for example, add 1 cup of table salt to the rinse cycle.

If It Ain't Dirty, Don't Wash It!

Just because you've worn a garment doesn't necessarily mean that it's dirty. When you undress at the end of the day, take a good look at your clothes. If they still look just fine, fold them neatly, or hang them up, and wear them another time or two before you toss them into the hamper. Besides extending the life of your wardrobe, you'll reduce wear and tear on your washing machine.

Unshrink a Shrunken Garment

Drat! When you washed your new pullover and tossed it in the dryer, it came out a couple of sizes too small. Now what do you do? Don't panic—follow these simple steps:

STEP 1. Fill a basin or sink with a solution of 1 tablespoon of either hair conditioner or baby shampoo per quart of water. Then insert the garment, making sure it's completely submerged, and leave it there for a few minutes so the fibers can relax.

STEP 2. While the item is soaking, find a similar piece of clothing that's the right size and trace its outline on a piece of paper (wrapping paper or an opened-up brown paper bag will work fine).

STEP 3. Remove the "swimmer" from the drink, squeeze out the excess water, and lay the garment on the paper.

STEP 4. Gently stretch it in all directions until it fits the traced outline. If the fabric is a little stiff, use a steamer or the steam from an iron to soften it up.

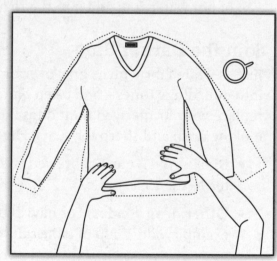

Lay the damp garment on the paper and gently stretch it until it fits the traced outline.

STEP 5. Set clean, heavy objects around the edges to secure them while the garment dries. (Coffee mugs, glass paperweights, or glass jars of food are perfect.) When it's dry, it should be as good—and as big—as new.*

While this "unshrinking" method will work with any fabric, knitted garments made of cotton, wool, or cashmere are easier to manipulate than woven materials or synthetic fibers like rayon or polyester.

4 Sweet Sweater-Saving Solutions

A sweater's basic construction makes it prone to a number of highly annoying mishaps. But fear not—you can put your favorite knits back in action with these fast fixes:

Stretched cuffs. Dip the cuffs in hot water, then blow-dry them on "High." This ploy isn't permanent, but it will put the cuffs back in wrist-hugging mode for a while. Then you'll have to repeat the fix.

Snags. Pick up an inexpensive snag-repair tool at a sewing shop, or order one online. Then simply push the end of the tool through the underside of the fabric at the site of the snag. Grab hold of the wayward strand(s) of yarn on the outside, and pull them back under. (You can also use a small crochet hook for this job.) But whatever you do, don't cut the snag off, or you're likely to trade it for a hole!

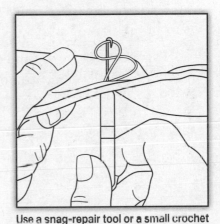

Use a snag-repair tool or a small crochet hook to pull wayward yarn back into place.

Pills. Gently, but firmly, run a pumice stone, comb, or piece of sandpaper over the sweater's surface. The unsightly pimples will pull right off.

Hanger bumps. You have two options here, depending on where you are when you notice the shoulder puckers:

- At home or in a hotel room: Lay the sweater flat and give it a blast of moist heat from a steamer or an iron. Or spread it out on a towel in the bathroom while you take a hot shower.

- At work or another place where you can't remove the sweater: Dampen (don't saturate!) the shoulders with cold water or an ice cube. Lightly press a cloth or paper towel over the bumps to press the fibers down into place and absorb the excess water. Then go about your business. As the water dries, the fabric will shrink back to its normal size.

And from now on, fold your sweaters neatly and keep them, and other knits, in drawers or on shelves—don't hang them up!

Snags, moth holes, or another malady ruining the body of a sweater? If the sleeves are still in good shape, turn would-be trash into treasure this way: Cut the sleeves off just below the shoulder seams, and hem the raw edges so they don't unravel. Then you (or a daughter, granddaughter, or friend) can wear those arms as leg warmers!

The Hole Truth about Clothes Moths

Almost nothing short of a fire or flood can demolish your wardrobe faster than an invasion of clothes moths. And contrary to what many folks think, wool clothing is far from the only potential victim. Any natural-fiber item in your closet, or elsewhere in your home, is fair game for the egg-laying mamas and their hungry offspring. So are furs, down pillows or bedding, pet hair, and even human hair in off-duty wigs or forgotten hairbrushes. The secret to closing down the maternity ward is to act fast. The minute you spot even a single moth, go on the offense with this three-part initiative:

▶ **Cook 'em or freeze 'em.** Either soaking infested fabric in hot water (greater than 120°F) for 20 to 30 minutes or running it through a dryer, set on "High," for an hour or so will kill moths and their eggs. So will tucking your clothes into the freezer for three or four days at a temperature that's below 18°F. The key to success here is dropping the temperature of the eggs as rapidly as possible, so the less packed the freezer is, the better.

▶ **Get 'em on a clean sweep.** Thoroughly vacuum every single nook and cranny in closets, dressers, armoires, and upholstered furniture, as well as places where any wall-to-wall carpet meets the baseboard. Then immediately seal up your vacuum cleaner bag, and toss it in the outdoor garbage can.

▶ **Trap 'em.** As added insurance, buy some commercial (and perfectly safe) pheromone-baited clothes moth traps, and hang them throughout your house to catch any culprits your DIY tactics may have missed. After that, to detect any future trouble in its early stages, keep a trap or two hanging in your closet.

Stay Moth-Free with These Savvy Strategies

Once you've gotten rid of the moths in your life—or if you simply want to keep the holey terrors from moving in—develop these four defensive habits:

- Clean or wash all of your winter *and* summer clothes and linens before you store them away. Moths zero in on anything that's sporting food or dirt stains, or even body oils that your eyes or nose can't detect.

- Whenever you buy a piece of clothing or any other natural-fabric item at a resale shop or garage sale, wash it or have it dry-cleaned immediately. Or simply give it some quality time in your dryer or freezer (see "The Hole Truth about Clothes Moths," at left).

- Vacuum your closets, drawers, and other storage areas frequently and thoroughly.

- Get rid of garments and accessories that you no longer wear. The less moth-enticing stuff you have in your closets or drawers, the fewer havens you'll provide for expectant moth mamas.

Get Unwired

Even with their zero-dollar price tag, wire hangers are no bargain because they can stretch your clothes out of shape, leave permanent creases in the shoulders, or send the garments slipping off onto the floor, where they then lie in a wrinkled heap. Those cheap tubular

---

AN OUNCE OF
PREVENTION

Create a Moth-Resistant Climate

One of the most effective moth-deterring strategies of all is to make the living conditions in your closets as uninviting as possible. The mother moths prefer the humidity to be on the high side—between 70 and 80 percent. Your simple mission: Put a dehumidifier everywhere you have clothing stored. You can buy a mini model for less than the cost of an average sweater—and a lot less than a high-quality wool or cashmere version.

plastic hangers can perform the same wardrobe-damaging feats. So protect your clothes by opting for these gentler options:

▶ Hangers with spring-type bar clamps for pants and skirts

▶ Padded hangers for delicate silk and lightweight cotton dresses, shirts, blouses, and anything that has thin straps

▶ Wooden or heavy-duty molded plastic hangers for coats, jackets, and flannel shirts

4 Secrets to Safe Storage

In addition to bypassing wire hangers (see "Get Unwired" on page 333), follow these guidelines to keep your clothes fresh and attractive—whether they're on active duty or taking an off-season snooze:

Even though you don't want to put your clothes on wire hangers, it is a good idea to keep one or two of them in your closet—that is, if you have any skirts or dresses that tend to cling to your legs. To get rid of static cling without resorting to smelly chemical sprays, just run the flat side of a wire hanger over the outer surface of your skirt, and then repeat the process on the underside.

• Don't store clothing—or any other fabric items—in plastic bags or containers (including dry-cleaner bags). Plastic traps moisture, providing a cozy home for a variety of molds and mildew. Instead, use clean cotton sheets, pillowcases, or breathable garment bags to keep your duds dust-free.

• Make sure the fabric is free of wrinkles. Lines and folds in your clothes are just like the ones in your skin—they become deeper and harder to get rid of with age!

• Before you store clothes (or any other fabric items), wrap them loosely in acid-free tissue paper. Then put them in a trunk or a box made of acid-free material. Never use plain old cardboard: It promotes an acidic environment that destroys fabric.

• For long-term storage, think horizontal rather than vertical. Although hanging does reduce wrinkling, over time it may result in stretched collars and misshapen shoulders.

STAIN REMOVAL 101

You can buy chemical stain removers, but some of the most powerful ones of all are right in your kitchen cupboards. Like these, for instance:

Stain	Material	How to Get It Out
Blood	Fabric	Blot, then pour on cold club soda.
Fruit or juice	Washable fabric	Pour salt on the spots, and soak with milk.
Grass	Washable fabric	Sponge with white vinegar, or apply a paste of water and cream of tartar, let it dry, and brush off.
Grease or oil	Smooth fabric	Cover the spot with cornstarch, wait 12 hours, and brush it off.
Grease or oil	Knit fabric	Pour club soda (cold or room-temperature) on the spot, and scrub gently.
Ink (ballpoint)	Washable fabric	Dampen sponge with milk, and dab until gone.
Mildew	Washable fabric	Moisten the spots with equal amounts of salt and lemon juice. Dry the item in the sun.
Mustard	Washable fabric	Soak the stain in a half-and-half solution of white vinegar and water. Blot with a soft cloth.
Perspiration	Washable fabric	Mix 4 tablespoons of salt with 1 quart of water, and sponge the stains with the solution.
Protein-based substances (e.g., milk, egg)	Washable fabric	Mix meat tenderizer with a few drops of water, work it into the stain, and launder immediately.
Rust	Washable fabric	Mix equal parts of salt and vinegar, and rub the paste into the stain. After 30 minutes, launder.
Tar	Fabric	Slather mayonnaise onto the spot.
Vomit	Fabric	Remove the residue, then cover the spot with baking soda, let it dry, and brush it off.
Wine	Fabric	Blot up any excess moisture, and saturate the stain with club soda. Rub lightly, and blot dry.

Note: *After you've treated the stain, launder or dry-clean the garment as usual.*

FASTENER FRUSTRATIONS

Zipper Dee Doo Dah

Few of us give much thought to the zippers on our clothes—until the danged things malfunction. Here are two of the most common zipping mishaps:

The slider catches on the fabric. First, enlist a helper for this fix-it ploy. Hold the garment taut along the length of the zipper while your pal pulls the fabric out from under the slider. Don't pull on the slider itself. That might damage it or cause it to stick more snugly.

The pull tab snaps off. You have two options here, depending on the zipper's construction:

▶ Replace it with a paper clip or safety pin pushed through the holes in the slider.

▶ If there is no hole, and the tab merely clamps into two slots on either side of the slider, here's your plan: Find an expendable garment with a similar zipper, use a pair of pliers to pry off the tab, and attach it to the broken zipper.

Curses—Jammed Again!

When a zipper gets stuck, as these dandy devices are prone to do, don't wrestle with it. The pressure could cause permanent damage to the zipper—and possibly the garment it's attached to. Instead, take a deep breath and use one of these two gentler fix-it strategies:

Lubricate it. Just use any of these common household products:

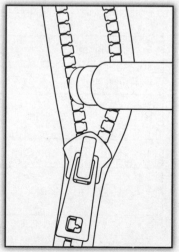

Rub the zipper's teeth with lip balm or another lubricant.

• A bar of soap

• A cotton swab dipped in olive oil

• Lip balm

• Petroleum jelly

• The point of a lead pencil

In each case, rub your fixer of choice along the teeth of the zipper, both above and below the sticking point (being careful not to get any of the stuff on the adjacent fabric).

Soak it. Add 2 cups or so of dishwashing liquid to a bowl or sink filled with warm water. Submerge the zippered area of the garment, and let it soak for about an hour so the concentrated soapy solution can penetrate both the slider and the teeth. Bingo—that dandy closing device should be back in business!

A Note-able Solution

You say your zippers are all working just fine, but your stiff joints or finger injuries make it nearly impossible to manage the zipper pulls? The simple remedy: Make the task easier by attaching a small notebook ring (available in office-supply stores) to each zipper's end tab.

Note: *This maneuver works just as well for small children whose tiny fingers have yet to master zipper management.*

How to Sew on a Button

Yes, I know this seems like a no-brainer, but the fact is that when most people perform this repair, they make one big mistake: They sew the buttons flat onto the fabric, which leaves no room for them to pass easily through the buttonholes. So every time you button up your overcoat (or whatever), it creates tension on the thread. Eventually, it snaps and the button pops off—maybe to be found, but maybe not.

The secret to keeping your buttons on the job is to give each one a small stem (a.k.a. shank) to hold it up, thereby leaving ample room underneath for the buttonhole side of the fabric to rest. Here's how to go about it using a typical four-hole button:

STEP 1. Thread a needle with a double length of thread and knot the ends together. Using a pin or marking pen, note the position of the button, set it in place, and hold it there.

STEP 2. From the underside of the fabric, poke the needle up through one of the holes. Lay a wooden matchstick on top of the button and stitch over the matchstick into the opposite hole and down through the fabric. Add three or four more stitches on each side, keeping the parallel alignment—never stitch diagonally from hole to hole or in a square pattern.

STEP 3. Pull out the matchstick, and push the button up to the top of the stitches. Poke the needle down through one hole to the underside of the button. Then make a shank by tightly winding the thread several times around the threads that hold the button to the fabric.

STEP 4. Push the needle through to the underside of the fabric and make a few stitches to secure the thread in place.

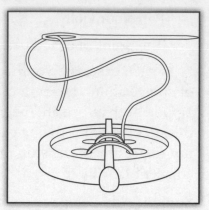

With a matchstick on top of the button, make four stitches through the holes on each side.

Make a shank by winding the thread around the threads that hold the button to the fabric.

* For a cotton shirt or other lightweight garment, a thin toothpick or straight pin will work fine.

Hold On to Your Buttons!

No matter how well (or how poorly) your buttons are sewn on, over time the thread will start to fray. So as soon as you add new buttons or bring home a new, buttoned garment, dab the strands with clear nail polish or white clear-drying glue. Either one will increase the fasteners' holding power.

End Snap Snafus

Even experienced seamstresses find it tricky to get snaps to match up on both sides of a garment. But it's a snap (sorry—I couldn't resist!) when you use this simple trick: First, sew on all the small "male" parts, and rub a stick of chalk over the little point on top of each one. Then put the second piece of fabric over them, making sure the snaps are in the right position. Then rub the back of the fabric covering each point—thereby marking the spot for the larger "female" part of the snap. That's all there is to it!

If you've got a bunch of buttons stashed in a jewelry box or drawer, don't let them sit there hogging valuable storage space—put 'em to work! Here's how:

- Use tiny buttons to stuff "beanbag" toys for kids or pets. Or, if your creations are small enough, sew a ribbon on top, and hang 'em on the Christmas tree.
- Glue decorative buttons of all sizes onto a plain wooden box or mirror frame.
- Recycle big buttons as markers for board games.
- Make a one-of-a-kind vest or jacket by sewing fancy buttons all over the front.
- String buttons together, then hang them in fruit trees. The noise they make as they jangle in the wind will discourage hungry birds.

ACCESSORIES

4 Fabulous Felt Feats

A wool felt hat is one of the best head warmers you can find. And it'll last for years if you follow these TLC tips:

▶ Use a soft-bristled brush for routine cleaning. For more intensive treatment, hold the hat briefly over a steaming pot or teakettle, then brush again to remove the soil. (This routine will also get rid of any creases.)

▶ When off-season storage time rolls around, clean your hat, stuff it with acid-free tissue paper, and tuck it, upside down, into a hatbox.

For good measure, toss in a moth-repellent sachet or two (see "Make Some Moth Chasers" on page 305).

▶ If you get caught in the rain or snow, blot up the water spots with paper towels or facial tissue. Then wad up a handful of tissue paper, and rub it over the marks in a circular motion.

▶ In the case of an overall soaking, let your topper dry naturally—don't try to speed up the process by perching it on a radiator or blasting it with a hair dryer!

Get Your Chapeau in Shape

Has your straw hat or wool fedora gotten bent out of shape? Here's a quick trick to bring it back into line. Boil a pot of water, and hold the bent part over the steam for a few minutes until the creases or misshapen fabric relaxes. Bend your hat back to whatever shape you desire, and set it aside to air-dry. Just mind your fingers—you don't want to steam them, too!

Restore Shine to Straw Hats

Over time, every straw hat loses its crisp, shiny appearance. But that doesn't mean it's ready to bite the dust. To bring back its youthful good looks, just give it a light coating of hair spray and let it dry. Then bingo—you're all set to sport that topper at the rodeo or the Easter parade!

AN OUNCE OF PREVENTION

Elevate Your Hats

Have you ever noticed that the brims of hats in stores never touch the shelves? That's because a brim that rests on a solid surface will flatten out like a pancake. So take a tip from professional milliners: Perch your headgear on hat stands, or overstuff each crown so that the filling sticks down below the hat, thereby elevating the brim. Hat shops generally use tissue paper for stuffing, but a plastic bag full of foam peanuts is a dandy alternative. You could also use bubble wrap, old panty hose, or a cast-off sweater.

Mouth Off against Mildew

Rats! You took your favorite leather handbag out of storage, took one whiff, and said, "P-U—mildew!" Don't despair. Just dampen a cotton pad with antiseptic mouthwash, and gently rub the bag's surface thoroughly. Wipe it dry with a soft cotton cloth, buff with a second cloth, then apply a commercial leather-nourishing cream.

Note: *This same trick works on any mildewed leather.*

Moo Juice Removes Ink

When ink leaks out of a ballpoint pen onto your favorite leather handbag, briefcase, suitcase, or jacket, don't panic. Just dip a clean, soft cotton cloth in milk and rub the marks away. Then rinse with a second cloth, dampened with clear, cool water, and dry the leather thoroughly using yet another soft, absorbent cloth.

How to Free Up a Stuck Suitcase Handle

I think every traveler would agree that the wheeled suitcase is one of the greatest inventions that ever came down the pike. There's just one problem: The telescoping handles on those babies have an annoying habit of freezing up. The good news is that getting them on the move again is nearly always a simple process. Whether your handhold is stuck in the up or down position, here's all you need to do:

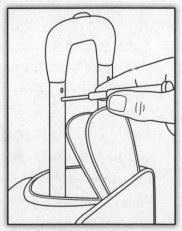

STEP 1. Using a small screwdriver, remove the screws that secure the handle to the sliding tubes. Put the tiny things in your pocket or a dish for safekeeping.

STEP 2. Look inside the hollow tubes. In each one you'll see a thin metal rod. When you press the release button on your suitcase handle, these babies convey the action signal to the lock-and-release mechanism at the base of the tubes.

Remove the screws that hold the handle to the movable tubes.

STEP 3. Grasp the tip of one rod and pull it up 8 inches or so beyond the tube's opening. Look at the open ends of the handle. In each one you'll see a small hole that accommodates the end of a rod.

STEP 4. Press the release button on the handle while you push one of the rods firmly into its hole. Hold on to it as you repeat the procedure with the rod in the other tube.

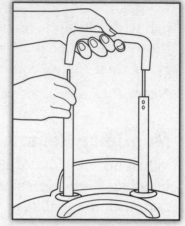

STEP 5. Hold the rods firmly inside the handle as you lower the assembly onto the sliding tubes. Line up the holes, replace the screws, and you're on a roll again!

Push the end of each release rod into its corresponding hole in the handle.

When Hard Knocks Ding Hard Cases

In the rough-and-tumble world of airport luggage handling, even the sturdiest plastic suitcase can pick up a dent or two. If your bag comes off the baggage trolley bearing a souvenir you hadn't bargained for, don't despair—just try one of these two tricks to repair the gouge:

- Open the case and pass a hair dryer back and forth over the raised area for about 10 minutes. The heat should flatten it out. (Just be sure to keep the dryer moving to avoid burning the plastic.)

- If your heat treatment doesn't work, cover a block of wood with a cloth, set it on top of the bump, and tap the wood gently with a hammer or a rubber mallet.

How to Reshape a Warped Purse

Leather shoulder- and handbags tend to get bent out of shape when they sit on a shelf too long. If that carryall is unlined, this three-step procedure will put it back in business fast:

▶ Make the leather more flexible by wiping down the bag's interior with a solution of 5 parts white vinegar to 1 part water.

▶ Stuff the purse with tissue paper until it's back to its natural shape.

▶ Let it sit for a couple of days, and then air it out to remove the odor.

Then, to prevent future warping, keep it stuffed with acid-free tissue paper between uses—or simply carry it more often.

Note: *To unwarp a lined bag, forget the vinegar and water treatment and just pack the interior tightly with tissue paper. The process will take longer, but eventually the leather will regain its original contours.*

3 Suede-Cleaning Tricks

Suede bags, shoes, and jackets are all magnets for spots. And the material is delicate and can be hard to clean, even for a pro. But the faster you act, the better your chances are of heading off permanent stains. Here's a trio of ways to go about it:

- Tackle grease spots by brushing them with a soft toothbrush dipped in white vinegar. Let the areas air-dry, then brush with a suede brush. If necessary, repeat the process a time or two.

- Remove ink stains and scuff marks by rubbing them with fine-grit sandpaper. Then use a dry toothbrush or nailbrush to bring up the nap.

- Treat general stains by rubbing the spots with an emery board or fine-grit sandpaper. Then hold the soiled area 6 inches

Don't Have a Ball

There's nothing more irritating than having to plow through a drawer in search of two matching socks. For that reason, lots of folks keep their foot covers paired up by folding the tops over together, forming a sort of ball. Well, take my advice: Don't do that! Granted, it does keep your socks together, but it also stretches the elastic, thereby reducing their life span. Instead, use one of these two hassle-avoidance strategies:

- Hold each pair together and fold it in half. Then carefully stack each set of twins in a drawer or in a basket on a shelf.

- Clip the two mates together with a spring clothespin.

LEATHER-WATERPROOFING COMPOUND

When you treat your outdoor shoes, boots, or work gloves with this old-time conditioner, they'll stand up to anything the outdoors can deliver.

2 parts beeswax

1 part mutton fat*

In a small pan, melt the wax and fat together, stirring well. Rub the mixture onto your shoes, boots, or gloves in the evening, and let them sit overnight. In the morning, buff them with a soft cotton cloth and get on your way.

* Ask your supermarket's meat department manager for mutton fat.

away from a steaming pan or teakettle until the suede warms up a little. (Don't let the steam saturate the leather!) Brush the marks with a tooth-brush or suede brush, let them dry, and then brush again to revive the texture.

Keep Your Gloves on the Go

After you launder wool or washable leather gloves, make sure they don't turn into shapeless lumps that you'll never wear again. How? Simply shove a rounded wooden clothespin into each damp finger! Got no clothespins on hand? Then roll up 10 paper towels to form tubes, and insert one into each digit. Either way, your paw covers will keep their shape as they dry.

If the Shoe Fits . . .

Use these five handy hints to keep it (and its mate) on the job for the long haul:

▶ Whenever you get a new pair of shoes, or have old ones reheeled, paint the backs of the heels with clear nail polish. It'll keep them scuff-free longer.

▶ Shoes that get wet and stiffen up will turn soft again if you sponge them off with warm water, and thoroughly rub castor oil into the leather.

- Remove stubborn scuff marks from shoes and boots by rubbing the leather with the cut face of a raw potato. Follow up with your usual polish.

- To cover scrapes and scratches on brightly colored shoes, use a waterproof felt-tip marker in a matching shade. If they are suede, disguise the marks with matching chalk.

- Silence a pair of squeaky shoes by spritzing lubricating oil on the source of the sound. Buff away any excess oil, and walk on. If you get any oil on the sole, remember to wipe it off before you track it onto the carpet!

Ouch—That's Tight!

We've all been there: You finally find the shoes you've been searching for, and they fit perfectly in the store—but they suddenly seem to shrink when you get them home. Or maybe you've ordered your usual size over the Internet, but when the package arrives, you find that the shoes are just a tad too snug. If you can't return them—or you simply don't want to—try any of these simple stretching tactics:

- Wear the shoes indoors for a few days with thick socks. That may be all it takes to expand the leather into your comfort zone.

- Spray the inside of each shoe with a half-and-half mixture of rubbing alcohol and water (test a small spot for colorfastness first). Then put the shoes on and go about your business for half an hour or so. Still too tight? Repeat the process a few times.

- Pack the shoes tightly with damp, bunched-up newspaper, and let the stuffing air-dry. That'll expand the leather enough to ease the fit.

While the techniques above should do no harm to your shoes, if you're dealing with expensive designer models—or maybe a vintage pair that can't be replaced—don't take any chances. Take your footwear to a shoe-repair shop to be stretched by an expert under more controlled conditions.

CALL A PRO

If you're of a certain age, you no doubt remember what happened on May 15, 1940. That's the day when nylon stockings first hit store shelves all over the U.S.A. Newspapers reported that no consumer product had ever caused such pandemonium! Women lined up for hours before the stores opened—after all, they'd been anticipating this day since the previous year, when DuPont introduced its "miracle fabric" at the 1939 World's Fair. By the end of the year, consumers had bought 36 million pairs of nylon stockings. And when did panty hose enter the picture? Nineteen years later, in 1958, courtesy of Glen Raven Mills of North Carolina. Seamless panty hose came along in 1965, just in time for the miniskirt craze.

Shore Up Your Shoelaces

As you're getting dressed for an outing, you discover that the little plastic cover—called an aglet—has come off one of your shoelace tips. Of course, you have no spare laces on hand. So what do you do? Just dip the naked end in white glue or clear nail polish. That'll stop the fabric from fraying until you can get a new pair of laces.

Liven Up Limp Lace

You want a lace shawl or scarf to be soft, but when it turns as limp as a wet dishrag, that's another matter altogether. To put the body back, wash the item as usual. Then dip it in a solution of 1 cup of Epsom salts per 2 gallons of warm water, and hang it up to dry. The salt will put life back in the fibers without making them stiff.

Note: *This trick works just as well on lace curtains.*

3 Handy Hosiery Hints

No, this isn't another list of uses for worn-out panty hose. (I'm sure you're already giving yours a gazillion and one new careers around the old homestead!) Here, I'm letting you in on three secrets that hosiery manufacturers would rather you didn't know about—because they'll keep your legwear on the job a whole lot longer.

▶ **Give 'em a briny bath.** Before you wear a pair of hose for the first time, soak them for 30 minutes in a solution of ½ cup of salt dissolved in 1 quart of water. Rinse in clear water and let 'em drip-dry.

► **Freeze 'em.** Dampen your new hose, fold them into a sealable plastic bag, and tuck it into the freezer for 24 hours. Then let the nylons thaw out naturally (not in the microwave!) and hang them up to drip-dry. The chilling-out period will harden the fibers, giving them the go power they need to last through many more wearings.

► **Rinse 'em softly.** Each time you wash your hose, add a drop or two of fabric softener to the rinse water. It'll make the nylon mesh more flexible and therefore less prone to runs. Then, instead of wringing the hose out, roll them up in a towel to remove excess moisture before you hang them up to dry.

JEWELRY

Clean Your Gems—Gently

Diamonds and other precious stones deserve all the TLC you can give them. So when your engagement ring, or any other elegant adornment, needs a little sprucing up, fill a bowl—not a sink—with lukewarm water and stir in a few squirts of mild dishwashing liquid. Put the jewelry in the bowl, let it soak for a few minutes, and scrub each piece very gently with a soft toothbrush. (One made for baby's first teeth is perfect.) Rinse with clear water, lay the pieces on a towel, and dry them with a hair dryer set on "Low."

Note: *This procedure works just as well on gold or silver jewelry, but don't use it on soft stones such as opals, pearls, turquoise, or jade. For them, use the fail-safe methods coming up.*

Pamper Your Pearls

Unlike diamonds and other gemstones, pearls are a perishable commodity. If they're not handled with extra-special care, they'll deteriorate. Here's your pearl-protection policy:

• Never touch them with any DIY or commercial jewelry cleaners

• Likewise, avoid harsh soaps, brushes, or abrasive cloths.

- For routine cleaning, wipe your pearls with a soft, damp cloth and let them air-dry completely before putting them away.

- When you're dealing with pearls that are visibly dirty (whether they're loose or in a piece of jewelry), put them into a panty hose leg. Dip the pouch in a sink filled with warm water and a squirt or two of baby shampoo. Tenderly massage each pearl with the panty hose fabric, being careful not to put stress on any thread in a necklace or bracelet. When you sense that the soil has been released, rinse with clear water, and remove the pearls from the pouch. Use a soft towel to gently absorb excess moisture, and let your treasures air-dry.

The Lowdown on Jade and Turquoise

These are two of the most popular stones used in jewelry—but that's not because they're rough and rugged hombres. Both of them are mighty picky about the care they get. Here are their demands:

▶ **Jade.** Mix lukewarm water with a few drops of mild liquid soap in a bowl. Dip a cotton cloth in the solution, and gently wipe your jade until it's clean. Don't scrub it, or you could scratch the surface. Then dip the cloth in water and remove any suds. Dry the stone with a soft, clean cloth and follow up with a polishing cloth.

> If you even suspect that your jewelry is antique—whether it's (let's say) an emerald-encrusted brooch or a silver and turquoise Navajo necklace—don't even consider trying any DIY cleaning routines. Instead, take the piece(s) to an expert jeweler, antique dealer, or museum conservator who can give you a positive ID and also advise you on the best way to care for your precious cargo.
>
> Likewise, consult a professional jeweler before you try to clean opals. That's because there are numerous types, they all require different cleaning methods—and it can be all but impossible for an untrained eye to tell them apart.

CALL A PRO

▶ **Turquoise.** Dampen a clean, soft-bristled child's toothbrush with plain water and gently scrub the surface of the stone. Do not use soap of any kind! Rinse the brush under running water and then—again gently—clean the gold or silver parts of the jewelry. Use a soft towel to dry the whole piece. Before you put it away, let it air-dry until you're sure it's completely free of moisture, which can dull the stone or tarnish any silver components.

Never immerse any jade- or turquoise-embellished jewelry in water, and never use a jewelry-cleaning product of any kind on the stone itself or on any metal surrounding it. Avoid tumblers and both ultrasonic and steam-cleaning machines, all of which can badly damage the stones. Finally (I hope this goes without saying!), always remove your jewelry before you go swimming or hop into the tub or shower.

Don't Cry over Sour Milk...

And don't dump it down the drain either. Instead, use it to clean your silver jewelry. Pour the milk into a basin, insert your pieces, and let them soak for half an hour to loosen the tarnish. Then wash them in soapy water. They'll sparkle like diamonds!

Conquer Noxious Knots

It can take the patience of Job to unwind a tangled necklace chain—unless you use this quick fix: Douse the knot with cornstarch, vegetable oil, baby oil, lubricating oil, or talcum powder—whichever you happen to have on hand. Then shove a straight pin or fine wire into the tangle to pry the links apart. Wash the freed-up chain with dishwashing liquid, rinse it in clear water, and pat it dry. Now you're good to go!

How to Make a Jewelry Frame

Costume jewelry that "lives" in a drawer or even a jewelry box can turn into a tangled mess in a hurry. And those baubles, bangles, and beads are all but guaranteed to pick up their fair share of dings as you rummage through them each morning. Here's a better idea: Make a holder that'll keep your bracelets, necklaces, and earrings safe—while doubling as a piece of one-of-a-kind wall art. Here's the simple five-step construction process:

STEP 1. Gather the goods. You'll need an attractive picture frame* (the size and degree of ornateness are your call), a tape measure, a roll of hardware cloth (available in any hardware store), tin snips or wire cutters, a staple gun and staples, and sawtooth picture hangers (also available in hardware stores). If you'd like to paint the frame, the wire mesh, or both, you'll also need spray paint in the color(s) of your choice.

Cut the hardware cloth to fit, and staple it to the frame (painting it first if you'd like).

STEP 2. Remove any picture and/or glass from the frame, along with any hardware that has held it (or them) in place.

STEP 3. Measure the inside opening at the back, cut the hardware cloth to cover it, with about ½ inch overlapping onto the back of the frame on each side. If you'd like, paint the frame and/or wire mesh. When the paint has dried thoroughly, staple the mesh in place.

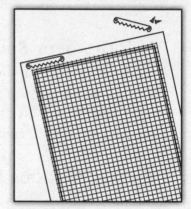

Attach sawtooth hangers to the top of the frame, and hang it on the wall.

STEP 4. Attach a sawtooth hook to each top corner of the frame, and hang it as you would any painting.

STEP 5. Attach the catches of necklaces, bracelets, and earrings to the wires, or dangle them from S-hooks or Christmas tree ornament hooks.

If you don't have a great-looking frame in your attic, look for winners at thrift shops or flea markets.

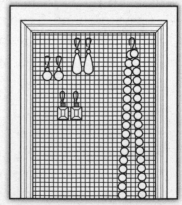

Dangle your jewelry from hooks, or attach the catches directly to the wires.

Personal-Care Products

Just like clothes, cosmetics and grooming gear will last longer and perform better if you give them some TLC.

Mind Your Makeup

Cosmetics differ in their normal life expectancy. But these guidelines will help them last longer:

- Don't store makeup in the bathroom. Cosmetics last longer in cool, dry conditions.

- Before applying makeup, wash your face and hands.

- Never dip your fingers into a makeup container. Instead, pour some of the product into the palm of your hand, or scoop it out with an applicator or cotton swab.

- Don't share your makeup with anyone else.

- Keep all containers tightly closed when you're not using the product.

- Don't moisten makeup with water or saliva. Either liquid could introduce destructive bacteria.

Note: *These same life-lengthening rules apply to medicinal salves or any body-care product that comes in a jar.*

Make Your Perfume Last

Perfume will not retain its fragrance longer if it's kept in the refrigerator. While perfume does fare better in a cool place, the fridge is too cold for the product to retain its scent. Plus, if the bottle isn't tightly sealed, the odor could be absorbed by fatty foods, like cheese and butter—and you could wind up with a grilled cheese sandwich that gives off the distinct aroma of Chanel No. 5!

Keep your perfume in a drawer or cupboard, away from light and high humidity. Normal room temperature is fine, but during hot weather, it's best if the area is air-conditioned.

Baby Your Brushes

Oil, dirt, and bacteria that get trapped in the bristles of hairbrushes can quickly turn these tools into germ-spreading clutter. So wash natural-bristle brushes once a month, and synthetic brushes three or four times a month, by soaking them (and combs, too) overnight in a solution of 4 tablespoons of baking soda per quart of water. Dry flat brushes on their backs, and stand round ones, heads up, on their handles in a container.

CHAPTER 14

Automobiles

In this day and age, doesn't it seem as though even the most minor automotive glitch demands a visit to the dealer's service department —usually at a hefty price? Well, don't fret, friends. Yes, it is true that today's computerized vehicles are more complex, and individual makes and models are far more specialized than they were a couple of decades ago. But there are still plenty of auto adversities you can fix yourself— and even more "preventive medicine" you can deliver to keep your cherished chariot on the high road for many years to come.

UNDER THE HOOD

Ladies and Gentlemen, Start Your Engines . . .

Slowly! One of the surest ways to shorten the life of your engine is to race it during start-up—especially in cold weather. Instead, start your car gently, and once you're under way, accelerate gradually. That's because you put the most wear and tear on your engine and drivetrain during the first 10 to 20 minutes of operation.

Don't Dawdle!

While your engine will suffer if you blast out of the driveway like a bat out of you-know-where, it is important to get on the road quickly. If you habitually sit in a cold car with the motor idling, waiting for it to warm up, you're asking for big trouble. That's because idling too often for too long results in incomplete fuel combustion, which in turn can lead to hefty repair bills!

Get Regular Checkups

You know that routine medical exams can help you stay in the pink of health by catching small problems before they turn into big ones. Well, periodic trips to the automotive "docs" can do the same thing for your car, and that can save you a bundle of money on future repair bills. It'll also help cut your gas consumption because a vehicle that's running in peak form burns fuel more efficiently than one that's suffering from even minor "health" challenges.

There's no doubt about it: Keeping a car performing and looking its best can take time and energy. But that may not seem like such an onerous chore when you consider this sobering statistic: The average price of a new car today is more than double what it was 20 years ago. Now, ask yourself this question: Has your discretionary income doubled over that time period, too? I didn't think so.

WELL, WHADDYA KNOW!

So keep this checklist handy and take it along whenever you visit your friendly neighborhood mechanic —or when you give your four-wheeled friend a once-over yourself.

▶ Get periodic engine tune-ups, and replace worn spark plugs. (Check with your mechanic for the timing of this service.)

▶ Keep the wheels properly aligned and balanced at all times.

▶ Test the brakes. If they're making any noise or dragging, have them fixed pronto.

▶ Check the transmission fluid (or have your mechanic check it) every time the oil is changed. It should be the bright red color of cherry soda pop; if it's any darker than that, it needs changing, too.

▶ Replace your air filter regularly. A clogged air filter can damage your engine—and cut your gas mileage by as much as 10 percent.

▶ When you fill 'er up at the gas pump, periodically add a gasoline-performance enhancer such as STP®. Besides helping to keep your fuel injectors clean, it'll increase your gas mileage by as much as 10 percent. (Ask your mechanic which brand is best for your car and how often you should add it to your gas tank.)

How to Jump-Start a Battery

Even if you belong to AAA or another roadside-assistance service, don't take any chances: Always carry a set of jumper cables in your car (they're available at any auto parts store). That way, no matter where or when trouble strikes, you'll be able to get your battery back in business quickly—or do a good deed for a fellow motorist. There are few automotive fixes that are simpler than jump-starting a dead battery—but it does need to be done in exactly the right way. Here's how to go about it:

STEP 1. Bring the "charger" car close to the "victim," but not touching it. Nose to nose, about 18 inches apart, is ideal. Set the parking brakes securely, and make sure both cars' engines are turned off, as well as headlights and all accessories (including those plugged into cigarette lighters and other power sockets). Automatic-transmission vehicles should be in "Park" and manual versions in "Neutral."

Position the two cars close together—ideally nose to nose, about 18 inches apart.

STEP 2. If your location permits, use an old rag or paper towels to remove any corrosion from the terminals of the dead battery.

STEP 3. Connect one end of the *positive* (+) cable (generally red or orange in color) to the dead battery's positive (+) terminal. Connect the other end of the *positive* cable to the *positive* terminal of the good battery. (The *positive* and *negative* terminals are clearly marked on all car batteries.) Never let the red and black jumper-cable ends touch each other once their corresponding ends are attached to a battery because serious arcing or damage to either car could occur.

STEP 4. Attach one end of the black, *negative* (-) cable to the corresponding terminal of the live battery. Fasten the other end to a solid, unpainted metal part of the dead car's engine, away from any moving parts (like belts or pulleys). Do not connect it to the battery because it could generate potentially hazardous sparks.

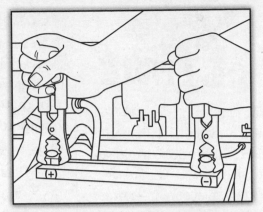

Connect the *positive* (red) cables to the *positive* battery terminals on both cars. Attach the *negative* (black) cable to the negative terminal of the *live battery only.*

STEP 5. Start the engine of the live car and let it run for a minute or two, pressing lightly on the accelerator to rev 'er up just a tad.

STEP 6. Start the dead car's engine. If it doesn't spring to life immediately, try again two or three times—but no more. The motor's reluctance to turn over probably indicates that you have problems elsewhere in your electrical system, and continued jump-starting efforts could cause major damage.

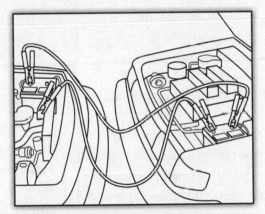

Attach the second end of the *negative* cable to an unpainted metal part of the dead car's engine—and not to the battery.

Note: *If the battery is cracked, whether fluid is leaking out or not, don't even think of trying to jump-start it! If you do, the battery could explode. Instead, replace it ASAP. (If you're a member of AAA, one of its mechanics will deliver a new battery and install it for you right on the scene.)*

Conquer Battery Corrosion

Getting rid of and preventing corrosion on your car's battery terminals is the easiest thing you can do to extend the useful life of that powerhouse. Here's a duo of dandy ways to cut through the crud:

• Mix 3 tablespoons of baking soda with 1 tablespoon of warm water. Then dip an old toothbrush in the paste, and scrub-a-dub-dub. Wipe the residue off with a wet towel and dry with a second, clean towel.

• Pour soda pop (any carbonated flavor) over the terminals. Give it a few minutes, and then wipe the sticky stuff away with a wet sponge. Rinse with clear water, and dry with a towel.

Whichever cleanser you've used, wait 10 minutes or so to make sure the terminals have dried completely. Then wipe a little petroleum jelly around each one to fend off future corrosion.

Give Your Car Key a Solo Role

Does your car key share a chain with a bunch of its counterparts? If so, you're all but begging for a dead ignition switch. How so? Because the weight of the keys, combined with their bouncing action as you drive, can wear out the tumblers inside the switch. The simple solution: Give your car key a lightweight "room" of its own—for example, a small carabiner that you can quickly detach from your main set—so you can drive with only the ignition key in that crucial slot. You'll add years of life to your ignition switch!

Note: *If your key sticks when you try to start the car, it means that your ignition switch is about to fail, so have it replaced—pronto!*

Unlucky Leaks

As we all know, it takes a number of liquids to keep the family car humming right along. With few exceptions (noted in the chart below), when you spot a liquid leaking from your vehicle, it could be a sign of serious trouble lurking just around the corner, so you need to have the problem looked at now. This handy fluid identification guide will help you determine what the mystery substance is, so you'll know what to tell your mechanic.

If the color is . . .	The fluid is . . .
Clear and odorless	Water from the air conditioner (and nothing to worry about)
Clear with a distinct odor	Gasoline
Black, brown, or amber	Engine oil or gear oil (In an older car, a little bit of oil leakage is normal, but larger quantities may signal a serious problem.)
Green	Antifreeze
Red	Transmission fluid or power-steering fluid
Yellowish or clear and slippery	Brake fluid

How to Replace a Blown Fuse

The next time your car's lights, radio, or other electrical devices suddenly stop working, there's a good chance the cause is a blown fuse. Don't rush off to the repair shop. Once you identify the culprit, you can replace it yourself in about five minutes. Here's all you need to do:

STEP 1. Check your owner's manual for the locations of your fuse boxes. (Most modern vehicles have at least two of them, containing a combined total of 40 or more fuses.) You'll generally find them in or around the instrument panel, under the hood, and sometimes under the rear seat.

STEP 2. Open the cover, and you'll see an array of different-colored fuses.* And on the inside of the cover you should find a diagram showing which fuse controls what function. There may also be several spare fuses and a little tool called (surprise!) a fuse puller that you can use to remove a blown fuse and insert a new one. (If you don't have a puller, you can pick one up at any auto parts store— or just use your fingers.)

STEP 3. Find the place on the diagram that indicates the relevant fuse. Then grab it and slide it out. You'll know at a glance if it's blown: The bridge wire between the two blades will be broken.

STEP 4. Insert a new fuse of the same amperage. Today's automotive fuses are both color-coded and differently sized to indicate their power. Plus, the amperage is printed on the top—so it's impossible to make a mistake!

If your car was made before 1980 or thereabouts, you probably have glass or ceramic tube-style fuses that look similar to the ones used in houses. A blown fuse will show

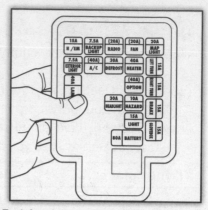

Each fuse box cover should have a diagram showing which fuse controls what function.

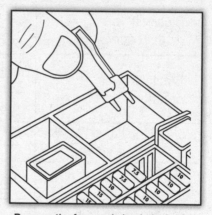

Remove the fuse and check the bridge wire to confirm that it's blown.

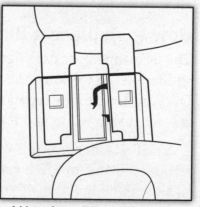

A blown fuse will have a broken wire between its two blades.

a broken wire, and the replacement process is essentially the same as it is for the newer blade-style fuses shown in the illustrations. The major difference is that the older models all look alike, with the amperage stamped on the fuse, so you need to check those numbers. Never—and I mean never—replace a fuse with a higher rating than the one you've removed.

Get in Line

The fuses for aftermarket accessories (that is, devices or systems that you or a previous owner had installed after your vehicle left the factory) are not usually in a box with their counterparts. Rather, each of these things—for example, fog lights or a CD changer—is governed by its own in-line fuse. The best way to find it is to trace the wire from the accessory

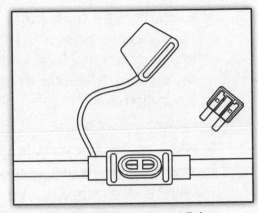

Aftermarket accessories usually have individual in-line fuses.

until you come to a container that resembles one of those shown in the illustration. It could be under the hood, under the dashboard, or even in the trunk, depending on the circuit it controls. Once you've found your target, simply open the housing, pull out the fuse, and give it the old eyeball test. If the wire inside is broken, pop in a new fuse of the same size and amperage. Then snap the housing back together, and you're good to go.

If you pull out a fuse and find that the bridge wire is not broken, or if a new fuse blows shortly after its installation, it means that you've got problems in the circuit. So take Old Betsy to your mechanic or auto dealer for an expert diagnosis and corrective "surgery."

CALL A PRO

TIRES & BRAKES

Keep the Rubber on the Road

The secret to long-lived tires lies in two words: smart maintenance. You can get the complete lowdown on that score from the Rubber Manufacturers Association website, www.rma.org. In the meantime, though, these are the basic guidelines:

▶ **Keep them properly inflated.** Your owner's manual will indicate the correct air pressure. If you no longer have the book, the tire manufacturer or a local tire dealer can give you the details. Check the pressure (when the tires are cold) once a month and before any long trip.

▶ **Conduct monthly inspections.** Look for signs of uneven wear, which could indicate improper inflation, improper balance, suspension problems, or misalignment. Any of these problems indicates that a visit to a mechanic is in order. Also, check for any stones, glass, or other debris that may have lodged in the treads because deeply embedded objects can cause a loss of air pressure.

▶ **Keep 'em moving.** Rotate your tires according to the specs from the manufacturer (generally after every 6,000 miles or so), or sooner if you see any signs of uneven wear.

▶ **Drive with care.** Don't make sudden starts, avoid sharp turns and quick stops as much as possible, and do your best to dodge potholes and other bumps. All of these actions will substantially increase the life of your tires.

Fluid Movements

You chose black-walled tires over whitewalls because you thought they'd stay clean longer. And they do—but they don't stay that way forever. So here's a simple way to keep those babies looking as good as they did the day you drove them out of the tire store: Just rub on a thin coat of brake fluid, using a soft, clean cloth. Then wipe it dry with a second soft cloth.

Baby Your Brakes

Every time you hit the brakes suddenly, a little bit of the life goes out of them. Granted, there are always going to be times when you have to come to a screeching halt, but there are some simple ways to keep those jolting stops to a minimum. To be specific, do your best to maintain a steady pace, monitor the traffic flow up ahead, and keep plenty of distance between you and the car in front of you. When you know there's a stoplight or a reduction in the speed limit coming up, ease off the accelerator, let your car coast, and, when you need to brake, do it gently. Hot tip: When you see a sign that says "Reduced Speed Ahead," immediately take your foot off the gas pedal. I've found that in most cases, by the time you reach the next sign, you'll be going at exactly the new, lower speed limit, with no braking needed.

Look, Ma—No Feet!

Never rest your foot on the brake pedal while you're driving. Even the tiniest bit of pressure can cause a drag that will wear out your brakes eventually. (This often-unconscious practice also wastes gasoline.)

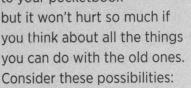

Outfitting your car with new tires can deliver a painful pinch to your pocketbook—but it won't hurt so much if you think about all the things you can do with the old ones. Consider these possibilities:

Cushion your arrival. Attach one to the end wall of your garage to soften the blow when you don't remember to stop in time.

Make a stand. For what? For all sorts of things. Fill the center of the tire with cement and, while it's still wet, insert an upright pipe that's 3 to 4 inches in diameter. Then either insert or attach whatever you need to hold up—for instance, a flagpole, post for a mailbox, kid-size basketball hoop, tetherball, or bird feeder.

Make a swing. Many of us grew up swinging on tires, and it's just as much fun today as it was back then. Tie one end of a rope to the tire, and the other end to a sturdy tree limb, and climb aboard!

Protect your boat. You have two choices here: Either hang whole tires from the sides of the dock, or cut strips of rubber from one or more tires, and nail them to the edges of the dock.

BODY BASICS

5 Terrific Tar-Removal Tricks

Road tar splotches may look as ugly as sin—and plenty intimidating—but it's actually easy to get the gooey gunk off your car without damaging the paint. Any of these common household products will do the job nicely. (Whichever method you use, finish up by rinsing with clear water and drying the de-tarred area with a soft, clean cloth.)

- Mix 3 parts baking soda with 1 part water, and apply the paste to the spots with a damp cloth. Let it sit for five minutes, and wipe with a second damp cloth.

- Spray the marks with a laundry prewash stain remover. Wait 10 to 15 minutes, then wipe it away.

- Rub creamy peanut butter onto the tar, leave it there for 10 minutes, and take it off with a soft cloth.

- Dip a clean cloth in regular cola (not diet!), and wash the globs off.

- Spritz the nasty stuff with WD-40®, give it five minutes to soak in, and then wipe with a soft cloth.

AN OUNCE OF PREVENTION

Buy a Car Coat

A car parked outdoors is a sitting duck for damage caused by everything from road salt to bird droppings, tree sap, and windblown branches. Not to mention the sun's UV rays that can destroy the finish and trapped heat that can ruin the interior. But even in a nice, cozy garage, dust continuously settles on your car, forming a layer of abrasive grit that can dull the paint. The simple solution: Invest in a good car cover. Prices vary greatly, depending (of course) on quality, as well as on the size and shape of your vehicle and what dangers you need to protect it from. For most automobiles, you can pick up a basic "overcoat" for about what you'd pay for a couple of professional car washes—and less than you'd probably have to shell out for a full-scale detailing job. For more information, search the Internet for "car covers," or ask about them at your local auto-supply store.

Chrome Sweet Chrome

Are you the proud guardian of an older car that has classic chrome on the outside? If so, then these TLC tips are just for you:

- For routine cleaning, rub the chrome with a cloth dipped in rubbing alcohol.

- To remove rust spots, crumple up a piece of aluminum foil shiny side out. Dip it in cola, and scrub the stains away. Rinse with clear water.

Let It Drain

Nearly all car doors have holes along the undersides to let rust-causing moisture drain out. To keep those openings free and clear, clean them out periodically using a pipe cleaner, wire coat hanger, or ultra-thin bottle brush. How often you need to perform this chore depends on the nature of the roads you drive on. If you spend most of your behind-the-wheel time on paved highways, once a year should be fine. But if your routine frequently takes you over unpaved roads or driveways—or your area is prone to mudslides—unplug the holes at least every few months.

POWERFUL POTIONS
WINDSHIELD-WASHER FLUID

Most commercial wiper fluid brands are made with methanol, and even a small amount of it could be highly toxic to a small child or pet. Also, the store-bought stuff will cost you three times as much as this DIY formula.

1 cup of rubbing alcohol*
2 tbsp. of dishwashing liquid
Water
Blue food coloring (optional)

Pour the alcohol and dishwashing liquid into a 1-gallon plastic jug, and fill the balance of the container with water. Cap the jug, and gently roll it around a few times to mix. Label the container. Add a few drops of blue food color to make sure that no one mistakes it for some other clear potion.

* If you live in cold-weather territory, make sure you use 99% isopropyl alcohol in the winter, and during periods of extreme cold, double the amount shown in the recipe.

Take the Plunge(r)

Got a smooth, shallow dent in your car? Before you shell out big bucks to a body shop, try this no-cost DIY trick: Moisten the rim of a drain plunger, and press it into the center of the hollow. Push on the plunger a few times if necessary to work up as much suction as possible. Then pull sharply as hard as you can. If you're lucky, your car's dimple will pop right out!

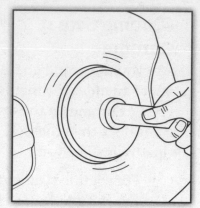

Often, a drain plunger can pull a shallow dent out of a car's body.

Tough Breaks

Whoops! You started to open your car's trunk, and your key broke off in the lock. Well, don't call a locksmith—at least not before you try this much less expensive option: Grab a curved tapestry needle (or go out and buy one if necessary). Then shove it into the lock and fish out the broken part of the key.

Polish Up Your Vision

Invariably, over time, headlight (and taillight) covers pick up minute scratches that dull the plastic surface—and reduce your ability to see the road ahead clearly. The simple solution: Squeeze a little dollop of white (non-gel) toothpaste onto a soft cotton flannel cloth, and firmly rub the scratched surface for several minutes, using circular motions. Wipe the paste away with a damp cloth, then buff with a fresh cloth to make the surface shine.

CALL A PRO

If you've locked your keys inside your car or trunk, don't try any DIY fishing tricks—call a professional locksmith. Contrary to conventional "wisdom," poking around with a wire coat hanger or similar improvised tool is likely to damage the weather stripping. That, in turn, will lead to leaks that could wind up costing you a whole lot more than the locksmith's bill.

Blowing Hot and Cold

If your vehicle has had an unfortunate encounter with no damage to the paint, this maneuver could save you from a costly repair bill, as long as the ding is on a flat panel.

STEP 1. Round up a hair dryer and a can of compressed air (available in office-supply and computer stores).

STEP 2. Set the dryer on "High," and move it over the dented area for one to three minutes, or until the surface is warm to the touch. To avoid damaging the paint, make sure you keep the dryer 5 to 7 inches away from the car at all times.

STEP 3. As soon as you turn off the dryer, spray the cold propellant onto the still-warm wound. The sudden change in temperature should make the metal flatten out.

Note: *If neither this nor the plunger ploy in "Take the Plunge(r)" (at left) works, bite the bullet and turn the "surgery" over to a professional body shop. Do not use any commercial DIY body-repair products. They don't work out complex dents, and what's worse, they use a glue that can damage the paint.*

POWERFUL POTIONS

AUTOMOTIVE ANTI-FROST FORMULA

There are few more annoying wintertime woes than waking up to find your car windows covered in frost or—worse—a thick coat of ice. This elixir can end your ice-scraping days for good (provided, that is, you remember to use it every time you have to park your car outdoors on a frosty night).

6 cups of white vinegar
2 cups of water

Mix the vinegar and water together in a bucket or pan, drench a cloth with the solution, and give all your windows and mirrors a good once-over. Or pour the potion into a spray bottle and spritz the solution all over the glass. The next morning, you'll wake up to ice- and frost-free windows!